The Virtual Worlds

Handbook

How to Use Second Life® and Other 3D Virtual Environments

Elizabeth Hodge
Sharon Collins
Tracy Giordano

All of East Carolina University

JONES AND BARTLETT PUBLISHERS

Sudbury, Massachusetts

BOSTON   TORONTO   LONDON   SINGAPORE

World Headquarters

Jones and Bartlett Publishers
40 Tall Pine Drive
Sudbury, MA 01776
978-443-5000
info@jbpub.com
www.jbpub.com

Jones and Bartlett Publishers Canada
6339 Ormindale Way
Mississauga, Ontario L5V 1J2
Canada

Jones and Bartlett Publishers
International
Barb House, Barb Mews
London W6 7PA
United Kingdom

Jones and Bartlett's books and products are available through most bookstores and online booksellers. To contact Jones and Bartlett Publishers directly, call 800-832-0034, fax 978-443-8000, or visit our website, www.jbpub.com.

Substantial discounts on bulk quantities of Jones and Bartlett's publications are available to corporations, professional associations, and other qualified organizations. For details and specific discount information, contact the special sales department at Jones and Bartlett via the above contact information or send an email to specialsales@jbpub.com.

Second Life is a trademark of Linden Research, Inc. Certain materials have been reproduced with the permission of Linden Research, Inc.

Production Credits

Publisher: David Pallai
Editorial Assistant: Molly Whitman
Production Assistant: Ashlee Hazeltine
Associate Marketing Manager: Lindsay Ruggerio
V.P., Manufacturing and Inventory Control: Therese Connell
Composition: Glyph International
Permissions Coordinator: Kesel Wilson
Title Page and Cover Design: Kristin E. Parker

Cover Images: Sky/Ocean 3D scene © Arenacreative/Dreamstime.com; 3D Earth Globe in Ocean © Olikli/Dreamstime.com; Second Life Screenshots featured on the cover are courtesy of the New Media Consortium and of Linden Research, Inc.
Printing and Binding: Malloy, Inc.
Cover Printing: Malloy, Inc.

Library of Congress Cataloging-in-Publication Data

Hodge, Elizabeth.
  The virtual worlds handbook : how to use second life and other 3D virtual environments / Elizabeth Hodge, Sharon Collins and Tracy Giordano.
     p. cm.
  Includes index.
  ISBN-13: 978-0-7637-7747-0 (pbk.)
  ISBN-10: 0-7637-7747-1
  1. Virtual reality in education. I. Collins, Sharon, 1956 Sept. 19- II. Giordano, Tracy. III. Title.
  LB1044.87.H64 2010
  371.39'7–dc22
                          2009033983

6048
Printed in the United States of America
13 12 11 10 09   10 9 8 7 6 5 4 3 2 1

Dedication

Elizabeth Hodge

To my husband Ronald for supporting and encouraging me to explore new methods for teaching and learning. To my children Gray, Tyler, and Mikeala for knowing that my promise to make them their own 'S' avatars when I finished the book would happen eventually with patience. To my mother Diana for the support, encouragement, and help in keeping my family sane throughout the writing process. And with special thanks and appreciation to my co-authors Sharon and Tracy, who challenged me to think outside of the box and who kept me grounded during the final editing phase.

Sharon Collins

To Brent, my fiancé, for always being there and helping me get through the hard times. To my children, Megan, Christie, and Nikki, for constantly supporting me and encouraging me to go my own way. I'd like to thank them for all the things they all took care of when I could not possibly move away from my computer.

Tracy Giordano

I would like thank my greatest supporter—my husband Tony—and my patient family who have walked with me through this journey. To my co-authors, who have truly felt the writing pains, I would like to congratulate and thank you sincerely for everything you have done for me and this book. And Tony, I owe you lunch…

Contents

Chapter 13: Your Moodle/Sloodle Connection 261

Chapter 14: Other Uses for Second Life 265

Chapter 15: Tying It All Together.............................273

Appendix A: In-World Educational Spaces and Virtual Hot Spots 287

Appendix B: Web Resources....................................293

Appendix C: Shortcut Keys 299

Appendix D: Glossary..303

Appendix E: Automatic Script Viewer Explanation.................309

Preface

Virtual worlds combine interactive 3D graphics, simulation technology, virtual reality, Voice over Internet Protocol (VoIP), and rich digital media to provide users the limitless ability to communicate, collaborate, and explore. During their infancy stage, virtual environments were largely based upon the gaming community and over time have been adapted to meet the needs of the growing number of educators who are integrating the use of virtual worlds for course delivery. Second Life® (SL) creates a social space for learners, a marketing opportunity for companies, and a source of income for hundreds of new entrepreneurs. Educators are exploring the vast capabilities available for social interaction, synchronous communication, simulations, and collaborations within this program. Several virtual software platforms exist; however, the SL platform will be the main focus of this book.

There are several books on the market that help you get acquainted with SL and the various features it offers its residents, but the authors of this book wanted to offer you something a bit different. This book will offer you everything you need to know, from the importance of creating a SL name to more advanced levels of rezzing objects to meet your specific instructional needs. This book highlights the importance of various instructional strategies and details the effective tools to help you incorporate these strategies into your virtual classroom. *The Virtual Worlds Handbook: How to Use Second Life and Other 3D Virtual*

Environments also includes several screenshots and step-by-step instructions that explain:

- Instructional assessments, training techniques, and strategies for integrating Second Life
- A simple, straightforward "orientation" process
- Tips and techniques for adding interactivity to objects
- Educational and training sites available in Second Life

By far the most amazing elements that this book provides are the objects and script for the immediate development and delivery of course material in an exciting, innovative virtual environment. So if you are ready to receive praise and acclaim from your administration, colleagues, and students, this book is a must-read for you.

The authors of this book will provide a unique perspective on learning the fundamentals associated with SL along with techniques for using SL as an educational and training tool. The authors of this book include their personal avatars Ekumu Ellisson, an associate professor and SL Consultant; Samia Karsin, Project Manager and SL Consultant; and Aolani Okelli, Virtual Early High School Coordinator and SL Consultant. Each of these authors provides a distinct view to teaching and learning with virtual environments. As you review the chapters you will note that readers will receive basic instruction on how to use the various tools within the environment and also instruction and discussion on how to use the environment to create a virtual learning community.

About the Authors

Elizabeth M. Hodge, PhD

*Content Advisor/Course Design
Expert
Associate Professor, Business
and Information Technologies
Education
East Carolina University*

Figure PR.1 Ekumu Ellisson/Elizabeth M. Hodge, PhD

Elizabeth M. Hodge is an Associate Professor of Business and Information Technologies at East Carolina University. Dr. Hodge has dedicated her professional career to integrating technology tools that will engage students in the learning process. She has published over twenty scholarly works on topics that incorporate innovative instructional strategies and the uses for Web 2.0 technologies for fostering communication and interaction in online distance education courses.

Sharon Collins
Content Advisor/Technical Advisor
Applied Management and Decision Sciences, ISM,
PhD Candidate
Project Manager, Academic Outreach
Online Learning Programs
East Carolina University

Figure PR.2   Samia Karsin/Sharon Collins

Sharon Collins is a Project Manager for Academic Outreach at East Carolina University. Sharon's expertise includes work on virtual environments as an estate manager, instructional designer, builder, scripter, technical support and mentor to students and faculty. Ms. Collins serves as a consultant on several grants that deal with collaborative technologies and distance education solutions.

Tracy Giordano
Content Advisor/Technical Advisor
Second Life Virtual Early High School Coordinator
Academic Outreach
East Carolina University

Figure PR.3   Aolani Okelli/Tracy Giordano

Tracy Giordano was the Virtual Early High School Coordinator for Academic Outreach at East Carolina University. Because Tracy is an experienced end user of MUDs, MUVEs, and MMORPGs, the crossover to the development of virtual environment content was a natural transition. Within Second Life, Tracy is an expert builder who customs designs and scripts tools for use within the educational sector.

Using This Book

Throughout *The Virtual Worlds Handbook: How to Use Second Life and Other 3D Virtual Environments*, you will find various elements to help explain and expand upon the information in this book, including tips, anecdotes from the authors, and assignments.

The authors' anecdotes reflect their personal experiences performing a certain task or expound upon interesting points. Each anecdote has a picture of one of the author's avatars, letting the reader know who is telling the anecdote.

Assignments are included to encourage readers to actively participate in the learning process and apply what they have learned in their own Second Life environment. Each assignment is accompanied by the SEA² logo. For additional resources and assignments, the reader can go to the SEA² website at https://sites.google.com/site/sea2sl/.

Companion Material

CD-ROM

The companion CD-ROM includes resources in conjunction with the book chapters that will be valuable for teaching and training purposes. For example, the authors often provide links to valuable resources on the web or SLurls to in-world locations. A full list of the CD content is provided below:

- In-world educational spaces and virtual hot spots
- Web resources
- Automatic picture viewer script and explanation
- Color figures necessary for comprehension
- Glossary
- Shortcut keys

SEA²

Figure PR.4   SEA² In-world Location

The most helpful resource for readers of this book is the in-world location SEA². The value in providing an in-world location is that it offers the reader the opportunity to access objects, tutorials, and resources in-world that will not cost extra L$ (Linden$™). For example, every time you upload an image or texture, it will cost you L$10. Therefore, the in-world location provides readers with the option of accessing the site to retrieve helpful items. The readers can access SEA² at http://slurl.com/secondlife/Teaching%208/235/109/23 and obtain in-world resources, objects, and tutorials.

SEA² Website

The website, which can be reached at https://sites.google.com/site/sea2sl, includes up-to-date information about Samia, Ekumu, and Aolani (SEA²) and additional resources, tutorials, trainings, and workshops.

Figure PR.5 SEA² Consulting Website

Acknowledgments

The authors would like to thank the Second Life community and the avatars that gave their permission to use their objects in the book, as well as extend their appreciation to the New Media Consortium for their support. The authors would like to recognize the building, scripting, and design expertise of their fellow SL peers, many of whom provided attire, objects, and images that could be used within the book to enhance the reader's comprehension of the material.

Furthermore, the authors would like to recognize the support East Carolina University provided in letting them explore new venues for the delivery of education.

Introduction

We have the power to transform learning through the use of virtual environments. Fundamental to all learning is the ability to communicate. Because speaking is the primary mode of communication, you will discover that there are many different ways to communicate, collaborate, explore, and socialize with other residents in Second Life (SL) and other virtual environments. The uses of SL are endless and are a hot topic in the business industry, federal government, health care organizations, and academia. Today's gaming generation views virtual environments as a strong social and interactive medium for communicating and socializing. Therefore, corporations can use this medium to promote and sell products or even conduct in-world meetings. Academia can use virtual worlds to offer students an enhanced learning environment with the power to alleviate feelings of isolation through the promotion of communication, interaction, collaboration, teamwork, feedback, engagement, and constructivist learning activities. However, SL was originally designed by Philip Rosedale to "demonstrate a viable model for a virtual economy or virtual society." Rosedale stated that, "I'm not building a game. I'm building a new continent" (Kohler 2009). This is just the beginning of the many different uses virtual environments can provide to their residents. *The Virtual Worlds Handbook: How to Use Second Life and Other 3D Virtual Environments* explores the many ways in which the average user can develop an interactive environment where different groups can interact, socialize, conduct business, and learn.

Figure IN.1   April 2003 SL World Map

The Book's Intended Audience

The intended audience for this book consists of readers who are new to virtual worlds, as well as returning residents who wish to learn more about corporate, government, health care, and educational uses for Second Life. The first half of the book will acquaint newbies or "noobs" (new in-world residents) to Second Life fundamentals. Whether you are a new resident or even a more experienced user, these chapters will provide you with tips and resources that will take your personal avatar, company, training program, or educational classroom to a new level. The second half of the book provides the reader with a more in-depth look at educational uses, training options, and in-world tools for communication, interaction, collaboration, and engagement between residents. Furthermore, this book will guide readers through learning about Linden Lab, virtual environments, economic matters, the culture of Second Life, and a list of resources and links that will make any noob an SL expert.

Second Life Fundamentals

The first half of this book will establish a solid foundation for the reader to understand virtual environments, learn basic techniques, and explore new ways for building and developing land. These chapters provide an extensive overview of the features available within the SL Viewer. Newbies will learn how to create an account, download the SL viewer, create an avatar, organize their inventory, and build a 3D environment. Readers who are familiar with SL will gain expert tips, assignments, and resources for improving their current performance and activity in-world.

Education and Second Life

The emergence and use of virtual environments to develop and foster learning in education is a new phenomenon that is growing at a rapid pace. Virtual environments give participants a sense of "being there" even when attending a class or social event in person is not possible, practical, or desirable. This in turn provides educators and students with the ability to connect and communicate in a way that greatly enhances the learning experience. The New Media Consortium reports that at any given time of day there are 80,000 residents logged into SL. SL continues to grow at an exponential rate. This can be noted by the more than 18,000 universities, community colleges, private institutions, and others in residence in SL, with more joining monthly. Furthermore, SL provides corporations, entrepreneurs, governments, and medical communities with the ability to explore new ways to promote products, conduct meetings, and sell objects for a profit in-world. Currently, more than 90 corporations have SL representation. Another area on the rise is the use of virtual worlds by the federal government to share best practices, policies, and objects associated with social networking software. The medical community also has a flourishing presence in SL. SLHealthy, which is an association for physicians and medics, is available in-world to promote better health and medical education to interested residents.

The second half of this book provides readers with questions that will assess the purpose and need for integrating virtual environments into their companies, training programs, and courses. Furthermore, these chapters cover instructional methodology and educational tools that foster communication, interaction, and collaboration.

Reference

Kohler, C. (July 15, 2009) "David Perry and the Infinite Money Loop." Wired Magazine. Retrieved from the world wide web on August 28, 2009 at http://www.wired.com/gamelife/2009/07/gaikaie

Virtual Environments

The Education Grid and Platform Ecosystem will "provide educators with a comprehensive end-to-end infrastructure for a new generation of virtual world learning environments." The three platforms the ecosystem will focus on are part of the highly developed Second Life® (SL™), including the Teen Second Life Grid™, Sun Microsystems Laboratories® Project Wonderland™ (under development), and Active Worlds. These worlds are prominent in the education, business, and industry fields and have been useful for teaching and learning because they are interactive and engaging.

Investigating platforms is an important step in choosing a virtual world. Following is a short description of each of these well-defined platforms. After this chapter we will provide you with an in-depth guide to help you learn how to work with the Second Life virtual world.

Second Life

Access Second Life as shown in **Figure 1.1** at http://secondlife.com/.

Second Life is a 3-D virtual world created by the residents who inhabit it. This platform was created by Philip Rosedale and the team at Linden Lab. According to statistics from December 1, 2008, there are currently close to 17 million avatars in Second Life, with a monthly count of 1,500,000+ and a daily count of 80,000+ "in world" at any given time. It is a unique place to discover educational opportunities, conferences, live music performances, games, interactive exhibits, and shopping experiences. At the time this book was written, Linden Lab was supporting an economy of $144 million a day in user transactions (Hale, 2009).

Figure 1.1   Second Life Virtual Environment

Examples of educational uses include the following:

- Classroom instruction
- Group interaction
- Office hours
- Role playing
- Peer review
- Collaboration
- Project development
- Faculty and administrative meetings
- Sharing videos and voice communication
- Text chat
- Interacting with the world
- Creating interactive objects
- Participating in communities, meetings, and conferences

Second Life enables you to create an avatar that can interact with individuals in order to learn and share. The world is your oyster, and there are endless opportunities to open your imagination and communicate with other residents in uniquely developed simulated areas.

Examples of SL users include East Carolina University, Princeton, North Carolina State University, the University of North Carolina at Chapel Hill, Harvard, Dell, IBM, Sun Microsystems, and the New Media Consortium.

Teen Second Life™

Access Teen Second Life as shown in **Figure 1.2** at http://teen.secondlife.com/.

This is another grid developed by Linden Lab for anyone from the age of 13 to 17. Linden Lab would like to protect its younger residents, so this land is restricted to teens only. Adults can gain access purely for educational purposes

Figure 1.2   SL Teen Grid

after a background check and approval for entry into an island. Teens from all over the globe meet here.

Examples of uses include the following:

- High school-to-college programs
- High school courses
- Educational programs
- Teen interaction
- Shopping
- Introduction to virtual worlds
- College fairs
- Dancing clubs
- Craft fairs

Examples of users include Pitt County School Systems, East Carolina University (North Carolina), Global Kids, Eye4YouAlliance, Ohio University, Virtual World Campus, and the New Media Consortium.

Project Wonderland

Access Project Wonderland as shown in **Figure 1.3** at https://lg3d-wonderland. dev.java.net/.

Sun Microsystems® Laboratories' Project Wonderland™ is an immersive-education virtual world built as a robust environment to provide scalability and security.

Figure 1.3   Project Wonderland

It is a free, open-source platform that runs on Java and has a large community of developers. Wonderland is currently under development and has new elements launching throughout 2009. The latest release provides additional functionality because Wonderland was designed to use the Education Grid and Ecosystem to develop a rich library of learning objects, digital media, learning games, and collaborative activities.

Examples of educational uses include the following:

- Writer's workshop
- Math help center
- Business applications
- Application sharing
- Software development
- Gaming
- Distributed collaboration
- Virtual theater
- Economics
- Share live applications
- Office documents

Examples of users include Essex University (UK), St. Paul College, the University of Oregon, the University of Zurich, the University of Missouri, the University of Rome, Sun Labs, and the New Media Consortium.

At this time, Project Wonderland is not as mature as SL and is not as widely used by educators. However, the open-source capability does make it a favorite of some educators because of the security of being able to run it on servers within the confines of their own environment.

Active Worlds

Access Active Worlds as shown in **Figure 1.4** at http://www.activeworlds.com/.

Active Worlds, another free, open-source software platform, was developed to create collaborative multiuser online applications with a community of thousands of users. Active Worlds was specifically designed to enable the creation and low-cost deployment of large-scale metaverses that can be run within your own environment. It is an older platform and is used by educators worldwide.

Figure 1.4 Active Worlds

Educational institutions, teachers, students, and individual programs can use Active Worlds in a focused setting. Via this community, educators can explore new concepts, learning theories, creative curriculum design, and new paradigms in social learning. More than 80 educational worlds are available.

Examples of uses include the following:

- Collaboration
- Meetings
- Classroom instruction
- Medical community
- Programming
- Shopping
- Quest Atlantis
- Active World teen site

Examples of users include the University of California at Santa Cruz, Cornell University, the University of Cincinnati, the Art Center College of Design, the University of Toronto, the Oslo School of Architecture, University College London, the Haags Montessori Lyceum, the Charters School, Sacred Heart Middle School, the Boston Museum of Science, NASA Ames Research Laboratory, the Center for Advanced Learning Technologies, and the United Nations.

Other Virtual Worlds

If you would like to read about all the other virtual worlds, you can find a comprehensive list at this website: http://www.virtualworldsreview.com/info/categories.shtml.

Some are simple means of communicating over the Web, and others are multi-user virtual environments with a purpose directed toward education.

Wrap-Up

Keywords/Definitions:

Active Worlds—a 3-D virtual world created by Active Worlds, Inc.

Ecosystem—habitats where a population lives and functions together as a unit

Linden Lab—the company that created Second Life

Main Grid—the system that serves and caters to all adult users of the Second Life virtual world

Project Wonderland—a virtual environment created by Sun Microsystems Laboratories

Second Life (SL)—a 3-D virtual world created by Philip Rosedale of Linden Lab in June 2003

Teen Grid—a separate server of SL that houses regions specifically geared toward Second Life users between the ages of 13 and 17

Virtual world (VW)—a 3-D computer-based platform that allows users to interact with each other in real time
Synonyms: virtual environment (VE)

URLs to Helpful Information and Tutorials

http://secondlife.com (create an avatar here)

http://secondlifegrid.net/

http://teen.secondlife.com/

http://www.activeworlds.com/edu/

Worlds Action Group—http://members.tripod.com/~LadyJude/

Andras's AW Tools—http://www.andras.net/

RenderWare Modeler—http://www.rwmodeler.com/

Accu Trans 3D—http://www.micromouse.ca/

PolyTrans—http://www.okino.com/conv/conv.htm

IngieBee's Dem2Rwx Tutorial—http://www.angelfire.com/de/IngieBee/

Dataman's Rwx Tutorial—http://www.synergycorp.com/temp/makerwx1.htm

Mauz's HagViewer Tutorial—http://mauz.info/hagviewer.html

Mauz's RWXMod Tutorial—http://mauz.info/rwxmod.html

Reference

Hale, T. (August 12, 2009). The Second Life™ Economy—Second Quarter 2009 in Detail. The Second Life™ Features Blog. Retrieved from the World Wide Web on September 1, 2009 at https://blogs.secondlife.com/community/features/blog/2009/08/12/the-second-life-economy-second-quarter-2009-in-detail.

Creating Your Account and Beginning Your Journey

Virtual environments provide access, communication, and interaction to learners from all over the world. The opportunities for using virtual reality are limitless, and they provide individuals with a unique chance to connect both physically and educationally to one another, the faculty, the university, and a worldwide market. Chapter 2 includes information on creating an account and all the components associated with taking your first steps "in world." This includes choosing your avatar's name, which is quite important because you cannot change it once selected. Although it might seem like a simple process, choosing a name in Second Life™ is the first major step in your entry into this virtual world. There are also certain naming techniques that should be addressed prior to selection.

Choosing your avatar is an important step. It begins with the Linden Lab default avatars, but you will find that you will change your avatar to match your personality or looks. This can be as simple as creating a "look alike" or as complex as choosing an avatar that represents your alter ego. While in world you always have the chance to change your avatar's appearance and to take on other personas for an hour, a day, or however long you choose. It can be exciting, and there is an entire psychological process around choosing your avatar's appearance. Read more about personas in the following anecdote.

Creating Your Account

Before you start exploring SL™, you must first create an account and a generic avatar. Linden Lab provides you with several avatars from which to select, and you can pick your sex. The avatar you select will change dramatically from the

W hile working on an SL project recently, I was visited by Snoopy and Woodstock. Imagine the possibilities when you can take on different personas for plays and other roles.

Figure 2.1   Get Started

original. It will evolve into a dynamic persona as you make it your own. Your avatar can take the shape of an animal, an object, a character in a play, or a professional once you begin your customization.

The first step is to go to the following website by entering the link in a browser such as Internet Explorer™ or FireFox™: http://secondlife.com/.

Click on **Get Started** (as shown in **Figure 2.1**), and remember, membership is free.

Here you will be taken to a page where you can select from male and female avatars. Currently, there are 12 in all. This will be your first decision: Will you be what you are in real life? Here is your chance to decide how your journey will begin.

Click on the avatar of your choice as shown in **Figure 2.2**, and you will see the entire avatar to the right of the selection.

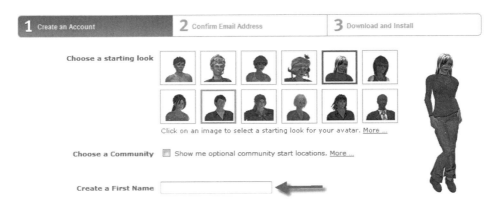

Figure 2.2   Create an Account

Now you can choose to enter into a community through the website's optional community start locations by clicking in the box beside "Show me optional community start locations." Linden Lab promotes selected communities. As a new SL resident, they help you get started, meet friends with a common language and interest, and attend a variety of events. These communities offer you a friendly environment for your first SL experience. By selecting Choose a

Community you will arrive in the selected community's welcome area.

For new SL residents, communities are a good place to start because these spaces focus on specific types of interests like geographic locations or educational uses. Selecting a community does not keep you bound to that space. Once you enter the SL environment, you are free to visit other locations wherever you see fit.

Figure 2.3 shows you some of the communities that are available for selection.

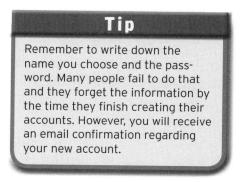

Figure 2.3 Communities

Culture of Naming

Create your first avatar name and type it in the box provided. Think carefully about the name you will choose. This name will be with you for the life of your avatar and will be how everyone in SL recognizes you. It will become your "second" name in life, as you will quickly see. Individuals who work in SL find that they sometimes do not even remember your real-life (RL) name once they get used to your SL name.

Create your last name from the list in the dropdown menu as shown in **Figure 2.4**. You can even do a search through Google to see the meaning of the name—you will be surprised how many are male or female oriented. For example, the name Halulu means "to roar, thunder," and the last name is Zsun. You can change your name here, but once you submit it, you cannot make any changes to your avatar name.

Finish creating your avatar by performing the following steps:

Tip

Remember to write down the name you choose and the password. Many people fail to do that and they forget the information by the time they finish creating their accounts. However, you will receive an email confirmation regarding your new account.

Figure 2.4 Avatar Name

1. Type your email address.
2. Confirm your email address. You should enter a valid email address because this is how Linden Lab will verify your account.
3. Select the arrow for the dropdown menu and pick your country.
4. Select the month you were born, the date, and the year (you should be honest here). Linden Lab uses your age to verify whether you belong on the Teen Grid or the Adult Grid.
5. Type in your real-life last name and first name in the next two fields. This should also be correct because Linden Lab may need to contact you later for actions within SL.
6. Select male or female.
7. Select a password and then confirm that password by typing it again.

8. Select the dropdown box and pick a security question so that if you ever forget your password, it can be retrieved.

9. The next section says, "Verify you are not a Robot!" Here you have to type the characters you see (**Figure 2.5**). Do not worry. Sometimes they are a bit difficult to read, but if you mess up, you get another chance, and the selection will change. That is why there is the line reading, "Problem? Try a different one." You can also choose "You can also try an audio captcha instead." Here text will be read to you, and you will type that text into the box.

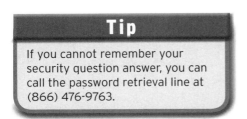

Tip

If you cannot remember your security question answer, you can call the password retrieval line at (866) 476-9763.

Figure 2.5   Robot

10. After reviewing the terms of service, check the box to agree and you will be taken to the next screen.

11. This screen, as seen in **Figure 2.6**, will tell you to check your email so that you can verify that you are the one creating the account. You should open your email account and see whether you have an email from Linden Lab. If you do not find one in your inbox, check your junk mail folder or spam folder.

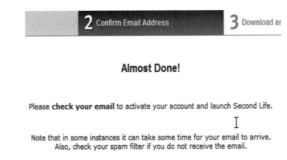

Figure 2.6   Almost Done

12. Once you click the link in your email, you are taken to the congratulations screen (**Figure 2.7**) to finish your verification.

Congratulations, Halulu Zsun!
Your Second Life account has been activated.

Figure 2.7   Congratulations

Figure 2.8   Download and Install

13. You can then download the software, which takes only a few minutes using a high-speed Internet connection (**Figure 2.8**).

14. Follow the download instructions, and you are now ready to launch the program and enter SL.

15. You must now launch the software that has been downloaded. Go to **Start > Programs > Second Life**, and the client will open when you click on it (**Figure 2.9**).

Figure 2.9   Second Life

You can also double-click on this icon on your desktop, as shown in **Figure 2.10**.

Figure 2.10   Second Life Icon

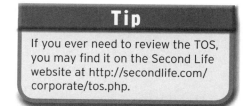

Tip

If you ever need to review the TOS, you may find it on the Second Life website at http://secondlife.com/corporate/tos.php.

Once the program loads, you must type in your avatar name and password in the boxes provided and agree to the terms of service (TOS), as shown in **Figure 2.11**.

Figure 2.11   Login Screen

Create Your Own Avatar

Follow the preceding steps to create a name, choose an avatar, and download the SL software. You are now well on your way to exploring SL and all it has to offer.

The TOS (**Figure 2.12**) is distributed by Linden Lab, and you may want to refer to this if you rent or own land.

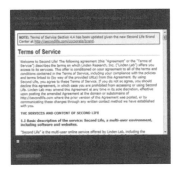

Figure 2.12   Terms of Service

Once you begin to use SL, if it has been awhile since you installed the software, you will have to update your client. If you see an image similar to that shown in **Figure 2.13**, you will need to download the latest version.

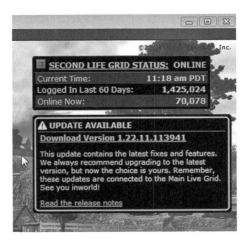

Figure 2.13   Update

Default Avatars

The avatar you choose in this initial setup is a default avatar. You will be able to change its appearance when you log "in world," but this lets you start with the basics. Some of the ways to customize your avatar are as simple as changing your hair. Other ways to customize your avatar are by changing your "skin," which is the total appearance of the color of your avatar, the shape of your body, and the color of your eyes. In SL, you can find many free skins, or you may purchase one that can be customized to a photo of you. Some of the skins available for purchase are fairly expensive, so finding a free one that you like is always a good option.

Figure 2.14 shows a first-time avatar with the default appearance. She will look like a different person after some customization, which you can do by changing the appearance of your avatar. You can take time to do that now, but it will be discussed in depth in Chapter 3.

Tip

Why am I completely gray?

Being gray means that you have not "rezzed" all the way. You should wait a few minutes, and if it does not correct itself, quit (Ctrl+Q) the program and log back in.

Arriving at Help Island or Your First Community Location

Depending on your previous location selection, your avatar will arrive on a landing pad at either Help Island or the community station that you chose earlier. Watch as your avatar rezzes, or appears, in world.

Once you arrive on the landing pad, you should try to "walk" off as quickly as possible. If you stay there, other avatars will arrive on top of you. They will soon be "swimming" above your head because they will not be able to land. Please make room for the new traffic. If you look in the upper part of your screen, you will see the name of the land where you arrived. For example, in **Figure 2.15** Hululu arrived on NMC Campus West.

Figure 2.14   Initial Avatar

NMC Campus West 248, 127, 23 (Mature) - NMC Campus West - The Aho Museum

Figure 2.15   Info Bar

Once you are on the landing pad, you should use your arrow keys to walk off the pad and move around. The next part of this chapter will cover moving your avatar.

Some of the things you will find on the island on which you arrive are listed next, along with the key screens to help you with your movement.

Click on Begin (**Figure 2.16**) to learn how to do initial movement in SL.

Avatars may start to chat with you the moment you land. If you do not wish to speak with anyone, just use the following information to move to another location.

Figure 2.16   Begin Tutorial

Tip

Communication: Should you chat with anyone in Help Island? Sure, if you are comfortable doing so, and the person wants to chat with you. Also, there are avatars That act as mentors there to help you and to answer your questions.

If you would like to chat, you can do so by selecting the chat bar in the toolbar at the bottom of the SL screen, as shown in **Figure 2.17**.

Figure 2.17   Communicate

You will learn more about chatting and all the related features in Chapter 4. Help avatars usually walk around a new space to see whether you need assistance. Usually the title above the avatar's head will indicate that he or she is an assistant or is available to answer questions. You may want to chat with him or her to get tips or assistance.

Basic Movement (Walking, Flying, and Teleporting)

As you move around (**Figure 2.18**), you will get used to the keyboard and will adapt quickly.

You can also use the Alt key and your left mouse button to change your avatar's view (**Figure 2.19**).

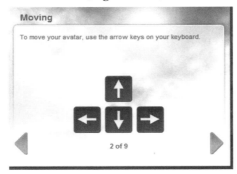

Figure 2.18   Arrow Keys

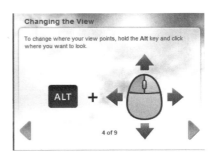

Figure 2.19   Movement

While in SL you can walk, fly, dance, and use other gestures to animate your avatar. Here are the first basic movements:

Use your arrow keys to move around in SL.

Practice moving around for a few steps. You will find that you can actually keep your fingers on the keys and move them simultaneously.

Now, let us try flying. By using the keys shown in **Table 2.2**, you can make your avatar fly through SL.

Tip

Pressing the Up arrow key twice will make your avatar run. Pressing it twice again will make your avatar walk. You can also run by pressing Ctrl+R.

Table 2.1   SL Movement

Up 	The Up arrow key makes your avatar walk forward.
↑	
Down 	The Down arrow key makes your avatar walk backward.
↓	
Left 	The Left arrow key makes your avatar walk left.
←	
Right 	The Right arrow key makes your avatar walk right.
→	

Table 2.2   Flying

Page Up 	The Page Up key makes your avatar fly up (or press and hold the "e" key).
Page Up	
Page Down	The Page Down key makes your avatar fly down (or press and hold the "c" key).
Page Down	

Figure 2.20 Fly

You will sometimes find that landing is not as graceful as you would like. There are times when you actually fall. That's OK though; your avatar will pick itself up and dust itself off. For a nice, soft landing, press the Page Down key the entire time that you are descending. You can also fly by clicking on the Fly button on the bottom toolbar of your screen, as shown in **Figure 2.20**. Chapter 4 will have more information and tips about flying.

Interesting Things to Do

While in your new orientation area, whether it be Help Island or a Community Island, there is a lot to do and see. Some areas will have changing rooms (**Figure 2.21**) (these may look different depending on the region). The changing rooms exist so that you can pick up some freebie items and perhaps try them on before you leave. Clicking on the door and walking inside will provide a private place to change your clothes.

Figure 2.21 Changing Rooms

Pick Up Some Freebies!

There are plenty of freebies on Help Island, that is, items other avatars leave for you to take without charging for them. When you see something interesting that you would like to pick up, just right-click to open the pie menu and click Buy (**Figure 2.22**).

Tip

L$0 transactions are actually deducted from your avatar's balance, but because they do not cost anything, no change is shown in your balance. These transfers are tracked so that you may have a record of them in your transaction log. To access your transaction log go to **World > Account History.** This will open an Internet browser where you will need to log in with the avatar name and password.

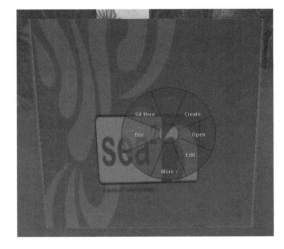

Figure 2.22 Buying

In **Figure 2.23**, this item can be purchased for 0 L$. L$ and Linden$™ are the abbreviated versions of Linden™ dollars, the SL currency. If the necklace did actually cost any L$, there would be a numerical amount in place of the "0." After you made your purchase, the cost of the item would be deducted from your avatar's balance.

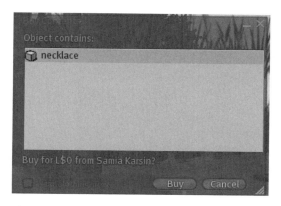

Figure 2.23   Buy a copy of a necklace

Figure 2.23 shows you what you will be purchasing. For this particular item you will receive a necklace. With some items you also receive what is known as a Landmark. You will learn more about Landmarks in Chapter 4.

Figure 2.24 shows that you are being charged 0 Linden$ for this transaction. You will learn more about Linden$ in Chapter 3: how to spend them, how to manage them, and how to give them to other avatars.

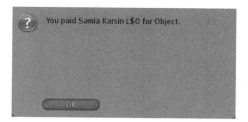

Figure 2.24   Paid

When making purchases or visiting sims, which is the name of islands in SL focused on helping new users, you should be careful of strangers that may try to pass you an object, notecard, or invitation. At this point, you should not accept anything from any avatars you do not know because you could become an unsuspecting victim of a *griefer*. A griefer is an individual who tries to negatively affect

Find an object, clothing, or tool that costs L$0 and purchase it.

your experience of the virtual world. These users may use an object with a script in it to negatively affect your avatar or your account. Feel free to chat with people and learn who they are before you accept anything. You can read more about griefers and how to handle them in Chapter 3.

Explore Your New World

Step into the world of virtual reality with your newly created avatar and begin to experience the tools that make this world interactive. This chapter will cover everything you need to know about getting through Help Island, your community, or other in-world location in SL and about moving into the rest of the virtual community.

There are a lot of places to visit in Help Island with tips and techniques for navigating through SL. As you walk around you will also see a store of freebies and exit signs that allow you to "teleport" out of Help Island. Teleporting (**Figure 2.25**) is how you move around in SL to get from one island or location to another. Click on the image, and you will see a blue box in the upper-

Figure 2.25   Teleport Signs

right corner of your screen. Keep this landmark by clicking on the "keep" button. A screen will open that has the word "Teleport" in the bottom-right corner.

If you did not go to a community, to leave Help Island, you must look for an "exit" sign (**Figure 2.26**) that will give you a landmark to the mainland. Click on the button, and you will be teleported to your next location in SL. These are chosen at random because if everyone were sent to the same place, the region would become overcrowded.

Enter
Second Life

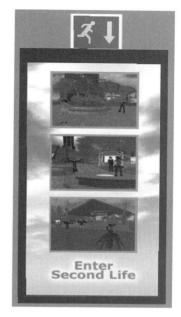

Figure 2.26 Teleport Station

In-World Communities

If you selected a community when you created your avatar, you will already be able to "search" for other islands. Here are some suggested searches (**Figures 2.27** and **2.28**) to enter so you can begin to explore your new world:

- **Vassar Island**—home of the Sistine Chapel.
- **Freebie**—a list of freebie sites to which you can teleport.

If you see a teleport that you would like to visit, left-click on its name, and you will see a screen simliar to that in **Figure 2.28**. You may then left-click the Teleport button to visit the space.

Search Second Life
All
Classifieds
Events
Showcase
Land Sales
Places
People
Groups
Back
Forward
freebie
Search
RESULTS 1 - 10 OF AB
Region: Freebie
FREEBIE WAREHOUSE 5,000+ Free FREEBIES - Est. 2006 - MLGHK.COM
Place: FREEBIE WAREHOUSE 5,000+ Free FREEBIES - Est. 2006 - MLGHK.COM. ... Freebie Drop Off Box (102, 157, 79). free. Freebie: 10 Buildings (68, 131, 87). free. ...

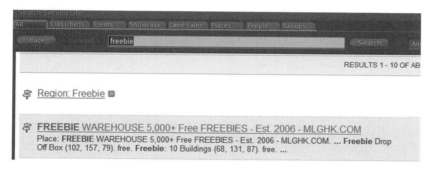

Figure 2.27 Freebies

Place: FREEBIE WAREHOUSE 5,000+ Free FREEBIES - Est. 2006 - MLGHK.COM
Category: NEWCOMER FRIENDLY
Region: Burns
HAPPY ST. PATRICK'S DAY!!! EVENT 120+ Exclusive St Patricks Day Freebie more FREE ITEMS!
Owner: Chrischun Fassbinder
Teleport

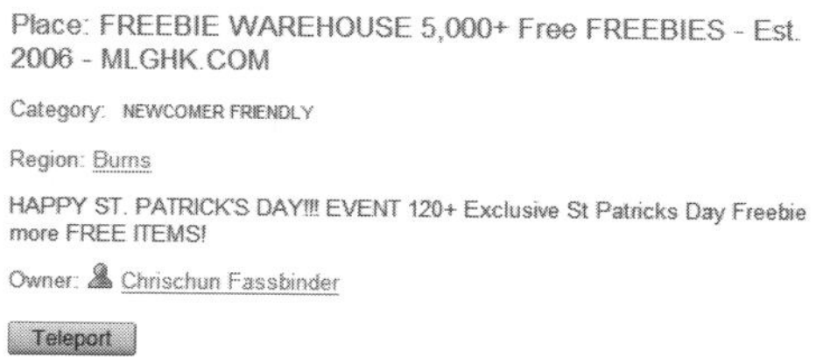

Figure 2.28 Freebie Teleports

Sloan-C is an educational island that contains material you may want to have if you plan on teaching in SL (**Figure 2.29**).

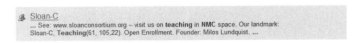

Figure 2.29   Sloan-C

Figure 2.30   The Teaching 8 Region

Teleporting

We briefly mentioned teleporting earlier; it is the ability to instantly move from region to region or space to space within SL. This is a feature in SL that is like *Star Trek*'s "Beam me up, Scotty" to the *Enterprise*. You can teleport to different locations around SL. If you bring up the search box and type a place in the box, SL will do a search (**Figure 2.30**), and if it is a parcel of land that you can visit, there will be a Teleport button.

Teleporting to Teaching 8 will bring you close to the SEA^2 land, where the authors of this book own land. If you would like to go directly to our teaching tools, you should use this SLURL: http://slurl.com/secondlife/Teaching%208/227/102/23.

Figure 2.31   SEA^2 Land

Map

Another way of locating places in SL is with the Map feature. Click on the Map button in the bottom toolbar, and the map will open for you with a menu on the right-hand side (**Figure 2.32**).

Figure 2.32   Map

Type "Teaching 8" in the search bar on the map menu, and you will see the region show up in the Search Results area. Clicking Teleport here will take you to the landing pad of Teaching 8 (**Figure 2.33**).

Other features on the map (**Figure 2.34**) are the icons that represent information you will see on the map from time to time. These are in the right-hand corner of the map: Person (a green dot on the map represents an avatar on the map), Infohub, Telehub, Land for Sale, etc. The symbols beside the word indicate what the symbols represent on the map.

Figure 2.33   Map Search

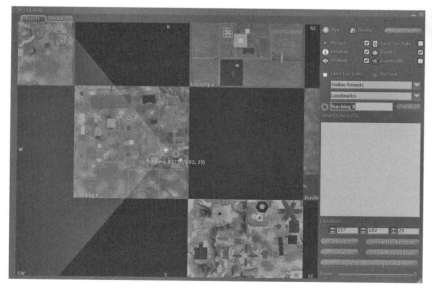

Figure 2.34   Map Light

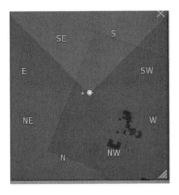

Figure 2.35   Mini-Map

Mini-Map

The mini-map will appear on the upper right-hand side of the SL screen. You can use it to get a good view of the island, to see whether there are other avatars on the island, and to see their general location (**Figure 2.35**).

Click on the Mini-Map icon (**Figure 2.36**) at the bottom of the screen in the toolbar, and you will see the map appear on the right side of the screen. You can also move it around by left-clicking on your mouse and by holding it while you move it around.

Figure 2.36   Mini-Map Search

The World Is Your Oyster—Exploring Second Life

Once you teleport off Help Island, you can explore any land you find intriguing. One way of finding a desired location is by using the Search Toolbar (**Figure 2.37**). By clicking on the search button on the bottom toolbar, or even by accessing it in the upper right-hand corner of your menu bar, you will be able to type in keywords to define the parameters of your search. The search button can be used to take you to different regions in SL as discussed before, and to search for other avatars, events, groups, etc.

Figure 2.37   SL Search

Searching for other avatars will become fun for you as well as beneficial. You will meet many avatars along your journey who will become not only your friends but also mentors as you learn the dynamic world of SL. Searching for friends, groups, and other locations is covered in more depth in Chapter 4 (**Figure 2.38**).

As you explore SL you will find a vast array of information, friends, social communities, and most of all a shared interest in learning. There is a wealth of information in this world, and we think you should take advantage of every resource.

Figure 2.38   Search Results

Avatar Groups and Friends

Avatars can belong to different groups and can be "friends" with other avatars. The advantages of adding others as friends is that you can see when they are online and that you can teleport them to your location quite easily. You can also give them some of your "inventory" or Linden$, as well as allow them to have full access to any objects you place down or build in world.

To add a person as your friend, you have to right-click on your avatar and view the pie menu (**Figure 2.39**). This menu will show you different choices for your avatar such as creating new Friends and joining new Groups. In the next image you will see that Samia Karsin belongs to SEA[2], which is the group we created for this book (**Figure 2.40**). You will also belong to SEA[2] if you would like to obtain some of our SL tools and educational material. Unless you are the one who created the group, you must be invited by other owners of the group or request to be invited. As you visit different places in SL, members of groups will ask you to join through an automatic invitation on their land or by personal selection.

There is also a Friends tab (**Figure 2.41**) for adding your friends. Clicking on that tab brings up a list of your friends. You can right-click on other avatars and ask them to be your friend, a request they must accept to complete the transaction.

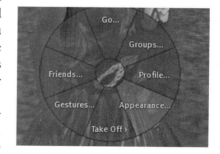

Figure 2.39   Group of Friends

Figure 2.40   Contacts

Figure 2.41   Friends

Using the Communicate feature, you have to search for them and add them as a friends. If they are not in world at the time, they will see the request when they log in. You can see that Samia has two friends at the time of this writing. There is so much more to learn about adding friends. Check out Chapter 4 for more information.

As educators, we are all aware that technology hardware and software can change faster than print in a book. Therefore the authors of this book would like to offer access to continuously updated tutorials for joining SL at SEA[2] located at http://slurl.com/secondlife/Teaching%208/246/114/23.

Wrap-Up

Keywords/Definitions:

Avatar—the virtual entity that represents a user in a virtual world
Synonyms: agent

Chat—the method of communication that avatars use to converse; can be either text or voice

Client—the SL program that is installed on the end user's account upon account verification; it is the portal through which a resident will login into the SL virtual world

Communities—special-interest sims that new users can choose to begin their journey in SL

Default avatar—one of the twelve generic avatars that a user may choose from during account creation

Freebies—objects such as clothing, furniture, or cars that any user may pick up for a minimal price ranging from L$0 to L$10

Fly—the action that an avatar performs when a user presses the Page Up/Page Down or the E/C keys on the keyboard

In world—the term used to describe the act of being logged into SL

Pie menu—the circular wheel menu that is accessed when an avatar right-clicks on an object, land, or another avatar

Resident—the generic name for a Second Life user

Rezz—to create or materialize in world

SL name (Second Life name)—the handle that is unique to a user's avatar; it is composed of a chosen first name combined with a last name picked from a generated list

Teleport—the act of instantly moving from one area of SL to another area of SL; can occur across sims or on the same region

Terms of Service (TOS)—A list of rules that every SL user must abide by

Walk—the action that an avatar performs when the directional keys or the ASWD keys are pressed on the user's keyboard

URLs to Helpful Information and Tutorials

SEA[2]—http://sites.google.com/site/sea2sl
NMC Second Life—http://www.nmc.org/keyword/second-life
SLOAN-C Why Teach in Second Life—http://www.sloan-c.org/node/1571

Customizing the New You and Your First Home

Customizing Your New Avatar

By now you are aware of the items in your Library inventory, and you may have collected more free items that are specifically for use with your avatar. These items are what you will use to change the appearance of your persona. This is where you really get to have some fun, be creative, and make the virtual you better. To do that, you will probably need some Linden™ dollars (Linden$). Linden$ is a form of money in SL™. It is used to purchase anything from clothes, hair, textures, and furniture to a variety of other objects. Although a great deal of these items are available free of charge, there are times when spending Linden$ will enhance your avatar, land, classroom, presentation area, and teaching.

Linden Dollars (Linden$)

To customize your avatar, your land, your classroom, or training room, it may be necessary to purchase Linden$. With Linden$ you can purchase land that can house your educational classroom, your personal store, or anything you desire. Linden dollars are the official method of payment and purchase that you use within SL to acquire items such as objects and clothing. Avatars can trade Linden$ whether they are purchased in American dollars, Euros, or other forms of currency.

Example: At the current time the exchange rate of Linden$ is 250 Linden dollars (L$) to the U.S. dollar.

Linden$ can be purchased on the Linden Lab site as well as other sites that trade money, such as the following:

http://www.ffxi-gil.net/SecondLife/Main-Server/Buy-Second-Life-Linden-USD.html

http://wiki.secondlife.com/wiki/L%24_Marketplace

https://secure-web6.secondlife.com/account/index.php?lang=en

https://secure-web6.secondlife.com/currency/index.php (click on the word "Buy")

Here you will be required to enter your method of payment and how many Linden$ you would like to purchase. Be aware that you will be charged a fixed fee of $0.30 per transaction regardless of the amount of L$ you purchase. If you have a basic avatar, you are allowed to purchase only a certain amount of Linden currency each day, depending on which grid you are in—the Teen Grid or the Adult Grid. You must first set up your account in Linden Lab, which includes putting in your credit card or PayPal™ information.

While in world, go to **World > Manage My Account** and click Go to open a browser window in SL (**Figure 3.1**).

Figure 3.1 Media Browser

Type in your avatar's first name and last name and your current password, then click on Submit. Another window will open that shows your current account information.

You will need to set up your account by clicking on Update Billing Information (**Figure 3.2**). Click on the appropriate option depending on what type of account you would like to set up. Your choices are a credit card or PayPal transaction. Follow the screen choices and fill out your information. Now every

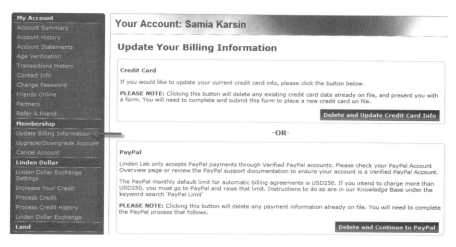

Figure 3.2   Account Info

Figure 3.3   Linden Exchange

time you make a transaction it will be processed to this account. If you need to update this information, return to this same screen.

Look for the information you see in **Figure 3.3**, and click Linden Dollar Exchange Settings.

For now on the next screen click on **Basic > Submit** and the following screen will appear. (**Figure 3.4**) You can now click on Buy L$.

About the LindeX™ Exchange

The LindeX™ is a Linden dollar exchange offering residents of Second Life the ability to either buy or sell Linden dollars. Charges are for purchasing Linden dollars and are placed on the same form of payment you have setup in your account settings for your Second Life account. If you have a credit on your US$ account balance that credit will be applied first. Prices at this site are set by the market price - I.E. the best price offered by the different sellers of Linden dollars.

For information about the LindeX exchange and billing transaction limits please click here

Figure 3.4   Buy and Sell

Figure 3.5 shows the screen on which to enter the quantity of Linden currency you wish to purchase in order to complete your transaction. The Linden$ will be delivered to your avatar.

There are limits to how many Linden dollars you can trade in a day, based on the account type

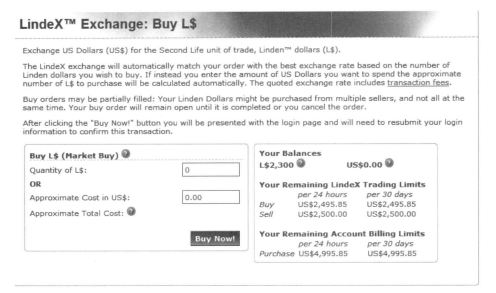

Figure 3.5   Exchange

that you have. Avatars in the Teen Grid are more limited than those in the Adult Grid. You will find the limits on your Exchange screen for your personal avatar. If you would like to see all the limits, you may visit https://secure-web20.secondlife.com/currency/describe-limits.php.

I think the limit chart can be quite misleading. I have had my work avatar for more than a year, but when I recently logged onto the Linden$ Exchange, my avatar was listed as having the purchasing power of only a Day 1 resident! I was very confused and curious, so I decided to research this phenomenon. Apparently, the "age" the Linden$ Exchange uses is the age you were when you made your **first** billing transaction—not your actual rezz day. Because my work avatar never purchased any Linden$ directly, the Exchange thinks she's still on Day 1. So if you want or think you'll need a higher purchasing limit, you should definitely start now.

From now on, since your account is set up, you can purchase Linden$ in world. Just follow these basic instructions:

Click on World at the top of the Toolbar in SL while you are in world (**Figure** 3.6). Then click Buy L$. The following screen will appear (**Figure** 3.7).

Figure 3.7   Currency

Figure 3.6   World

On the next screen (**Figure** 3.8) click OK, and your transaction will be processed. Originally Samia Karsin had L$1,300, and she now has L$2,300, as shown in Figure 3.7, and the cost was US$4.15.

Tip

You can also get to the buy screen by clicking on your L$ balance in the top-right corner of your client.

Figure 3.8   Transaction

Figure 3.9   Linden Dollars

This amount shows up in the upper right-corner hand, where you can visually track your Linden$ spending as well (**Figure 3.9**).

Other avatars can also give you Linden$ in world, but you can earn Linden$ by "camping out," too. There are many sites in SL where you can sit in a chair or perform some type of action such as take a survey to earn more Linden$. Usually the amount of Linden$ paid out is minimal, but it is enough to get you an outfit, a script, or a new tool for class.

There are so many freebies in SL that you do not always need to purchase Linden$ to acquire items and tools. However, to build your environment, Linden$ will be necessary to upload textures. Uploading a texture in SL will cost you L$10. This is a small price to pay to personalize your area and objects.

Your account settings in SL will enable you to trade quickly and efficiently. There is also a Transaction History where you can look at all the transactions your avatar made for the lifetime of your account.

Selling Linden$

Linden Lab will also sell your dollars for you on LindeX™ (**Figure 3.10**).

About the LindeX™ Exchange

The LindeX™ is a Linden dollar exchange offering residents of Second Life the ability to either buy or sell Linden dollars. Charges are for purchasing Linden dollars and are placed on the same form of payment you have setup in your account settings for your Second Life account. If you have a credit on your US$ account balance that credit will be applied first. Prices at this site are set by the market price - I.E. the best price offered by the different sellers of Linden dollars.

For information about the LindeX exchange and billing transaction limits please click here

Figure 3.10   LindeX™

Click on Sell L$, and you will see another transaction screen to sell your Linden$. Remember: There are transactions going on worldwide in SL; it has become a business for many of its residents. Currently $1.6 million is traded daily in SL, and you can get current economic statistics from http://secondlife.com/statistics/economy-data.php.

Uses for Linden Dollars

Some of the items you can purchase with your Linden$ include the following:

- Textures
- Clothes
  - Shoes
  - Shirts
  - Pants
  - Dresses/skirts
  - Jackets
  - Swimsuits
- Objects
  - Exercise equipment
- Furniture
- Paintings
- Fruit
- Plants
- Rocks
- Scripts
- Sounds
- Skins
- Body parts

These items will help you customize your avatar, help you build your space no matter how large or how small, and give you a more personal feeling about your SL experience.

Buying Guide for Your Avatar
Freebies for Your Avatar

The Bazaar Free Stuff
  http://slurl.com/secondlife/Stillman/146/90/23

The Free Dove
  http://slurl.com/secondlife/Gallii/113/53/33

Iwo Jima
  http://slurl.com/secondlife/Iwo%20Jima/224/96/36

NMC
  http://slurl.com/secondlife/Learning/169/176/24

Gnubie Store
  http://slurl.com/secondlife/Powder%20Mill/121/142/34

SL is an open world with a lot of different cultures and personalities involved. There are times you would like to collect some "fun" things and times when you need professional clothing and objects. Here are some spaces to find different kinds of attire.

QUENTIN Professional Clothes
  http://slurl.com/secondlife/Alpha%20Centauri/8/46/28

StarSong Business Suits and Business Wear
http://slurl.com/secondlife/Liberty%20Central%20N/231/80/51

Marzipan's Closet
http://slurl.com/secondlife/Poidor/222/170/133

Buying Clothes, Objects, Scripts

One of the best ways to customize your avatar and space is to purchase objects, clothes, scripts, and other items. In Chapter 2 we briefly mentioned buying items or picking up freebies. Get ready to expand your SL experience as we cover this topic more thoroughly.

There are several ways to purchase items within SL. Some of your options include in-world purchase and SL Exchange.

To purchase in world you can teleport to many locations where creators make their objects available for free or for Linden$. Using the search feature, you can find lands that are relevant to your topic and item. Teleport to these locations, walk or fly around, and discover the wealth of objects that avatars have placed there for your use. Doing so is especially beneficial if you purchase items such as presentation screens, movie projectors, training items, and customization for your space. You will find out more about the use of all these items in Chapter 4.

Once you find an object you would like to own, you have to right-click on it when you are in world. This step will open the pie menu that has several choices. In **Figure 3.11** the pie menu indicates that you can buy this flower. When you click on the item it will appear highlighted. This highlighting helps you make sure you selected the correct item. If there are several items around, you might want to click on Edit and look in the General tab to ensure that the name of the object is the object of your intent.

Figure 3.12 shows the buy dialog of the tiger lily flower. Take note that the dialog mentions that

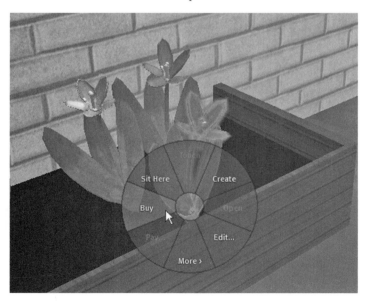

Figure 3.11   Pie Menu

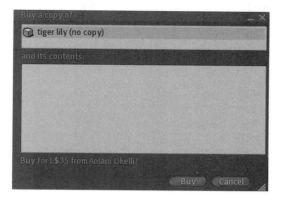

Figure 3.12   Prim Object

the object does not allow copy rights. Items that you pick up in world have different permissions. The creators can set these permissions to allow you to transfer items to other avatars, to copy the item, or to modify the item. They can also edit the permissions to make sure that you cannot perform these functions. Disallowing these permissions is a useful tactic to protect the creator's intellectual property rights and profits. If you plan to supplement your income from a business in SL, it is wise to pay attention to these permissions.

The Buy dialog will always display the price of the object and will tell you which avatar placed it for sale. Returning to Figure 3.12, you can see that this particular item cost L$35 and the avatar who is selling it is Aolani Okelli. To complete the transaction, click on the Buy button, and SL will put the item in your inventory. SL also sends a confirmation notice (**Figure 3.13**) that details the name of the item you bought, whom you paid, and how much it cost.

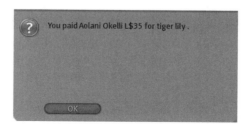

Figure 3.13   Payment

Tip

It is a good idea to write down what you purchase as you go along. Managing your inventory can become cumbersome, and if you purchase a lot of objects during a day, you may forget the name of what you purchased. Some items are named appropriately and others may have a tag name or shorter description.

In **Figure 3.13**, you can see that the object cost L$35, which the purchaser paid to Aolani Okelli.

Now that you have the object in your inventory, you need to check to be sure it arrived. Open your inventory by clicking on the Inventory button in the bottom right of your screen. Once the inventory window is open, type a keyword from the object's name in the search bar, and it will pull up any item you possess that contains that keyword. In **Figure 3.14**, you can see that the buyer would type "tiger lily" to find the flower she bought.

Figure 3.15 shows a purchase of avatar hair. This gives you a good example that one purchase may contain multiple objects. Some bundled packages can contain pieces of the

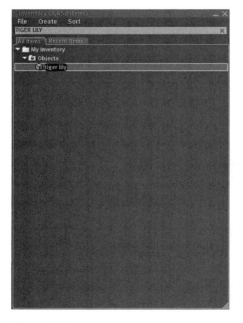

Figure 3.14   Inventory

Figure 3.15   Buy Contents

same object that must be combined for the total product, whereas other packages just offer different options. For instance, this item offers different hair colors and instructions on how to wear the hair. At times there is even a landmark, so you can return to the region where you purchased the item. All of the listed items are put into your inventory once you complete your purchase. This particular item is L$195, which is still not a bad price when converted to US$.

You can immediately wear the product if you like, but because there are so many objects, it is best to put it into your inventory and then select the color you would like to wear.

As soon as you purchase an item, the Linden$ will be deducted from your account. You will see the transactions in the window on the top right of your SL screen. When you are shopping you may sometimes encounter an object that does not give you the Buy dialog box. Instead, you will see Pay or Fast Pay. These are two other sales transactions that you may encounter that are intended to simplify the buying process. The Pay dialog will have the listed prices and box for you to input your payment.

The Fast Pay dialog will provide you with one or more buttons from which to choose. These buttons will list the amount of Linden$ you agree to pay.

Regardless of whether the vendor presents you with a Buy dialog, a Pay dialog, or a Fast Pay dialog, you will always receive a confirmation notice in the upper right-hand corner of your screen.

Educational Tools

Educational tools are an important part of making sure your classroom space is set up for the optimal learning experience. Learn more about which tools to buy in Chapter 12.

Appearance

Your avatar's appearance is an important part of making the entire SL experience feel more personal. As you begin to use SL more frequently, you will really want a representation of yourself. Whether you choose to be a fox, a cat, a gamer, a winged creature, or just a close version of your real self, the avatar you choose makes you feel like you are walking, talking, and making new friends in both another dimension and in real life. Several studies concerning this topic have been carried out. You can locate some of them at http://wiki.secondlife.com/wiki/Other_Second_Life_Studies.

Let us continue work on the new you that you began in Chapter 2. Right-click on your avatar, and the pie menu will appear with several selections (**Figure 3.16**). Click on Appearance, and your avatar will spin around to "face" you, and you can see its front. The Appearance window (**Figure 3.17**) has many details that you can adjust to customize yourself, and doing so can take some time. Remember, you can always save what you

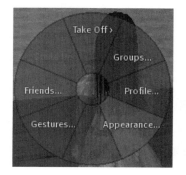

Figure 3.16 Appearance

Figure 3.17   Edit Appearance

have done and come back to it later. In fact, you might make adjustments daily such as changing your hair color, shirt color, nail color, the size of your feet, and your body fat.

As you explore SL, notice the different personalities and representations of "self" you come across. Remember, each avatar you come in contact with has a person on the back end. It is your decision whether to trust the person behind

Whenever I do training, one of the first things I do is have people create their avatar. It is always amazing to see how much time people want to put into changing their clothes and hair. Usually time is limited and there are so many things to do, but I have learned to schedule at least 30–45 minutes for letting students personalize their new personas.

Getting "ruthed," or altered in appearance, is quite common. While writing this chapter, Samia was "ruthed" and had to take off the object that changed the avatar. Fixing it is sometimes as easy as just removing a skin that has been placed on you or a tattoo. Sometimes it is a bit more difficult, but there are fixes—so do not despair if you look a bit strange at times.

the avatar and make him or her a friend or to add the person to your group. However, there are other avatars in SL that are placed there for your convenience. These avatars are called "bots" and are put on a space to be greeters or to pass out general information in the form of notecards.

Once you click on Appearance, the window appears (Figure 3.17).

This screen gives you information about your skin and allows you to make changes. For instance, Samia has on a "Jaimee" shape called "Eclipse." This is also where you select a female or male shape if you would like to change from the original avatar you selected. For any selection, move the sliders back and forth and watch the alterations as they occur. After you are happy with the changes, you can save them. You can also save your avatar selections to your Inventory by clicking "Save As" and giving them a name. Doing so creates a new avatar skin that you can keep and put back on anytime you need to refresh or retrieve it. A great example of why you would need this saved skin is that when your avatar gets "ruthed," you can easily return to your previous appearance. Being "ruthed" is when something gets put on your avatar that alters its appearance in a negative fashion.

The following is a list of the items you see on the screen and a brief description of what you can do under each tab.

All these selections change the shape, height, thickness, size, length, and other general features of your

---

Tip

The size of your feet actually affects the way your shoes fit on your avatar. If your shoes do not look right, come back to this selection and change the size of your feet.

avatar. They all work about the same way, by moving the slider under along the scale. Change the following:

Body parts

Body	Mouth	Face detail
Head	Chin	Makeup
Eyes	Torso	Body detail
Ears	Legs	Hair
Nose	Skin	

> **Tip**
>
> Shirt is one of the selections you will use often because quite a few shirts are very short waisted. This enables you to make your shirt longer and a bit more professional looking.

> **Tip**
>
> Undershirt and underpants are one of the few garments we recommend that female and male avatars keep on at all times–if you desire a professional look.

Your avatar usually arrives with hair that you can alter through the appearance menu. As hair is purchased for your avatar, this hair will be minimized to a scalp or bald head, and few of these changes will work. The beauty of SL is that you can change your hair, eyes, and appearance whenever you like.

Clothes

Shirt	Gloves
Pants	Undershirt
Shoes	Underpants
Socks	Skirt
Jacket	

Have some fun with your avatar, and make the changes that you feel personalize the avatar. You will soon find that you are protective of this persona and may even be a bit more daring than with your own appearance.

I have been in a few situations where I was trying to alter my shirt in front of a group of other avatars. Here again is a word of caution, as we mentioned earlier; this is not always a wise thing to do. I did not have an undershirt on and was adjusting my collar and midriff. This exposed some "skin" I would not normally show.

Profile

You can find the profile section by right-clicking on your avatar and choosing Profile from the pie menu. Your profile holds information about your avatar as well as about your real life—if you choose to provide it. It shows your avatar's "rezz day," or birth date, which informs other users of how long you have been using SL (**Figure 3.18**). You can also click on another avatar and choose his or her profile selection to find out information about this person.

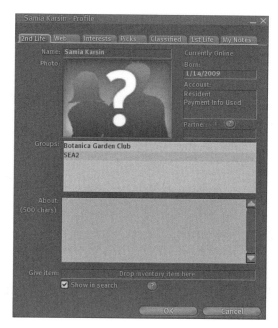

Figure 3.18   The "2nd Life" Screen

If you would like everyone to see a picture of your avatar, upload it under the 2nd Life tab. SL generates your group list here, but in the "About" section you may enter your likes and dislikes or whatever you want to share with another individual. Figure 3.18 shows you a profile without a picture. Simply click on the image and pick a texture you would like to upload as your photo.

You can also upload your RL picture under the tab 1st Life and put information in here about what you do in RL such as your job, organization, and interests (**Figure 3.19**).

Figure 3.19   The "1st Life" Screen

Some people have duplicate avatars, so even though the birth date of their avatar is young in SL days, you may find as you chat with them that they seem more experienced.

When approached by an avatar, the first thing I do is right-click on the avatar and check out the profile. Even if it has limited information, you still feel a little more comfortable talking to this person if you see the groups he or she is associated with and perhaps some of his or her interests.

The next tab is the Web (**Figure 3.20**), where you can put a website that is associated with your avatar, company, institution, or whatever you choose. Type in the URL of the website in the space provided. If you do not have a website or do not want anything displayed in here, you can simply leave it blank.

Click on the word Load, and the website will load (**Figure 3.21**) into the window after you click Go. Clicking on the dropdown arrow brings up two other selections, which will load the website in an external screen or to return to the profile website if you have navigated away.

The next tab is the Interests tab. It is where you can select items you would like to share with others, to use to build in SL, or to sell in SL. You can also click

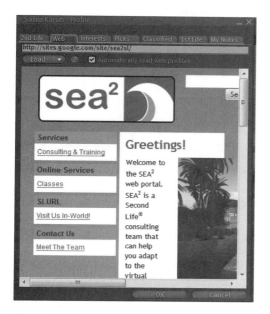

Figure 3.20   Web

Figure 3.21   Web Load

on your skill set, which will give other avatars an idea of how experienced you are in this virtual world. Many avatars do not put anything in here, but if you are looking for someone with experience in SL or in a particular occupation, you may find it listed here. For instance, if you needed a builder for SL, checking someone's Interests tab might provide that information.

One of the most informative tabs is the "Picks" tab, which tells everyone about your favorite places in SL. All this information is specifically for other avatars to see and browse so that they may get to know more about you.

The Classified tab enables you to place an ad in SL's classified listing. Clicking on New enables you to put your ad on the SL Classified section, but there is a fee for this service. You will be asked for a price upon clicking "publish." If you pay for this activity, your ad will appear in the Search feature of SL, which is located on the bottom of the SL client in the toolbar.

The next tab is where you can store your 1st Life information. Put as much as you would like to share here, but remember that others can read it. If you do not wish for other avatars to know who you are, then you should leave this blank. SL is a social place, and you may find that you are more comfortable giving others information here than on other social spaces such as Facebook®, Twitter®, or MySpace®.

The tab with My Notes is the final tab, and you are not allowed to write things here on your own avatar. However, if you select someone else's profile to view by right-clicking on the avatar, you can make notes about that person. These notes are only for you, and you may put any information that you would like to remember about that avatar. The next time you see the avatar, you can look at the My Notes, and your note will appear.

> In the My Notes section I usually put an avatar's real-life name if I know it. It becomes a bit confusing when you have so many avatar friends and some names can be similar. It is quite helpful to put someone's RL name and organizational information here. After you have been in SL for a bit, it is common to be remembered by only the avatar name. Even in RL, I have a hard time remembering RL names and have introduced people as their avatar name.

After changing each selection, simply, click OK, and all your changes will be there. The profile is a useful tool, and you should use it to make SL a bit more personal for yourself.

Now that we have personalized your avatar, it is time to find out how to personalize and build your land. We will cover many topics here, and we will expand on those topics in Chapter 9.

Buying Land after You Purchase Linden$

Did you know you can purchase or rent land in SL? All the estates and islands you visit are owned by individuals, corporations, universities, and/or groups. Anyone can use their Linden$ to purchase real estate in SL by fractions of 1/4, 1/8, 1/2, 3/4, or by a full sim or parcel. You can also purchase virtual real estate through your normal purchasing channels for your company or university. Once you purchase or rent, you become the manager of a sim. This gives you certain rights on the space you rent or own. If you buy land from Linden Lab, it will remain yours until you release it. There are some additional fees that come with buying land, depending on what type of account you have. Renting is a great way to check out the region and to be sure it is where you want to call home. It is advantageous for institutions or educational entities to rent. There are other groups to purchase land from, or you can also pick it up on eBay or another resell location. Just do a search in a search engine browser on "resold SL sims" or "rental in SL."

See http://secondlife.com/land for more information.

I'm Not Ready to Commit—Is There a Free Place for Me to Call Home?

The SL community is very open and usually shares information, resources, and space. Before you invest in land, you can also ask whether there is a space someone else owns that you can use for a short time. This approach enables you to practice in SL and to estimate how much land you might need for your project. Public sandboxes are popular in SL and can be located on various sims throughout the grid. Sandboxes are spaces where you can practice building. These parcels are usually set so that anything you build will be returned in your inventory within any increment of time that the parcel owner designates.

> ### Tip
>
> When building in a sandbox, it is important to take a copy of your work into your inventory. When the parcel returns it, you should find it in your Lost and Found folder, but it may end up in pieces. If it is something you really want to keep, just right-click on the object and select Take in the pie menu. You can always return to this sandbox and build on that same object again.

In some sandboxes you are allowed to test-run scripts in an object, but like the building feature, that setting is managed by the owner of the parcel. These areas are also usually a good place to make some contacts and to ask questions. There are a lot of building shortcuts you can find by simply reaching out to others.

sea^2

If you have a parcel or sim, practice making your own sandbox. You will find more information about this in Chapter 9.

Freebies for Your Home

With the open community in SL, there are always items known as "freebies," which you have learned about in the previous chapters. Some of these freebies will be useful in building your space. Browse your inventory and see the wealth of items you may have already collected, or go to the following freebie spaces to find them and pick them up. Furniture, buildings, plants, trees, scripts, and other objects are all readily available. It is wise to use some of these; trying to create all your own objects can feel overwhelming. It is also a great way to see how others built their objects because you can inspect the object to see how many prims the creator used, whether the build is made of linked objects, what texture was used, and whether the object uses any scripts. Sometimes the scripts and similar information are locked, but knowing the scripts helps you better understand what is possible.

Setting Your Home Position

Orientation to SL space and finding a home can be important. It seems only natural that we all have a point of reference. This reference is your SL home, which can be the parcel you own or a favorite public space. To set your home position, go to **World > Set Home to Here**. Now every time you log in to SL, you can set your preferences to arrive at your home. If you visit other areas, you can also press Ctrl+Shift+H on your keyboard to return to your home. You can Set Home to Here only if you own the land or belong to the group associated with that land.

> I have been to several spaces that I found uncomfortable and wanted to teleport out quickly. If you have your home set, instead of searching for another landmark or struggling with your inventory, press Ctrl+Shift+H and be teleported immediately back to your safe haven. Once I searched for something quite simple and ended up in a place with avatars who were pretty aggressive. It was so nice to take my avatar out of this situation quickly.

Estate Management—Managing Your Space and Changes to Make to Prepare your Land for Building

In the previous section, you learned a bit about purchasing land. We will now explain in greater detail the advantages and disadvantages of owning and renting as well as how you manage your own space.

There are actually several ways to divide out land in SL. One is through a region, and the other is through different sizes of parcels. Region owners have more control over their space. Parcels give you some options but not others. In the next section, you will learn what those options are, and this may help you decide what type of space you should purchase or rent.

Region versus Parcel

A region is an entire island that is 256 m × 256 m, or 65,536 square meters, and each region has an allotment of 15,000 prims.

A parcels is a portion of the island that varies in size but always stays below 256 m × 256 m, or 65,536 square meters. SEA[2] (http://slurl.com/secondlife/

Teaching%208/234/107/23) is a parcel on the Region of Teaching 8 that is actually owned by an organization known as the New Media Consortium. It sits on a little more than 6% of the region at 4,095 square meters.

Parcels receive a portion of the 15,000-prim allotments. SEA[2]'s limit is 937 prims—also a little more than 6% of the region's allotment.

As with everything else in SL, it is easy to control your region or parcel with some of the menu options. To see the Region/Estate window, go to **World > Region/Estate** to see the tabs you can set depending on your status on the region.

Following is an explanation of the items you will see under the Region/Estate feature.

Region

As you can see in **Figure 3.22**, most of the areas under Region are grayed out. This is because we are only the owners of the parcel, SEA[2], not the region, Teaching 8. But, you can see that it is an Estate/Full Region; the region is Teaching 8. Only the owner can set the items seen here.

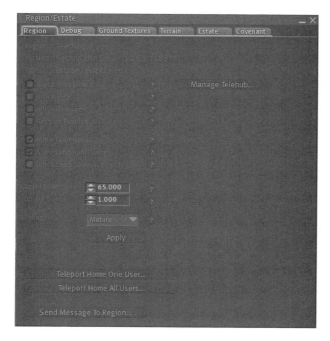

Figure 3.22   Region/Estate

The titles at the top give the region information such as the name of the region; the version; which server the region is on with Linden Lab; and the type, which is Estate/Full Region. An explanation of the other menu items is follows.

Block Terraform

Terraforming is how you sculpt the land. You can make land similar to your own geographic area, such as making it resemble a beach or a mountain area. This process involves raising and lowering the land as well as selecting texture you put on the land to give it a more 3-D appearance. Terraforming is covered more thoroughly in Chapter 9.

An alternative to in-world land editing is to upload raw files. You can create these files in an outside program such as Adobe Photoshop. Using this method, many developers can make a quick transition between land forms. In-world terraforming can be a long process. As a land owner you may find that the work you put into terraforming can be destroyed in moments by griefers or oblivious new users. Fortunately, you can block terraforming completely by performing the following simple steps:

1. Go to **World > Region/Estate** in the Menu bar.
2. Click on the Region tab.
3. On the left side there is a box titled "Block Terraform" that you can toggle to turn terraforming on and off.

Manage Telehub

Controlling where your visitors appear on a region can be important. You can control where visitors appear with two basic approaches. You can either make all your visitors teleport to a preset location, or you can have them teleport wherever they wish on your space. **Figure 3.23** shows the selection for setting

Figure 3.23   Telehub

your Telehub. The following settings are applied to an object you place on your region.

To connect your telehub you should carry out the following steps:

1. Right-click on the object and select Edit.
2. In the Region/Estate window, click the Region tab that you see in Figure 3.22.
3. Click Manage Telehub.
4. Click Add Spawn.
5. Click your telehub object again, and click Connect Telehub.

> ### Tip
>
> Using a telehub means that you must disable Allow Direct Teleport on the Estate tab of the Region/ Estate window because it will interfere with the telehub. You must also clear any Landing Points that might be set for the parcels on your Estate. You will learn how to set these further on in this chapter. Also, if you choose to allow direct teleporting, you cannot use a telehub and must remove any object you placed on your estate for that purpose.

Block Fly

Avatars will not be able to fly to this region if this option is checked. You might use this setting if you are having a conference and do not want people flying over each other.

Allow Damage

This option runs a health system on the island that allows avatars to enable damage objects to affect them regardless of parcel settings. Damage objects are ones with scripts that can bump into other avatars or other objects.

Restrict Pushing

This setting disallows pushing from any object set to group. Yes, an avatar can actually push an object off of your region or parcel. You will see a message that your object has been sent off world or that it has been returned to your inventory.

Allow Land Resell

This setting allows an owner to resell the land to another avatar or group. If you rented your land, you will not see this option. These transactions can take place in world, through a transaction website or on eBay.

Allow Land Join/Divide

This option allows the region to be parceled out so that an owner or group-owned piece can be divided. You can divide a region into as many smaller parcels as you wish. The advantage to this setting is that it allows you to show various videos or to set permissions per parcel. With the standard SL options, you are allowed only one video per parcel.

Block Land Show in Search

This setting blocks owners from showing their land in the search menu.

Agent Limit

This region is set to allow 65 avatars simultaneously. This is usually set at a default of 40, and most people do not change this. If you allow more than 40, you can have serious lag time, and other avatars will have a negative experience. However, if you are going to be sitting still and not doing a lot of moving, such as hosting a conference, it is wise to bump this number up to allow a certain number of visitors.

Object Bonus

This option deals with the prims that are allowed on any given parcel. The default is 1.0, and unless you are familiar with Region settings, you should not change this because it may cause objects to be returned or deleted.

Rating

Adult, Mature, and PG are the selections under the rating scale. At the time of the writing of this book, there is much discussion on what regions should be rated, where they should be located in the great scheme of regions, and how to handle certain content. Educators in particular are concerned that their voices will not be heard and that their regions will be placed among the masses and not given a specific area. Mature content is a pretty general category given to a lot of educators. There is also talk of making an "Adult" section for places that have some type of sexual reference or objects. If you would like to keep up on what is happening with ratings, join one of the list-server discussion groups on http://secondlife.com.

Teleport Home One User

Choosing this option is the same as Kick User From Estate, and when you do so you must type in the name of the user and do a search. You have to get the name exactly right, and then it will teleport that user home.

Teleport Home All Users

All avatars will be teleported home if you select this option.

Send Message to Region

Any avatars on the Region will receive a message. It is best to do this by group settings, though, and to send a message to a group if you own a large region.

Debug

This setting is controlled by the owner.

- **Disable Scripts**—this would disable any objects from having interactivity set by scripts. For instance, if you have an object that is a "greeter," the greeter will stop chatting to others not in your group if you disable scripts.
- **Disable Collisions**—the default would be "off" for this selection, which will prevent objects from colliding and perhaps will help with poor performance on the sim. For example, if you have objects that move and bump into each other, this action would stop if you selected Disable Collisions.
- **Disable Physics**—this setting will be one you do not want to use unless all others fail. This will stop objects from colliding but will also stop avatar movement. Potentially it could be a negative experience.

Source: http://wiki.secondlife.com/wiki/Estate_Tools_test.

Object Return

Figure 3.24 shows how you can have any object returned that you do not wish to be on your Estate and how you can control others regarding objects.

Figure 3.24   Object Return

Residents

You can select an avatar name, and you can return all objects belonging to that avatar within the entire estate. This helps if you have a griefer who is wreaking havoc on your space.

Options

These settings allow you to "hone" your selections and are self-descriptive:

- Return only those objects with scripts
- Return only those objects on someone else's land
- Return objects in every region of this estate

Figure 3.25 shows you some of the other selections.

Figure 3.25   Collide

Get Top Colliders

This choice will give you a list of the objects that are experiencing potential collisions.

Get Top Scripts

This setting will give you a list of all the scripted objects, the name of the object, the owner, and the location.

Restart Region

Only Region owners can perform this action. The region will restart after a two-minute warning, and all residents will be disconnected. One should do this only when directed, by Linden Lab.

Ground Textures

Let us move on to Ground Textures, which can really change the way the land looks. In addition to creating levels on your space, you can also change the type of terrain your island has by changing the ground textures. This setting is available to you only if you are an Estate Manager. The following are some of the options you have available as Estate Manager:

Select the Terrain Textures

By clicking on each block, you can select a texture that will become the terrain texture. As you select the texture, keep in mind that it is controlled by the height of the land and the directional coordinates. As you see in **Figure 3.26**,

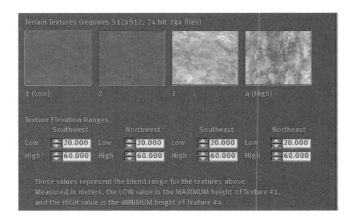

Figure 3.26   Terrain Textures

Although all of this sounds a bit easy, I remember when I was first managing my estate—it was a bit difficult to get the land looking like I wanted it. A single adjustment could turn my beach into grass. In some places, I never achieved the look I really wanted. If you have a region, you will spend a lot of time changing the textures and creating your land—especially if you want to change it for the season or customize it for a specific class or training session.

there are four elevation ranges, and each requires a texture. For instance, in this image you see that the Southwest is set to 10.000 for the low land parameter and 20.000 for the high land parameters. As the figure tells you, the low value is the maximum height of Texture #1, and the high value is the minimum height of Texture #4.

This will take a bit of getting used to and a lot of practice. You can also change this for the season: add snow, for instance, for the winter, or add a bit of green and flowers for the spring. As you raise and lower the land, the features described next will be seen. You can change these to any texture you have in your inventory.

Use your imagination and create new textures to use for your land. Creating a beach area is common in SL. You can make this by dropping the land down and selecting a sand texture that you can either buy or create through Photoshop, Gimp, or other image-editing software.

Here we have discussed the terrain textures and elevations, but there is much more you can do with the land under the Edit Terrain feature, which is discussed in depth in Chapter 9.

Region Lighting

Like changing ground textures, you must have Estate Manager permissions when changing the daylight settings of your region. To access this menu, go to **World > Region/Estate Tab** and click Terrain. Here you have the

> ### Tip
>
> Although you can set lighting for your region, users have the option to set permanent light through the **World > Environment Settings**. This would override any daylight settings you put on your region.
>
> You can use keyboard shortcuts to two of these settings by pressing the following key combinations on your keyboard:
>
> Midday—Ctrl+Shift+Y
>
> Sunset—Ctrl+Shift+N

option to set a permanent setting at sunset, midday, sunrise, and midnight, or you can choose to have the region transition through the day on its own.

Estate Sun

This setting (**Figure 3.27**) makes the sun position in this region the same as the sun in the rest of the estate. If you are not the estate owner, you cannot control the estate settings. The default is set to "on."

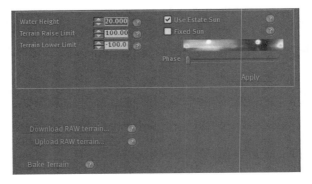

Figure 3.27   Terrain Changes

Fixed Sun

This setting sets the sun position to the position in the Phase slider and stops the sun from moving. The default is set to "off."

Estate Water and Terrain Settings

You can also set the following to further enhance your land:

- **Water Height**—this is the height in meters where water appears. The default is 20 meters.
- **Terrain Raise Limit**—this is the distance in meters that parcel owners can raise their terrain above the "baked" terrain default height. Baked means that the land reverts to the last saved level of the region. For many sims this may be when the island was first created.
- **Terrain Lower Limit**—this is the distance in meters that parcel owners can lower their terrain below the "baked" terrain default height.
- **Download, Upload RAW Terrain, and Bake Terrain**—unless you are an owner of a Region, this setting will be grayed out.

The next tab is the Covenant tab, which you can find under the Region or the Land tab.

Estate

The settings under this tab are some that you will use often as an Estate Owner. It gives the name of the Estate, the Owner, and the Estate Managers (**Figure 3.28**).

Use Global Time

This option makes the sun in your estate follow the same position as on the mainland estates controlled and operated by the Lindens.

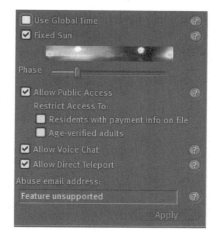

Figure 3.28 SL Sun

Fixed Sun

This option sets the sun position to the one selected in the Phase slider and stops the sun from moving.

Allow Public Access

This option determines whether residents who are on other estates can enter this estate without being on an access list. The settings also include restricting access to avatars with payment information on file and to age-verified adults. There is also a setting under About Land that deals with public access that will be explained later in this chapter.

Allow Voice Chat

This option turns off voice chat on your island, which could be necessary if you have griefers shouting unwanted language in your space.

Allow Direct Teleport

Residents, or avatars, are allowed to directly teleport to any point on the estate. If this option is not checked, they will be teleported to the nearest telehub.

Abuse Email Address

If this option is set, all abuse reports on the estate will be sent to a specific email address. If it is not set, the abuse reports go to Linden Lab. It is unsupported in some regions, and if you cannot set this, the abuse reports default to Linden Lab.

Allowed Residents/Groups

On this list you may enter the residents whom you would like to allow on your estate. You can do so by individual avatar name or by a group name. It is available only when Public Access is unchecked.

Banned Residents

If you are the region owner, you may add any resident's name here that should be banned from the region. If not, you can send the names to the region owner and they can add them here.

Send Message to Estate

An Estate Manager can send a message to the entire estate.

Kick User from Estate

An Estate Manager can kick any user from the estate. You can also do so under Eject User.

Covenant

Because SEA^2 is actually on the New Media Consortium region, we have to abide by their covenant and rules of order (**Figure 3.29**).

Tip

Whether you own a region or a parcel, it is a good idea to post rules of conduct on your space. You can also put the Covenant in a note card for other avatars to take. As in RL, people need to know your expectations.

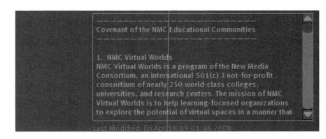

Figure 3.29   Covenant

Now, let us cover the About Land features, which are a bit different from the region settings.

About Land

General Tab

In the General tab (**Figure 3.30**) you will see the name, description, type, rating, owner, and group for the Region or Parcel. The owner can be an individual or a group. If it is a group, more avatars will have access to advanced features.

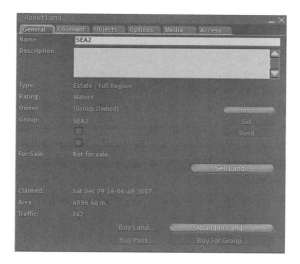

Figure 3.30 General About Land

If it is an individual avatar, that one avatar will have several controls over the parcel that others do not have. You can click the Info button to find out more about the owner or owners.

Allow Deed to Group

This option will deed the land to a specific group. You should be sure you want to do this because it may be difficult to undo.

Owner Makes Contribution with Deed

This setting is available only if you set the deed.

Info

The land owner's name will be listed under the Owner, and the Info box beside it will give you information on that avatar when you click it.

Set

This button will set the land to a group.

For Sale

This option will be set to "not for sale" if you do not own your land. A lot of land is rented in SL. If this is available for sale, it will be highlighted, and you can select "Sell Land."

Claimed, Area, Traffic

This feature gives information on when the land was claimed for ownership or rented, how many square meters the land is, and how much traffic is on the land.

Buy Land, Abandon Land, Buy Pass, and Buy for Group

These settings all allow you to perform operations on your land. If you do not own your land, the only setting that will be available to you is Abandon Land. If owners have chosen these setting, you can find some of the land for purchase on websites through Linden Lab.

Covenant

Here is where you put the general information about what you expect if you are the Region owner.

Objects

Under the Objects tab there is information that is important to the parcel owner or the estate owner. You can control many features of your land through this area (**Figure 3.31**).

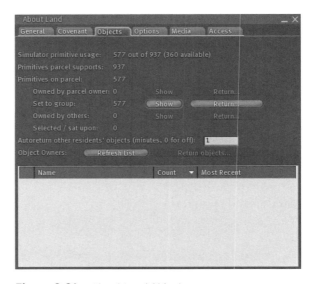

Figure 3.31   About Land Objects

Simulator Primitive Usage

As mentioned before, each region or parcel is allowed a certain number of prims. In Figure 3.31 you see that SEA^2 has 577 of 937 used prims, with 360 left that are available for use. This means that we can place only 360 more prim objects on our space. If we try to place more than that, a message will tell us that the parcel is full. Building with prim-light objects is something you should try to do—it will come with experience as you learn how to build.

Primitives Parcel Supports

This is the maximum number of prims that you can have on your space.

Primitives on Parcel

This is a list of how many prims are on your parcel.

Owned by Parcel Owner, Show, Return

Clicking on Show will highlight or show all the items placed there by the parcel owners. You can also return those items. The same is true for the Set to Group and Owned by others options (**Figure 3.32**).

Figure 3.32   Parcel Owners

Autoreturn

When this option is set you can actually return objects from avatars that are not in your group. If you allow building on your parcel to any avatar, this can help you control when the objects are returned to their creator's inventory. If this is set to "0," the objects will remain; if it is set to "1," the objects will disappear after 1 minute; if it is set to "2," the objects will disappear after 2 minutes, and so on. If you have a large estate you do not want to go around and clean up objects continuously. Also, if avatars leave objects on your parcel or estate, you are using up your prim allotment.

Be careful to watch this setting, because if you are a Region Manager and parcel out pieces of your land, the default is "0." All pieces on that region will return to the "0" setting.

> **Tip**
>
> Be sure to watch this setting. Griefers can take advantage of this by placing objects made of multiple prims on your space. This is done as a prank, but with a script an object can duplicate itself fairly quickly. If you find that your sim is almost full, try searching for this object and clean it up by returning it or deleting it.

Object Owners

If you select "Refresh List," you will be given a list of objects and their owners by avatar name. It shows the count of objects and the most recent date that an object was placed on the space.

Options

Everything under this list of options controls settings on your land. You get to decide what other avatars can do on your space. For the most part, anywhere you go in SL, these settings are all turned on except for Edit Terrain (**Figure 3.33**). You can also allow others in your group to control these settings.

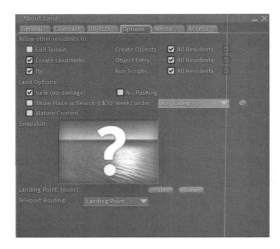

Figure 3.33   About Land Options

Edit Terrain

This option allows avatars to change the topography of your land. This action should be restricted to land owners. We covered editing land both previously in this chapter and in Chapter 9.

Create Landmarks

This option allows residents to create a landmark in your space, which allows them to easily return later.

Fly

This setting allows all residents to fly when on your land. Turning this feature off would be done only when you are having an event and you do not want disruptions during class or training events.

Create Objects

All residents or groups can create objects if this option is selected. This feature can be controlled through the Return Objects setting.

Object Entry

This feature is more restrictive and relates to pushing an object on your space. If this option is on, you cannot reposition the object onto the parcel. However, if you sit on the object, you can push the object to the other parcel. If you are in another region, you can slide objects from another region. This is not a perfect setting, but it does help with having too many objects from unwanted avatars.

Run Scripts

Only residents and those in the group associated with the land can run scripts. If this option is set to all residents, then other avatars may then run scripts. If this setting is off, other avatars can use objects with scripts. However, if you fly high enough, the script will work: this does not block everything, but affects only things on the ground.

Land Options

Safe

A land that is not safe is land you can be hurt on. This option is usually unchecked if you are in a war zone area or more of a game area where you can crash into things and get hurt as an avatar. Once an avatar's health has gone to 0%, that avatar will be returned to its home location.

No Pushing

Avatars cannot push you if this option is selected. If it is not selected, an avatar who has a gun can actually affect the other avatar by involuntarily pushing him or her backward. Keeping this option on helps keep events safe.

Show Place in Search for L$30/week

This feature enables show in the Linden search, but there is a charge to perform this function.

Mature Content

You would select this option if you have mature content on your island that should be restricted.

Snapshot

You may put a picture of the land or anything you would like here as long as the texture is in your inventory.

Landing Point

A landing point is where an avatar will appear when it teleports to your parcel. To set the landing point, position your avatar over the entry point and click Set.

Teleporting Routing

The Teleport Anywhere feature leaves avatars free to teleport anywhere on the parcel. If you block this, avatars will have to teleport in manually by running or walking onto the parcel.

Media

The media section is the place where you set different types of media to play on your parcel. This setting is useful and is one with which you should practice and become proficient. It gives presenters the right to show movies, to play sounds, to play a radio station, and to enhance their presentations (**Figure 3.34**).

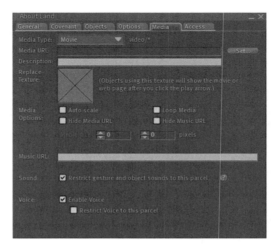

Figure 3.34   About Land Media

Media Type

Select your media type by choosing one of the five items from the dropdown menu (**Figure 3.35**).

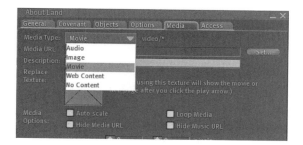

Figure 3.35   About Land Selections

Media URL

Set the media URL (**Figure 3.36**) by typing in or pasting in the URL of the media you want to play on this parcel.

Figure 3.36   Media URL

Click on Set and type in or copy the URL you desire to use. There is more information about this in Chapter 9.

Description

You can type a description here of what the media is about, or you can leave this blank.

Replace Texture

To play media, you must choose a media texture that will instruct the parcel to turn any object with this texture into a media player. To set the media texture, click on the box to pull up your texture-picker window. Type the word "Media" in the selection box, and you will find a default media texture in your inventory (**Figure 3.37**).

Figure 3.37   Media Inventory

Media Options

Auto Scale

This option sets the size of the media; this is the normal setting.

Hide Media URL

This option will hide the URL so that residents do not see it.

Loop Media

This setting will play the media over and over again once the resident hits the play button on the bottom of his or her screen.

Hide Music URL

This option hides the music URL you select.

Media Size

This option shows the size of the media you will be using.

Music URL

You can grab music from several local channels. This feature is explained more detail in Chapter 9.

Sounds

This setting will restrict sound and voice to the parcel or will enable avatars from a farther distance to hear what is being said or played.

Voice

- **Enable voice**—this option enables all avatars to have voice capability on a parcel. If you are having an event, or if someone is being disruptive, you may want to turn this feature off.
- **Restrict voice to this parcel**—if this feature is selected, it does not allow voice to travel off the parcel.

Access

Allow Public Access

This feature opens the island up so that any avatar can visit. This setting is also on Region/Estate.

Block Access By

You can block access for residents who have not given payment information to Linden Lab and to residents who are not members of age-verified groups. Again, this feature can also be set on the Region/Estate tab.

Allow Group Access

Our parcel is set to the SEA[2] group, and we could check this so that only our SEA[2] group could visit. We want visitors, so this setting would be open most of the time for the island unless we wanted to close it while we were changing out some of our instructional tools or fixing our land.

Sell Passes To

This option will be grayed out unless you are the region owner. The owner can sell passes to avatars for a certain Linden$ amount and for a certain period of time.

Allowed Residents

This is the place to specifically allow only residents you want to visit your island. In this section you can type the avatar name, or you can do a search to find the name and add it to this list.

Banned Residents

Here you can ban any residents you do not want to visit your island because of disruptive behavior. If you are part of a region, you can also ask the region owner to ban them from the region.

As a parcel owner on a larger sim, you may Eject and Ban a griefer from your space by right-clicking on the avatar and selecting **More > Eject and Ban**. This option will push the offending avatar to the outer bounds of your land. If the avatar tries to enter your land again, the user is given a 15-second warning until he or she is pushed away to the outer bounds again.

To prevent instances of griefing, you have the option to block the user from your land. To do this, open the About Land Window and right-click on the Access tab. In the bottom-right corner, click on "Block User." After clicking on this button you will be given the option to search for the user by entering the griefer's avatar name and clicking Search. Once you find his or her name on the generated list, click Select to add him or her. With this option the user will not be given a warning and will only be able to hover around your space. On their screen, your space will be surrounded with "No Entry" unless the parcel boundary borders the edge of the region.

Also, if you are the estate owner, you may Eject and Ban a user from your entire region by opening your Region/Estate window and selecting Add User under the Banned User list. Like blocking a user from a parcel, the griefer will not be able to access any portion of your region. If you only own a portion of the parcel, you should contact your estate owner or managers to ask how to regionally ban an offending user.

Duplicate Permissions in Region/Estate and About Land

We covered the permission in Region/Estate and About Land, and as you can see some of them appear to be the same. There are slight differences in the settings, and they will be covered in **Table 3.1**.

Table 3.1 Permissions

Duplicate Permissions	
Region/Estate	About Land
Block/Allow Voice Chat	Block/Allow Voice Chat
Allow Direct Teleporting	Landing Point/Teleport Routing
Banned Residents Teleport removes offending user from land and restricts him or her from returning to the entire region. User will be unable to teleport or return to the region. User is added to Ban list in the Region/Estate Window	**Banned Residents** User from parcel and is "pushed" to the edge of the parcel. Upon entering, user is given 15-second warning to leave and is ejected again. User is added to the Block List in the About Land Window.
Restrict Public Access Disallows all residents who are not on the Allow List in the Region Estate window. Overrides the public access of the parcel owner.	**Restrict Public Access** Blocks residents who are not on the About Land's Allowed List; however, even allowed residents can be blocked if Region Public Access is not enabled.
Allow Damage	Safe
Restrict Pushing	No Pushing

You can find many overrides and tips by doing a search on http://secondlife. com. Those shown in Table 3.1 are just some of the settings that can be different between regions and parcels.

Types of Estates

Open Estates

Open estates are public spaces that allow all residents to visit, with no restrictions. As an open estate you can have any visitors from any culture come and explore your space. It is interesting to see how many visitors you receive and where they are from, as if globalization is happening right in front of you. There are thousands of parcels in SL, so visit as many as you can. It is a wonderful place to meet interesting individuals who can teach you about their culture.

Some advantages of having an open space include the following:

1. Ideal settings for holding conferences, socials, or seminars for corporations.
2. A virtual portal for residents to learn about your institution, company, corporation, or store.
3. Less maintenance to manage group (unless land is usable only by a certain group).

Having an open space can also have some disadvantages.

As an estate owner, there are also some considerations you must take into account if you do plan on keeping a full open estate.

Review and adjust your region settings to ensure that griefers have limited access to important features. Some of the features you should protect are these:

- Blocking terraforming
- Disallowing outside scripts
- Restricting pushing

All of this is managed through the Region/Estate window, which is accessible through the World menu as previously mentioned. With the aid of griefing tools, unwanted residents can tamper with your hard work. Griefers are generally drawn to sims where new users congregate because these users may not realize how to deal with a griefer's offenses.

Establish a Code of Conduct for Residents to Follow on Your Space

Creating ground rules for all visiting residents is a good practice to start at the debut of your space. Anticipating potential concerns and detailing consequences of poor actions can serve as an effective deterrent. Creating these may be as simple as linking out to a Code of Conduct, or it may entail crediting an edited version that is specific to the virtual world environment like, establishing a dress code.

Evaluate Whether You Want to Restrict Privileges to a Certain Group

Privileges such as building rights and script running can be restricted to a certain group. If your space is primarily for your class, but you would like to allow visitors only to observe, you may want to associate your land with your group.

From here, you will have to add each new user to group. Be sure to pay attention to the role that you are assigning to each avatar. Generally, the "Everyone" role is sufficient.

Closed Estates

If you would like to restrict visitors, it may be easier for you to start with a closed estate. These estates are strictly private and do not allow anyone other than approved members to visit. To create this environment, you will need to create a group for you and other avatars in your institution, business, corporation, etc., and you will need to associate this group with the land in the **About Land > Access** tab.

You should also disable "Public Access" to your space.

For an Estate Owner

Open the Region/Estate tab and uncheck the box titled "Pubic Access."

For a Parcel Owner

Open your About Land Window > Access tab and uncheck the box titled "Public Access."

Advantages to designating closed spaces include the following.

- Control variables if you are conducting research
- Access to griefers and unwanted users

However, creating a closed estate naturally requires more work and regular maintenance of your group. If group members are phased out, such as semester or quarter changes, you will need to remove these users manually.

Also, you may only have 100 members in a group, and each Second Life resident may belong to only 25 groups at one time.

Daily Maintenance

Managing your estate also entails some daily or weekly maintenance. As mentioned previously, there are a certain number of prims that you are allowed to have on your sim. Because prims are a limited resource, you will want to ensure that any unnecessary prims are removed from your space. One of the ways to monitor prims is through the autoreturn feature that was discussed earlier in this chapter.

> **Tip**
>
> You can create a mixed estate by separating your space into smaller parcels. For example, if you would like visitors to visit only your island's presentation hall, you can parcel out the land and set this area to "Allow Public Access" in the About Land Access tab.

Designate and Enforce a Building Sandbox

Another useful feature is that of creating and designating a parcel as an official sandbox to contain all the building that residents do on your space, including your group members. To create a sandbox perform the following steps:

1. Create a new parcel on your space.
2. Right-click on a space on your land and select Edit Terrain.
3. Choose the "Select Land" option and left-click and drag a portion of your space to become your new sandbox.
4. Click "Subdivide" and confirm the message box that comes up.
5. In the new parcel, right-click on the land within the borders and select About Land and enter the amount of time objects will be returned.

Most sandboxes leave a 3-hour (120 minute) window. As a measure of courtesy, you may want to leave a sign or a message reminding all builders to take a copy of their work into their inventory and informing them of the amount of time that is set in the autoreturn.

Use Rezzers to Build Temporary Spaces

Rezzers are scripted objects that can build out buildings or items for your use. These items can also de-rezz when you no longer need the structure. For example, if you only need an amphitheatre for a two-day conference, you can use a rezzer to build it out for the two days. When your conference is over, you can de-rezz the building and use the space for another purpose.

Tip

If you find yourself running out of spaces on the real estate, think up. Sky labs can give you greater privacy and can be as simple as creating a 30 × 30-meter platform. However, if you build it above 300 meters, be sure to give residents a flight feather. An advantage of building above 300 meters is that your space will not be visible on the map.

Rezzers are available at a variety of locations and are available online at the SL Exchange. One such tool that can temporarily rezz items such as chairs, tables, and sky labs is Cookie Designs Mysti-Tool. Outside of the Rezzers, the Mysti-Tool is a great tool, but it is especially useful for any educator. With this tool you can set break reminders, keep a teleport history, and scan the sim for surrounding avatars.

To learn more about this tool and its uses, check out Chapter 12, which focuses on Educational Tools.

Wrap-Up

Keywords:

Appearance—the process through which a user may edit the visual attributes of an avatar's body to include height, weight, pigmentation, hair, clothing, etc.

Building—the act of constructing an object or primitive or item by manipulating size, texture, or other object manipulation features

Buy—the initial action an avatar must imitate to enter a buying transaction; this action may be accessed through the pie menu

Camping out—a generic phrase used to describe the newbie practice of playing out an action to receive a minimal payment of Linden$. Camp sites are a business gimmick used to attract users to a sim.

Closed estate—a private sim that is available only to the owner and residents he or she selects

Estate—the entire virtual space that an avatar owns; may be one or more regions

Estate manager—resident who can set land permissions through the Region/Estate menu

Griefer—an individual who intends to cause harm or discomfort toward other avatars and their property

Home (Ctrl + Shift + H)—the location that your avatar remembers as its origin; the default is the first island the user rezzed into upon coming to the Main grid but can be changed by going to World > Set Home to Here

Inventory (Ctrl + I)—a system that saves and stores an avatar's property, which includes all assets such as landmarks, notecards, calling cards, objects, clothing, etc.

Land—a generic term to refer to the virtual real estate of a business, institution, or store within SL
Synonym: space, area, sim

Linden dollars (L$, Linden$)—the SL currency used in world

Linden Dollar Exchange—the system through which an avatar can trade Linden dollars for real-life currency

Object—a term commonly used to refer to SL items that have been built out of one or more primitives

Open estate—a sim that is open to all SL residents

Parcel—a portion of a region that can vary in size

Parcel media—audio, images, video, or web content that an owner may link to a certain space

Parcel music—an mp3 or live stream of music that a parcel owner may add to his or her space

Permissions—settings that can restrict or allow other users to copy, modify, or transfer SL assets

Picks—a tab on the SL profile where the user may list sites that the user believes are noteworthy to visit; a common business strategy for stores and businesses is to offer rewards to users who display the store's site in the users' Profile picks

Prim—a fundamental shape used and manipulated in the building process to create objects *Synonym:* primitive

Profile—a listing that describes information about a particular user and his or her avatar such as rezz date, groups that avatar belongs to, and information about the user's 1st life

Region—a piece of virtual real estate that is 256 meters by 256 meters

Rezz—to create or materialize in world

Rezz day—the actual date that a user created a certain avatar; this information is automatically generated on the user's profile under the 2nd Life tab

RL—"real life"

Sandbox—a designated space set aside for building; these spaces usually reset after a certain amount of time

Search (Ctrl+F)—the process of looking for sims, objects, or other SL elements by entering keywords into a query system

Sell—to offer an object or asset for sale in exchange for a certain amount of Linden dollars

SL Exchange—an online system through which users may sell or buy SL items through the Web

Textures—images that are uploaded into SL to use for building or sharing information

Telehub—a specific location that estate managers may set to force all avatars to rezz into a particular location when visiting a region

Terraform—to make adjustments or modifications to the actual land of a region or parcel

Resource

http://wiki.secondlife.com/wiki/Video_Tutorial/Land/About_Land_options.

Chapter 4

Let's Go Virtual

By now you have learned a great deal about Second Life™ and have begun the journey by searching for a home in this environment. The next step is putting the new skills you have learned into practice so that you can uncover more of the exciting opportunities that are available when you fly, communicate, and share ideas in world. This chapter provides an overview of all the options available in the various menu bars. You will also receive helpful hints and assignments for improving your SL™ techniques. What you have probably already discovered is that the tools available in SL are user friendly and are similar to the tools designed to look like the Windows or Macintosh environment. Before we begin exploring each of the toolbars available, keep in mind that depending upon the version of SL you downloaded, some toolbars and skins might look a little different. Just as you would expect with any software program, toolbars can be hidden or peeled off for easier access and placement within your screen. Do not worry if your screen does not appear exactly like a figure in the book; in this world you have to be ready to adapt to anything.

The menu bar is an area you will want to become familiar with because it provides access to a variety of real life (RL) and SL resources. In **Figure 4.1**, you will see the various options available on the menu bar. Becoming familiar with each menu will allow you to access information quickly.

Figure 4.1   Menu Bar

Tip

What would a software program interface be without offering a person ten different ways to complete the same task? Second Life is no different. The processes and directions that are provided to complete a particular step have been made available to ease your transition into exploring SL. However, please realize that many shortcuts exist and are too numerous to outline. So if you find a better way of completing a familiar task, do not hesitate to use it. You will find that on most toolbars shortcut keys exist. You will also find that by right-clicking you can open a pie menu that provides you with tools to select. Whatever process you choose, it is our intent to make you comfortable with living and working in SL.

Tip

If you plan on holding an event or class or even just setting a time to meet someone in world, be mindful of the different time zones because this could cause confusion.

The menu bar contains many options for accessing material; however, it also contains helpful SL information. For example, as you can see in Figure 4.1 after the Help menu, three icons are present. These images denote (from left to right) building/rezzing, scripting, and object-pushing capabilities. If the land that you are currently on does not allow any of these actions to take place, a red circle with a line through it appears to the right of the image.

The next element on the menu bar is your current in-world position. The numbers associated with the location are coordinates that allow you to teleport to different locations in world. In Figure 4.1 you see the following: Teaching 8 228, 106, 22 (Mature) SEA^2. Teaching 8 is the region and 228 is the east–west coordinate, followed by 106, which is the north–south coordinate, followed by 22, which denotes the elevation. Mature means that the location may contain mature content. Second Life has two options available: X-rated and G-rated. Mature means that there might be X-rated content available at the location, whereas the G-rated location would be acceptable for all residents. SEA^2 on the menu bar is the name the owner has given to the land.

After the coordinates is the current time based on PDT, which is based on the Pacific Time Zone (**Figure 4.2**).

Figure 4.2   Menu Bar

Next on the menu bar is L$ followed by an amount. Figure 4.2 shows L$1,590. As you learned in Chapter 3, L$ is the Second Life currency, known as Linden dollars. L$ allows you to upload or purchase anything in world. The amount on the menu bar indicates how many Linden dollars your avatar currently possesses.

The last area on the menu bar is an open area for you to input keywords to complete a search in SL. When you key in your text and press Enter, the search dialog box will open with your term, and you can then define the parameters for the type of search you want to complete.

Now that you have learned about the elements available on the menu bar, let us dive into each menu and review some of the processes. The File menu option is actually the one area where you will upload RL images as textures into SL.

In **Figure** 4.3, you will see the various options available on the File menu. This figure also shows the shortcut keys.

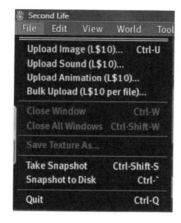

Figure 4.3   File Menu

Tip
Learning the shortcut keys associated with many of the commands is also helpful. It will make accessing the features easy for those of us who like to alleviate extra steps. For example, if you wanted to conduct a search, you could use **Edit** > **Search** in the menu bar, or you could simply hold down Ctrl+F, and the Search menu will automatically open.

Upload Image Feature

The Upload Image feature allows residents to import an image created in RL. These images can be modified with any graphics-editing software and uploaded into SL for L$10, or ten Linden™ dollars. L$10 is equal to 4 cents in U.S. currency at this time. To modify the image you can use Paint, the image editing software on your PC, or you may use Microsoft Office® PowerPoint™ or Word™. You can also use other more complex image editing software such as Adobe® Photoshop™ to edit images. No matter the software, the important element is that when you edit/create an image you may upload only images with the following extensions into SL: .tga, .bmp, .jpg, .jpeg, and .png.

Targa, or .tga, is an uncompressed 24-bit flat texture. The 24-bit TGA images are relatively simple compared with several other prominent 24-bit storage formats. However, TGAs may also be created as a 32-bit format, which enables an alpha channel. The alpha channel is the portion of the image that allows textures to have a degree of transparency.

Tip

Be careful to choose the best image file format for the intended purpose in world. Choosing the wrong format could reduce the image quality. We suggest you save images as .tga or .png for uploading to Second Life.

Bitmap, or .bmp, requires padding rows to 4-byte boundaries. The .bmp is an image file format used to store bitmap digital images and is memory heavy.

JPEG, or .jpeg, allows you to adjust the degree of compression. This approach allows for choosing which is more essential, image quality or size of storage.

Extensible file format, or PNG, is a metadata container that does not place the image data or attributes at a fixed location within the file.

Before you upload your image, realize that SL supports only certain dimensions. Therefore, if you want a good-quality image that is not distorted in the transfer stage, you need to make sure that it has a power of 2. This means that the height and width of the image must be in even multiples of two. For example, an image that is 900 × 500 pixels is not a power of two, whereas an image that is 400 × 200 pixels would be a power of two and therefore would not be distorted when uploaded to SL.

Process for Uploading an Image

The process of uploading a single image is simple. Click on **File > Upload Image**. Locate the image on your computer hard drive, USB, or other storage space. Once you have found the desired file, select it by highlighting it within the dialog box and left-click the Open button. In the Upload window you may choose to input a new name for the image, or you may keep the file name. In the form box you can enter a description if you would like to add clarification. Finally, when you are satisfied with your texture, you may press the Upload (L$10) button to begin the transaction.

Next you will receive a notice of payment and a copy of your texture to preview. The texture will be placed in your My Inventory Texture Folder.

Upload Sound

You can upload sound (.wav) files into SL for L$10. Sound files can be used in combination with objects or avatars by scripting the sound to run. For example, you might script an avatar to say "hello" in combination with a gesture to "wave." Another example is scripting an object to make a sound such as causing a cup of coffee to make a sizzling noise.

In Chapter 9 we will continue our sound discussion by providing information, techniques, and helpful examples for adding sound to your space. You will also learn how to use different types of audio that can be streamed into your SL space.

We once purchased a crocodile to place on our SEA[2] island that had a scripted sound. The problem was that the sound traveled through a 20-meter distance and disrupted other residents. So be careful to set your sound range; if you do not, you might receive a few, shall we say, interesting messages from other residents.

Upload Animation

In SL, an animation is a set of instructions that causes an avatar to exhibit a particular set of motions. In world you will find several animations that already exist that you can choose to set in a pose ball, attach to your HUD (Heads-Up Display), or simply wear to allow your avatar to become animated. Different types of animations exist in SL. Animation can be as simple as a pose or as complex as customizing a gesture to include animations, sounds, text chat, and pause/stop features. If you choose to create your own animations, SL provides you the option of uploading these animations in world just as you have uploaded images. To upload an animation, you will follow the same process discussed under uploading a sound, except this time you will be selecting an animation file that ends with the extension .bvh. Uploading an animation costs L$10.

Once your animation has been uploaded into SL, there are several important parameters that must be set to make the animation work properly in world. Several tutorials exist to help you define the parameters; they can be found online.

Bulk Upload

The bulk upload feature will allow you to select all the images at one time and upload them for L$10 each file. If you are organized, and you wish to complete a bulk upload, this option is best suited for you. For educational purposes, we often have a series of images (presentation slides) that need to be uploaded at one time to SL. It is the same process as an individual image upload except that when you choose/select the image, you will choose the first image in the series, hold down the shift key, and select the last image in the series. This allows you to select all the images in the series.

It is important to name your files with a distinct name that is associated with the purpose. If you upload an image or bulk upload a series of images to SL without naming them appropriately, they will automatically be given the name of that file. In the past students have done this quite frequently, and when they place these images (now deemed textures) into a presentation screen in SL, these textures are sorted out of order. It is difficult to give an effective presentation when your textures are mixed together with other residents' textures.

sea²

Suppose you were to assign students a presentation project that required them to create a PowerPoint presentation that consists of 20 slides. What would the L$ cost be to upload 20 images, and what would be the cost to the student in U.S. currency?

- **Close Window**—just as the name insinuates, close window will close a window you have opened in SL.
- **Close All Windows**—another simple process, but Close All Windows will close multiple windows you have open. For example, you might have your inventory, search, and map open all at one time. Using the close all windows command will do just that: close the windows.

Take Snapshot

What would SL be if we did not have the same type of opportunities that we do in RL? If you have ever wanted to take up photography but did not have the money to purchase RL photography gizmos and gadgets, now is your chance to step into SL and become an advanced photographer by using the Snapshot feature. Taking a snapshot in world gets easier and easier as each new SL update offers residents more complex features. At one time taking a snapshot in SL cost L$10 and meant clicking on a button, but now SL offers you options for adjusting the quality of your image and zooming in for a more focused shot, as well as for improving the storage options available. The process does not cost any Linden dollars if you simply save the images to your hard drive.

What is most exciting about taking a snapshot in world is not only that you can find a career in world but also that this job can translate those images into RL money.

To become an experienced photographer or even if you wish to just stay a novice, it is important to explore the different features available. Within the

Snapshot dialog box you can set the image size, zoom in for a close-up, angle the camera in a specific direction, and even change the angle of the sun so it creates a shadow or creates a focal point for a specific feature you want to emphasize in world. There are many shortcuts for changing the snapshot features. A few simple steps might include the following:

- **Ctrl+Shift+Y**—shortcut for having the midday sunlight. This helps to brighten a snapshot. In the World menu, **Environmental Editor > Advanced Tabs** will allow you to adjust a variety of settings from the color of the sky to limiting the amount of fog in the snapshot. Or better yet, you can change the angle of the sun or moon to create different shadows or focal points.
- **Mouselook**—if you are tired of getting pictures that have the same view, you can try using Mouselook to give you a new perspective.

Whatever your reason for taking a snapshot, be sure to use some basic design principles. By creating a focal point with images, you will cause residents either to remain on your land or to quickly teleport to other locations. Determine the purpose for the snapshot and who your audience is and why you are trying to capture their attention. The following are some simple design principles you can use as you determine the appropriate position for the camera.

- **Alignment/Simplicity**—the way the objects are aligned on the land. The most important element to keep in mind is to align both vertically and horizontally because you will want to create a balance between avatars and landscape in your snapshot.
- **Proximity and Balance/Movement**—refers to the relationships that items create when they are close together. You will want to create appropriate connections between objects in the snapshot. You will also want to create a balance and to use white space effectively. Also note the direction or movement of the avatars and objects in your snapshot. You should never have an avatar facing out of the image; when possible change the angle, or when editing the image you can flip it to change direction.
- **Contrast and Clarity**—what is the focal point of your image? Make it bold, make it big, make it small, and think of how to make a great focal point. This does not mean that you must have bright colors; rather, it could be how you adjust the environment's sun and create shadows within the snapshot.

Once you have taken that snapshot, you need to determine where you plan to store it. In SL you can choose from saving the snapshot to disk (hard drive), sending it to your inventory (L$10) and placing it in your photo album, or sending it to an email address.

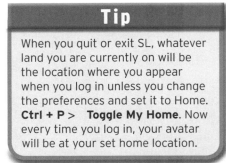

Tip

When you quit or exit SL, whatever land you are currently on will be the location where you appear when you log in unless you change the preferences and set it to Home. **Ctrl + P > Toggle My Home**. Now every time you log in, your avatar will be at your set home location.

Figure 4.4 Search Menu

Snapshot to Disk

The Snapshot to Disk feature will take a snapshot, and the only prompt you receive is the Save location dialog box on your computer.

Quit

When you are finally ready to exit SL, you may click on Quit. You are given another opportunity to quit or cancel before you exit the SL program.

Edit

In **Figure 4.4**, you will see the various options available on the Edit menu. This figure also shows the shortcut keys.

As we began to work on this chapter, we thought it important to cover as many features as possible to orient you to the SL environment. When we began to reviewing the features available on the toolbars, we realized how time-consuming covering each option would be and we knew that our readers would understand the basic functions that are normally associated with many software programs. So as we begin to outline the options available in Edit, we may not highlight a few we knew you would understand, such as Undo, Redo, Cut, Copy, Paste, Delete, Select All, and Deselect.

Search

As mentioned in Chapter 2, the search engine can provide a wealth of information with the strike of a key (Ctrl+F). The strange thing about search engines is that, although they give you instant feedback, you must sift through the returns that you receive to find the one element you are searching for in SL. As you begin your search process, you should think about what it is you want to find. Try to determine what type of keywords you could input into the search to get the best return. Luckily in SL, the search engine allows you to define parameters that allow you to narrow the returns. As shown in **Figure 4.5**, many tabs are available to delineate the area in which you wish the search to take place.

In Figure 4.5, you will see the various options available on the Search menu.

Figure 4.5 Search Menu

You can search All, Classifieds, Events, Showcase, Land Sales, Places, People, and Groups. There is also a category section that allows you to define the search parameters further by cross-referencing. These include Any Category, Linden Location, Adult, Arts and Culture, Business, Educational, Gaming, Hangout, Newcomer Friendly, Parks and Nature, Residential, Shopping, and Other. So as we once said, the world is your oyster, and all you need to do to find what you are looking for in world is to spend some time searching. Once you have found what you are looking for, you may access it by clicking on the Show on Map button, or if you feel it is the appropriate location in world, you can click on Teleport.

If you are unsure where to begin searching, you may want to start off by searching for a mentor. Several exist in world, and we have found them to be valuable resources. Often the mentors will even provide a goody bag, backpack, or other neat, free tools that will get you started on your way. One of the most important things to remember is that if you ever search and teleport to a location where you feel uncomfortable, all you need to do is either teleport home (Ctrl+Shift+H) or X-out and quit.

Tip

Once you teleport to a location in world that you like, you may want to create a landmark to it so that you can repeatedly have easy access to the location. To do so, click **World > Create Landmark**. The next step after you have created all the landmarks will be to organize them in your inventory. But that is a topic for Chapter 5.

Attach Object/Detach Object

The process of attaching and detaching an object is simple. As a newbie you might ask yourself, "What type of object would I attach to my avatar . . . don't most things come in a box?" That is true, and at one time or another every resident has mistakenly attached a box to his avatar. The reason is that when you purchase a product, there is often a series of items that comes with it. Somewhere, someone was a marketing genius. How clever to not only place the object being purchased, directions, and often a notecard that provides a SLURL that links back to the location you purchased the product; the object might also contain information about the designer(s). Most avatars have, at some time or another, worn a box; certain objects can be placed on avatars in a variety of locations. The list of places is endless; you can even place something on an individual body part. Suppose that you want to be a pirate for the day. You can place a patch on your right eyeball, a sword in your left hand, boots on both your left and right feet, a bottle of rum in your right hand, and a hat on your skull. As you can see, attaching an object is easy. Choose **Edit > Attach Object > Choose body part location**. Detaching an object works the same way.

Taking Off Clothing

The option to take off clothes is not something most people would think about in RL, certainly not unless it was in a locked dressing room. For SL, this might not be a bad idea at times. The ability to remove clothing is an important feature in SL because you may often change the look of your avatar (as presented in Chapter 2). The one suggestion we have for residents learning this new feature is first to buy undergarments, and second, to go to a location that is either safe or enclosed.

Gestures

In Second Life we often find that our avatar is not as fluid or seamless as we are in RL. The ability to incorporate gestures allows our avatar to take on a more RL-like persona. Adding a gesture might include animations, sounds, chat, and wait features. The gesture you attach to your avatar could be as simple as typing in a predefined gesture in text chat that will automatically trigger a motion such as waving or clapping your hands. Other gestures can be more complex and are kept in your inventory. These gestures might include a series of commands that trigger an action from your avatar such as dancing. Of course, you have the option to create your own gesture. When you access the Gesture menu, it pulls

Once we were providing an academy for faculty interested in learning more about the uses of Second Life for teaching and learning. The academy covered not only the basics of SL but also how to teach in world. During the "basics" section we wanted to show faculty that they could design their own shirts for their students to wear so that they could represent their university. Somehow, and I do mean that, I clicked on Detach All so that I could change the appearance of my avatar. There in a room full of educators, my avatar stood totally naked. I tried to run away and then to fly away to hide. Unfortunately, there was just no getting off the projection screen. I have never been more embarrassed in my life. I have also never put clothes on so fast. The situation taught me several valuable lessons about SL.

First, undergarments are a must; second, you should always change in a location that is comfortable, better yet somewhere that has a door to close. The other thing that it taught me was how real feelings are in SL. Although this was only an avatar, I personally felt naked and truly embarrassed. I had not expected that teaching and learning in SL would expose me to these types of feelings.

up current active gestures that you have stored in your inventory. You have the option of editing these gestures or making new ones. Creating a gesture is a simple process. The key is to have sounds and animation that you want to use available in your inventory to use with new gestures.

In **Figure 4.6**, you will see on the left-hand side the list of current active gestures. On the right-hand side you can see the New Gesture window. At the top of the New Gesture window you can see an area where you can key in a description of the gesture you are creating. Trigger means what you need to type into the text chat or what shortcut key to press to make the gesture run. The Library contains animation, sound, chat, and wait features. Animation was discussed previously in the chapter. When creating a gesture, you can use animations you have developed or freebies that you found in world. As you can see, the Start Animation is highlighted, and below that you have a dropdown arrow next to the Wave option, which will allow you to choose the animation you want to trigger. The same is true for each element. Sound will allow you to assign

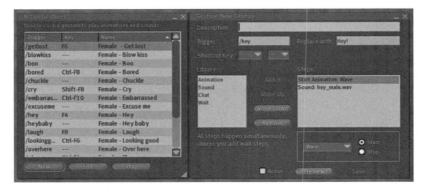

Figure 4.6   Gesture Menu

a sound to the gesture you are creating. You may use any of the default, purchased, or uploaded sounds that you have in your inventory. Chat and wait are the easiest features. Chat allows you to key in text that you want to appear in the local chat log when your gesture is triggered. The wait feature allows you to choose the duration of time between each element of the gesture. So, for example, you might place a short waiting period between the animation wave and your sound so that your avatar will actually wave before it verbally says hello.

Creating new gestures is fun because it allows you the freedom to customize the movements you want your avatar to make in a certain situation.

Preferences

The preference feature in SL has two advantages: You can access the preferences to edit a particular feature to improve the performance of the features, or you can edit a particular preference to adjust the settings to your personal liking. This section on Preferences will show you how to edit particular settings in the Preference dialog box to improve the performance of your computer in conjunction with particular features that you may want to adjust based on your personal preferences.

SL Performance and Personal Preferences

Many factors associated with your computer affect the performance of SL. To improve the performance of SL, you must begin with an understanding of the vital components that make up your computing system. The vital pieces include the motherboard, the hard drive, the computer processor, ROM (read-only memory), RAM (random-access memory), video/graphics cards, network cards, disk drives, and other optional devices that are run by a power supply. Certain components of your computer are essential to the level of Second Life's performance.

For example, if you do not have a certain processor speed, computer memory, or graphics card, it is possible that SL might run more slowly or not at all. Therefore, it is important to review the system requirements prior to downloading SL. You can find these at http://secondlife.com/support/sysreqs.php.

Once you have adequate computing power, the next element that affects SL's performance is the preferences that you set. To open the Preferences dialog box, access the **Menu Bar > Preferences**.

General Preferences

In **Figure 4.7**, the left-hand panel contains a column of tabs that you can click to edit specific preferences in SL. Figure 4.7 displays the General tab. The General tab contains several personal preferences along with the UI Scale, which will adjust the magnification of the user interface. Moving this slider up will increase the size of the font and buttons on the interface of the Second Life client.

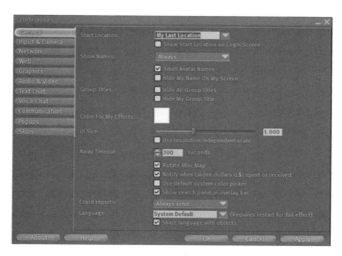

Figure 4.7   General Preferences

Other Preferences

Several other preferences can be changed in the General tab, such as the start location that your avatar will rezz log in at, preferences for identification bubbles, away status timeout, and crash report preferences.

Input and Camera

In **Figure 4.8**, the Input and Camera tab is displayed. This tab is where you may modify the preferences for your input peripherals and camera properties. The peripherals managed in this tab are your mouse and a joystick. You can also toggle whether you want your Page Up and Page Down keys to control your avatar's flight.

Figure 4.8   Input & Camera Tab

The camera option section is helpful when you are getting ready to produce an video called a Machinima. Filmmaking in SL is quite a hobby and provides a successful transition for plays and other artistic projects created within SL. These camera options help produce a cinematic effect without using an outside product.

Network

In **Figure 4.9**, the Network tab is displayed.

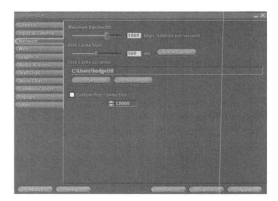

Figure 4.9   Network Tab

Within the SL viewer, your cache serves as an important element; it stores information about your settings for fast access and retrieval. For example, your cache will store information on your friend list so that it can be retrieved faster. If you clean your cache (which is important from time to time), it will take longer to load the information you are requesting until your cache is set again. To clear your cache, Ctrl+P > Network Tab > Clear Cache button.

Web

In **Figure 4.10**, the Web tab is displayed.

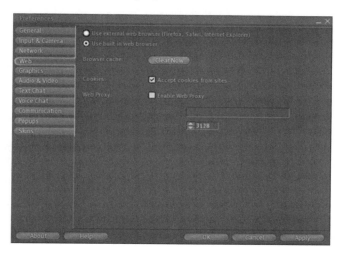

Figure 4.10   Web Tab

The Preferences menu allows you to set your personal preferences for SL, and here you may want to determine whether you want to browse a webpage by using an external browser such as Microsoft® Internet Explorer®, Mozilla Firefox®, or Apple® Safari®. However, you can choose to use the built-in SL browser.

Graphics

In **Figure 4.11**, the Graphics tab is displayed, but be sure to toggle the Custom box because it will open the full advanced-setting screen.

The Graphics tab contains several settings that will adjust the quality of the graphics you view and the amount of detail you will view in world. The first element is the Quality and Performance and although there is no "standard," you will want to be sure that at whichever level you choose, from low to higher quality, your avatar movements are fluid.

Be sure to check the Custom box because it will provide you with settings that will help you improve the appearance of SL.

- **Draw Distance**—draw distance is calculated from your avatar and camera view. This setting allows you to see the objects within a certain "drawn" area. The higher the draw distance, the more objects you can see in SL.

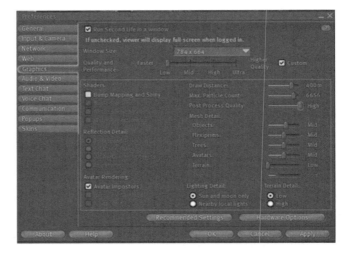

Figure 4.11   Graphics Tab

- **Bump Mapping and Shine**—this setting affects objects that have a bump or shine texture panel.
- **Reflection Detail**—controls what objects are reflected on the water surface. If you have trees or buildings, the area can be set to show the reflection in the water surface.
- **Max Particle Count**—controls the number of particles when near a particle script (water, snow, etc.).
- **Mesh Detail**—this setting determines the amount of detail shown in an object.

Hardware Settings

Within the Graphics tab is the Hardware Options button that you should click on to access the dialog box shown in **Figure 4.12**. To increase SL's performance be sure **not** to select Anisotropic Filtering.

Figure 4.12   Hardware Settings

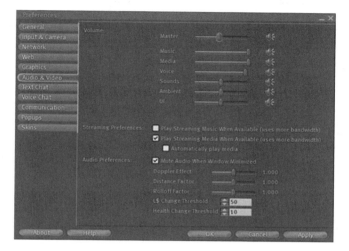

Figure 4.13   Audio & Video Tab

Audio and Video

In **Figure 4.13**, the Audio & Video tab is displayed. In this tab you can control the different types of audio that your SL produces. The top portion of this menu is also available through your main interface when you click on the up arrow next to the speaker. To adjust these options, move your slider left or right to decrease or increase, respectively, the stated volume. You may also mute it by pressing on the speaker icon located to the right.

Table 4.1 details the types of audio sounds.

Audio Sounds

The Streaming Preferences control your ability to hear streaming media and streaming audio.

Text Chat

In **Figure 4.14**, the Text Chat tab is displayed. In this box you can change all the features associated with your text chat. The chat console is the background box that appears when you read the text chat.

The chat bubble option is a neat feature that makes the chat float above the head of the avatar who just spoke. This helps you see which avatar is speaking but can be overwhelming if there are many avatars speaking at once.

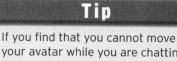

Tip

If you find that you cannot move your avatar while you are chatting, make sure that the "Arrow keys always move avatar when chatting" option is checked.

Table 4.1   Audio Sounds

Sound Type	Description
Master	Controls the master volume of all audio. This does not change the varying degrees of your audio, but it does change the maximum volume that these different audios may reach.
Music	This option refers to the music that is played or streamed on a parcel.
Media	This option refers to the volume of a video, web page, or other media option that is toggled through the parcel media.
Voice	Voice adjusts the volume of all the voice chat that can be heard within SL.
Sounds	Sounds refer to the 10-second sound bites that an avatar or object may play in SL.
Ambient	Ambient sound controls the volume of environmental noise.
UI	This option controls the sounds caused by interaction with the SL client's user interface, such as when you click a button or close a dialog.

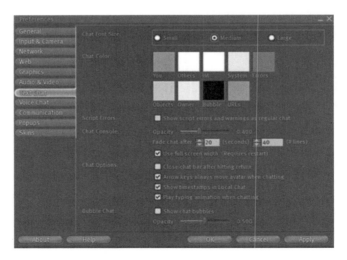

Figure 4.14   Text Chat Tab

Voice Chat

In **Figure 4.15**, the-ice Chat tab is displayed. This tab will be discussed in depth later in this chapter.

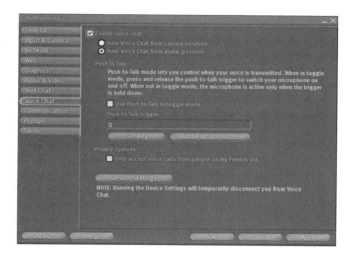

Figure 4.15   Voice Chat Tab

To use the voice chat feature, you must enable it first by checking the box at the top of the screen. Next you can either use the Push to Talk feature or you can set a key on your keyboard to press when you wish to use voice chat.

In **Figure 4.16** you see the lock next to the Push to Talk feature. The lock feature will lock your talk button on and will allow all residents within a certain distance to hear what you are saying and any background noise. We suggest that you do not lock the Talk button because it increases background noise and static.

Figure 4.16   Lock Talk Feature

Device Settings

Device Settings is a feature that allows you to optimize your input source. To begin, choose your input and output devices (i.e., Logitech microphone headset). Next you can test out the devices and settings by speaking into your microphone and setting the desired volume.

Communication

In **Figure 4.17**, the Communication tab is displayed.

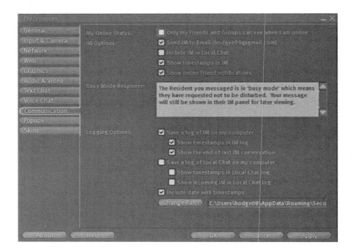

Figure 4.17   Communication Tab

In **Figure 4.18**, the Popups tab is displayed.

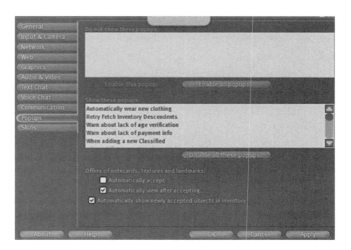

Figure 4.18   Popups Tab

In **Figure 4.19**, the Skins tab is displayed. The Skins tab allows you to choose what skin your SL viewer uses.

Figure 4.19 Skins Tab

Figure 4.20 View Menu

View Menu

In **Figure 4.20**, you will see the many different options available for changing your avatar's view in SL.

What makes SL special is that, as the SL world evolves, it is based on the individual designer's view. Therefore, if you have never physically been somewhere in RL, you can go there in SL and see the recreated location based on the designer's view. What is also important is not only that are we seeing one person's perspective of how to design his or her space, but also that we have many different tools available for altering the space we are in by modifying the view we use. In **Figure 4.20** you can see the list of tools to help you change the layout of your screen. A simple switch from camera controls to Mouselook can change the entire view of the SL world.

In **Figure 4.21**, you will see the view of SEA[2], using standard camera controls.

In **Figure 4.22**, you will see the view of SEA[2], using Mouselook.

However, if switching from one view to another causes your avatar to fly into things or zoom in too close, a good shortcut to remember is the Escape (Esc) key. This will reset your view back to normal. If Esc does not work the first time it is pressed, just try it again.

Figure 4.21 Camera View

Figure 4.22   Mouselook View

Build

When you access Build in the View menu, the Build window opens, and your cursor becomes a wand. At this point, you may rezz several shapes called primitives, which are the basic building blocks of any SL object. All residents can build their own environment with these tools, and in Chapter 6 we will introduce you to the fundamentals of basic building.

Communication

In 1999, the SL initial program used text-based chat as its only means of communication. In the past 10 years, SL has become a virtual platform that encompasses both tradition and innovation to deliver immersive tools for its residents. Communicating in SL has taken on a whole new meaning as the infusion of various Web 2.0 technologies have made this activity far more interactive. This section will provide you with an overview of traditional communication methods, innovative Web 2.0 technologies, and tips for making your in-world interaction fun and exciting. But before we can review the various communication methods, it is important to understand the basics of how residents communicate with one another.

If you are new to SL, you may not have had the opportunity to meet a lot of people in world, but eventually the occasion will arise where you will need to communicate some type of message. Whether you are a student taking a class in world or an SL resident intent on starting a business, you will need to understand the fundamentals of this interaction.

Contacts

However, if you happen to be in SL and you are all alone at your location and you feel like chatting, you can click on the Communicate up arrow to choose from a menu of Contacts, Local Chat, Redock Windows, and Mute List. The Contacts menu contains a list of your friends and groups.

Figure 4.23   Chat Button

In **Figure 4.23**, you will see the Show Chat button, which toggles the apperance of the text chat bar. You will also see the Communicate button with an up arrow of choices.

When you wish to communicate with someone who is standing near you in SL, you can click on the Show Chat Bar button. Once this is opened, you can type in text, gesture commands, links, and the like. The text chat will appear in the window and will remain there for roughly 15 seconds before disappearing. Another option you will have is to use the Local Chat log, which allows you to see the entire threaded discussion.

Friends

In **Figure 4.24**, you will see a Friends tab and a Groups tab that provide lists of all your in-world contacts.

Figure 4.24   Contacts Menu

> **Tip**
>
> If you want the local chat to stay on your screen for a longer (or shorter) time, you can change the 15-second default under the Text Chat tab of your Preference window. **Ctrl+P > Text Chat > Fade** chat after 60 seconds (60 seconds is the maximum amount of time you can set before the text fades).

> **Tip**
>
> You can use Ctrl+C to automatically open the chat window.

Using this list, if you want to start a conversation with a friend in world, you can highlight the friend's name and choose IM/Call. Doing so will call the contact. But if you do not have any friends listed, then you will need to go out and meet some in SL. There are many ways to make friends in SL. The best way to start is by using the Search menu to find areas of interest. You can teleport to these locations to find out more about what the locations provide. You can also attend SL events. These events could be educational or fun in nature; it will all depend on who you want to meet. Listed at the end of the chapter are a few newbie-friendly spaces where you can make friends and even find mentors.

When you have found someone in SL that you would like to be friends with, the next step is to offer friendship. When making friends, you might want to build a rapport with someone prior to offering friendship. Be sure that you ask them if they would like to be your friend prior to choosing Add a Friend, because it can be considered rude and is often intimidating to people who do not know you well enough. If you are at the stage of offering friendship, you can follow the simple process of doing so.

In **Figure 4.25**, you will see the list of friends and the option to add a friend.

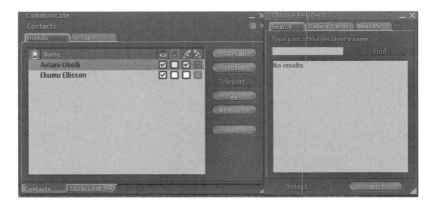

Figure 4.25　Add Friend Option

> ## Tip
>
> A simple way to offer friendship if you and the other resident are in the same location is to right-click on the resident and select Add Friend from the pie menu.

If the contact you want to offer friendship to is not in the same location, you can click on Add and type the name of the resident in the form box. Next, click the Find button, and a list of matches will appear in the box below your entry. From here you may highlight the correct resident's name and left-click the Select button. A friendship offer will be sent to the resident for him or her to either accept or decline.

Another element that is important to understand about creating a relationship with someone and accepting friendship is that are various degrees of friendship available. **Figure 4.26** provides a look at the options for friendship.

Figure 4.26　Contact Menu

In Figure 4.26, you will see different options for friendship. Next to the name of your new friend you will see that there are four icon options available to toggle on or off (check mark).

As you can see in **Table 4.2**, there are a variety of friendship levels, and although these might seem harmless at first, it is important that you reserve the rights to your objects. You might also find that, although you like to chat with this friend, you might not want this person to know your exact location on the map every time you log into SL.

Now that you have made a friend, you can also use the other contact tools to communicate.

Table 4.2   Friend Options

Option	Description
Online Status	The eye option allows a friend to see when you are online.
Locate	This option lets the friend locate you on the map.
Edit My Objects	This option lets the friend edit, delete, or take your objects.
Edit Friend's Objects	This option indicates that you can edit your friend's objects.

The IM/Call feature will allow you to send the friend a request to chat. The profile button will allow you access to the profile that your friend has created. Teleport allows you to offer a teleport to a friend so that you can be in the same location. Pay allows you to give some of your Linden$ to a friend. Delete is, of course, deleting a friend from your contact list.

Go to NMC Castle and offer friendship to a resident (http://slurl.com/secondlife/Braunworth/232/214/271).

Using the profile button, learn more about this friend's SL and RL interests.

Groups

Depending on your purpose, joining or creating a group will add value to your SL experience. If you are looking for another way to meet residents and add friends to your contact list, joining a group on the basis of similar interests is a great place to start.

Joining a Group

If you thought making friends in SL was going to be difficult, all you need to do to change your mind is access the group list available on SL's Wiki, Flickr's SL Pool, or ProfilesLive.com, which list more than 700 groups. What you may find difficult is adhering to SL's limit of 25 groups. Although joining a group is easy, and finding people with like interests is easy with more than 700 groups from which to choose, what exactly does belonging to a group entail?

Groups Tab

Whether you have joined a particular group or have set up your own, the following tools exist to help you organize and stay in contact with current members.

IM/Call

The IM/Call feature allows you to contact particular members within the group or to send out an IM/Call to the entire group at one time.

Activate

The Activate feature allows you to activate the group(s) you belong to and to make your avatar active. It also allows you to deactivate specific groups without leaving the group entirely.

Leave

The Leave feature allows you to leave the group and become an inactive member.

Info

The best feature available for groups is the Info (Information) button, which will open a dialog box filled with features. What makes the Group feature so phenomenal is the intuitive choices that are available to users to formalize groups, assign roles, give voting rights, and many other options that make groups a great feature for any company, organization, or academic class.

General

The General tab will provide basic information about the group, current members, and SL accessibility to opening the group for others to join.

Members and Roles

The Members and Roles tab will list current members, current roles, and abilities while also providing the group with the ability to invite new members or even eject members who behave inappropriately. Within the group environment you can create and send notices to your members.

Notice

The Notice tab will archive notices should the group need to recall previous messages. The Proposal tab allows the group to create a proposal and send out notices to have each member place his or her vote.

Lands and L$

Finally, the Land and L$ tab provides you with details on your land, as well as any sales or L$ earned by the group.

Creating a Group

As demonstrated by the number of groups already formed in SL, you do not necessarily have to create your own. However, there are several benefits of creating a group in world. In some instances you might want to create a group simply to stay connected with your SL friends. However, groups can provide structure for companies, organizations, classes, etc.

To create a group in SL, access the **Menu Bar > Edit > Groups > Groups Tab > Create**. Once you click the Create button you will need to determine a group name, develop roles, assign roles, list members or invite members, and determine whether the group will be open to all SL Residents.

Each class in SL, my students are required to join at least two groups. They are required to join the university group as well as their class group. The purpose for the class group is so that the instructor can send notices, assign roles and abilities for land, and develop proposals for the students to vote on. A proposal might be something as simple as a set of dates and times for students to vote on for delivering course content synchronously. It is also a great way for the instructor to track the last time a student logged into SL because the Members and Roles tab provides the last login date.

Search Groups

The search feature allows you to search for SL groups in world, to view your current groups, or to create a new one.

Local Chat

In **Figure 4.27**, you will see the chat log along with all the residents who are participating and the time of the comment.

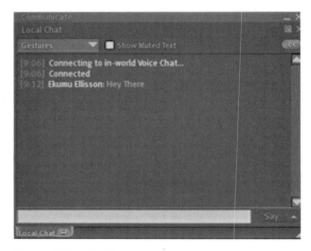

Figure 4.27   Chat Log

The local chat that takes place in world will automatically appear in the bottom left-hand corner of your screen. However, as groups of residents join in on the chat, this chat can sometimes become overwhelming and can be easier to digest if you open the local chat dialog box. As you can see in Figure 4.27, not only is the local chat showing but also IM (instant messaging) conversations that are taking place between yourself and one other resident. These are private discussions that allow you to click on the tab to keep up to date with the conversation. Another important element about the local chat feature is that you can copy and paste it into a document. So if you happen to be having a meeting that someone could not attend, that person could then go back and view the chat log to see what discussions took place. Copying a chat log is simple. First make sure the chat log is active. Then press Ctrl+A on your keyboard to select the entire chat. To copy the text into your clipboard, press Ctrl+C, and open any type of document and press Ctrl+P to paste the text. At this point, you may choose to edit your text to filter out any unnecessary comments or save the document as it is.

IM/Call

As we mentioned earlier, instant messaging is a form of text chat that takes place between "invited" residents who have been called. When the dialog box opens, you will see a chat log similar to your local chat; however, this time it includes only you and other invited residents. Within the IM screen you can text chat using the same features as in the local chat. The IM/Call dialog box does contain options to Call, which is a private voice chat between you and your party. To the left of the call button you may click on the "Profile . . ." button to view the resident's profile. Profiles were mentioned in Chapter 3, but a resident's profile is a menu that contains various information about the avatar's SL likes, RL likes, etc.

Calling Cards

If you want to continue the tradition of networking, SL is a great place to develop friendships, collaborations, and even to seek out job opportunities. The calling card feature is similar to receiving a business card in RL. It provides a resident with your profile information and any other item you might want to give a potential contact.

Voice Viewer

The Voice viewer option entered the SL playing field in August 2007. Since its inception, residents have been using it in many different ways, from simple conversations about merchandise to purchases, dating activities, board meetings, training procedures, and university classes.

Voice Comm

The voice communication feature allows residents to communicate verbally using tone and inflection, which makes the interaction more dynamic and fluid.

Voice Viewer

When you first download the SL viewer, you will find that the voice chat feature is disabled. However, prior to activating the voice chat function you will need to purchase a VoIP (Voice Over Internet Protocol) headset. The VoIP headset provides the best quality audio and sound over a traditional microphone and speakers, although these can be used.

To activate the voice chat feature click on **Edit > Preferences > Voice Chat Tab**.

In **Figure 4.28**, you will see the Voice Chat setup menu.

Here you should toggle (check) Enable voice chat and click Hear Voice Chat from your avatar position.

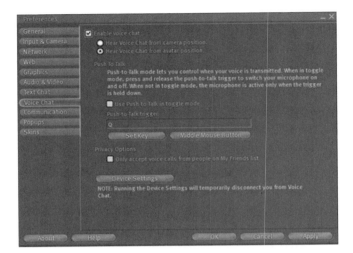

Figure 4.28   Voice Chat Tab

The Push to Talk feature allows you to either use the preexisting Talk key or set your own key. For instance, you can set the preference to use **Set Key > Q**. This allows you to hold down the Q key when talking, because it isn't something often keyed into the text chat.

Privacy Options

The Privacy Options feature allows you to accept calls only from people in your contact list. We do not suggest selecting this feature if you plan to attend open SL events. It will keep you from communicating with other residents in world.

Device Settings

The next button is the Device Settings. If this is your first time using the Voice chat feature or if you ever have problem with voice, you should run through the process of setting up your device.

Figure 4.29   Voice Chat Device Settings

In **Figure 4.29**, you will see the device settings setup menu.

Before you go to set up your device settings, make sure that the headset cables are plugged in to the proper location.

Once you have done so, you may run through the process of testing out your microphone headset system. Should you run into problems and not be able to communicate with other residents by using voice chat, you can return to the Preferences menu to check that your settings are correct. Sometimes people use other desktop conferencing devices, and when they return to use their headset system it does not recognize the set. Another issue that often arises in SL voice chat is a firewall complication. You can address any voice chat issues you may come in contact with by accessing the Second Life Wiki on Voice Chat FAQs at http://wiki.secondlife.com/wiki/Voice_FAQ#SL_Voice_FAQ.

Amazingly, once residents used the voice chat feature, more questions arose about making the communication more seamless, fluid, and natural. In response to this need for a natural speaking "look," many residents created poses and gestures that can be worn by avatars during conversation. These features, known as "speech gestures," can be found in your inventory library. To use the gestures, you can drag the folder onto your avatar; then be sure to activate the gestures. Now, as if gestures were not enough, residents wanted more, and with the release of the Second Life Candidate 1.20® you now have the capability to lip sync. Just be sure to enable it in the Advanced menu screen (Ctrl+Alt+Shift+D) (**Figure 4.30**).

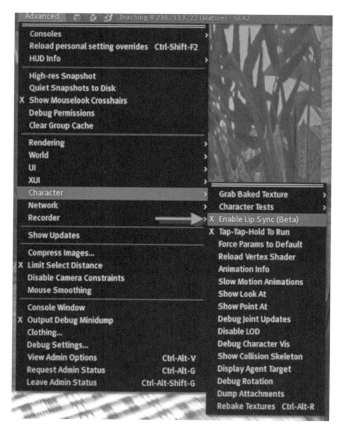

Figure 4.30   Character Setting

Figure 4.31 Lip Sync Feature

In **Figure 4.31**, you will see the avatar's mouth open as she begins to use voice chat with the enabled lip sync feature.

The lip sync feature runs from the SL viewer, whereas the voice chat is run on a parallel SL viewer written for Linden Lab. The two elements running parallel does make it a bit difficult for the voice and lip movements to be synchronous. However, the lip sync feature adds a great deal to the look of your avatar as it speaks. If you want to increase the level of synchronous movement, you will find a helpful resource link at the end of the chapter that provides information on setting variables to increase or decrease mouth movement.

Active Speakers

Another element available in world that helps when you are holding an event or conducting a session is the Active Speakers Button. To access Active Speakers you can click beside the Talk Lock button, where there are speech bubbles that look like a popup message like those shown in Figure 4.16.

The Active Speakers window displays a list of residents who are currently speaking on a particular voice (Talk) channel. In the Active Speakers dialog box a dot appears beside each speaker's name indicating who is currently speaking. As each avatar speaks, his name jumps to the top of the list to indicate that he is the most recent speaker. To sort the speaker list alphabetically, you can click the Name Header; this will also lock the names in alphabetical order.

Web 2.0 Technologies

Fundamental to all learning is the ability to communicate. Because speaking is the primary mode of communication within RL, adaptations must be made to foster relationships and interactions in a virtual environment. For example, when determining what type of communication method to use in a virtual environment, residents should evaluate both the synchronous and asynchronous platforms. By determining the type of interaction residents are trying to foster, they can enhance their social presence and communication method by infusing Web 2.0 technologies that are now available to use in conjunction with Second Life.

Web 2.0 can be defined as advanced Internet applications, tools, and technologies that are generated, refined, and published by active Internet users. The active users can be categorized as contributors that help to customize what is being generated for public consumption on the Internet. Some of the popular Web 2.0 technologies include blogs, Wikis, RSS, and social networking applications and tools.

Blog

A blog is a website that contains regular updates and entries about different subjects deemed important by the individual maintaining the blog. Subjects can range from emerging technology to how the individual enjoyed her dining experience at a particular restaurant. At times it might seem that there is no rhyme or reason for what might be posted on a blog because the content it is entirely at the discretion of the user/creator. In SL, blogs can be found as an object with a script that when triggered will access a weblog, or it could be an actual BlogHut in world. Whatever your reason for searching and reading blogs in SL, you will easily come to find that there is an abundance of residents that have a lot to blog about on in world activities.

Twitterbox

To understand Twitterbox, you must also understand what Twitter® encompasses. Twitter is a way to communicate, interact, and stay connected with people who also "Tweet™" (communicate) using the application. When you create a profile in Twitter you can search for friends or family, or you can do a general people search. These actions will allow you to follow someone's communication thread. While others can choose to follow your communication thread, provided access is granted on both ends. Simply put, Twitterbox is an object in SL that allows you to receive Twitter feeds in world. Several uses for Twitterbox are presented in Chapter 12.

Facebook

The latest mashup to hit the Second Life scene is Second Life Link™. The Second Life Link application integrates Facebook® and Second Life, but with only minimal features in its current beta format. Second Life Link's current integrated applications include seeing which of your Facebook friends are in SL, what their avatars look like, what their SL online status is (with the ability to teleport to their current in world location) and what their favorite SL locations are.

Several other Web 2.0 applications and technologies exist, and further information and links are provided in Chapter 12.

Camera and Movement Controls

Although previously discussed in Chapter 2, camera and movement controls will be used differently from one person to the next depending upon your level of skill, level of comfort, and personal preference. The best way to determine your preference is by testing each method available. Four different methods exist: mouse, keyboard, camera and movement controls on screen, and 3D Mouse.

Many users find that once they choose a particular way to control the movement of their avatar, it is difficult to switch to a different method. Whatever your preference, you will find that flying, walking, and even running will become easy the more you spend time in world. Keep in mind that lag can affect the movement of your avatar. You may find your avatar not moving immediately when you try to fly or walk, and then the next thing you know your avatar is flying past the location you wanted because the movement is finally processing. Lag is caused by the number of prims, particles or, the convergence of many avatars in one location. Lag can also be caused by the number of items you have in your inventory, so be sure to clean and organize your inventory, as presented in Chapter 5. If you want to keep abreast of what is going on with the SL viewer, you can view the statistics bar. To access the statistics bar quickly, you can hold down Ctrl+Shift+1.

Another feature that relates to camera controls is the ability to zoom in and out. The feature not only helps when you are moving about the environment but more so when you are building and rezzing objects. Within the Menu bar > View, you will find the Zoom features. If you use the zoom features within the View menu, it will allow you to zoom in only to a certain degree. The zoom will "jump" your camera control closer and then back to its original position. An easier and more precise way to zoom is to use Ctrl+0 to zoom in and Ctrl+8 to zoom out.

> **Tip**
>
> Here is a simple way to manipulate the view in SL.
>
> Alt+left mouse button will allow you to pan horizontally while being able to zoom in and out.
>
> Ctrl+Alt+left mouse button will allow you to pan vertically while being able to zoom in and out.

As you move around the SL environment, you will find that many objects in world provide a tip. The Hover Tip provides the name of the object, the owner, the description, and the price. The hover tips do provide help when you are shopping or possibly looking around a location to find particular information on a piece of land. You can toggle the Hover Tip feature on and off by accessing the **Menu Bar > View > Hover Tips** and then select the tips you wish to view.

Avatar Movement

This section presents the many different ways in which an avatar can get from here to there in the SL environment. Many of these concepts have been presented in previous chapters, and they will probably be presented in subsequent chapters because it is not common to stay in one location in SL—there are just too many exciting places to explore and friends to meet. What this section does provide that you might not find elsewhere are the ways to move your avatar and, we hope, ways to alleviate embarrassing moments.

Walk

The best way to describe your first steps in world would be to equate it to your first steps as a toddler. Your avatar is moving right along when, BAM, you walk right into a building, you fall back, and you pick yourself up and start walking again. Just as you would imagine, a child might cry in a situation like this, and you, too, may have feelings of embarrassment. That is one thing you will find using SL, that no matter how many times you convince yourself that your avatar is separate from you, it just is not the case. You will also find that you begin referring to your SL self in RL conversations. But let's get back to walking. As explained in the controls section, there are several different ways to move your avatar by using the movement controls, shortcut keys, or even the 3D mouse. There are no simple solutions to improving your walk other than practice, practice, practice.

There are, however, different ways to move. So if walking does not work, you can try running, Ctrl+R. This will get you moving at a fast pace.

Another way to get your avatar moving is what Will Ross notes as the Long Jump (http://travelingavatar.quickanddirtytips.com/flying-in-second-life.aspx).

This fancy footwork requires a bit of dexterity. You will be combining a simple walk while taping the fly movement, and when you are ready to land, you may slow down the taping to start bringing your avatar down from the jump.

Flying, of course, is a preferred method of travel in SL. However, like most avatars first trying to fly, you will fly too far, hit buildings, and fly through objects such as trees—and that is before you even make a face plant when you stop flying and fall to the ground. Do not let the thought of all these embarrassing moments stop you; remember that with practice comes wisdom. But if you do not want to wait for that, you can try these flying tips to help you fly and land more gracefully.

To begin flying you can either click on the Fly button, press the Home key on your keyboard, or simply use Page Up. Clicking on the Fly button will only get your avatar into the fly mode, whereas using the Page Up key will allow you to keep flying higher and higher until you reach the clouds at 70 meters. The highest altitude you can reach without the assistance of a flight feather or flying gadget is 70 meters, whereas once you have attached a flight feather you may fly up to an altitude of 200 meters. While in the air, you can use your movement keys to move in any direction. Should you want to return to the ground, you can click on the Stop Flying button, which will bring you crashing down to the ground with the inevitable face plant. However, we suggest using the Page Down key for a more graceful landing.

Teleport

Nothing brings us back to the days of the starship *Enterprise* more than the concept of teleporting. Plus, the analogy to this mode of travel could not be more on target. Therefore, if you feel like traveling from there to here and here to there quickly, by all means teleport. Teleporting will allow you to move immediately from one location to another. You have several different options for teleporting to a new location. When you choose to teleport as opposed to walking or flying, you can do so by using one of the following: landmark or teleport object, search, map, avatar offer, landmarks set in your inventory, or an Internet SLURL (Second Life uniform resource locator). When you teleport, you should arrive at the parcel's associated landing point if one has been defined.

To fully understand the benefits of teleporting, you should review the following features:

Coordinates allow you to teleport to specific locations in SL. Coordinates are used on the SL Grid, which is broken down into regions. The regions include three coordinates: east–west, north–south, and elevation. You can find the coordinates of your current location on the menu bar after the name of the region in world. For example, Teaching 8 228, 106, 22 (Mature) SEA[2]. Teaching 8 is the region and 228 is the east–west coordinate, followed by 106, which is the north–south coordinate, followed by 22, which denotes the elevation. When you open the Map feature, you will see coordinates next to the location section that indicate where you are currently located. You can copy coordinates in the Map location to your clipboard as an SLURL.

An SLURL is often provided on web pages, blogs, Wikis, etc., to denote a link to a specific in world location. When clicked, the SLURL will open a browser and indicate the location to which you will be teleported in SL. When you click on the Teleport Now feature, your avatar will teleport to the new SLURL location, making travel simple and access easy through RL Internet applications.

Home is the location you set as your preference for residence when you enter SL. Anytime you wish to set your Home coordinates you can access the **Menu Bar > World > Set Home to Here**. This allows your avatar to quickly teleport home at any time (Ctrl+Shift+H).

If you are on another resident's parcel and want to set the Home location to that resident's coordinates, you may find that you must become a member of the group prior to setting the Home location.

Landmarks are coordinates (assets) that are maintained in your inventory. Landmarks are the locations in world that you have "landmarked." A good analogy would be to equate a landmark to a bookmark or your favorites that you set in an Internet browser. You create a landmark to an SL location so that you can

---

Tip

Once you have set a landmark, open your inventory (Ctrl+I) under your **My Inventory > Landmarks**. Click on the region coordinates you just landmarked and right-click. From the dropdown menu, choose Rename. Rename the landmark to something that describes the location. For further organization you might want to create site-specific folders within your Landmark folder so that you can drag landmarks into specific folders. For example, some of the folders you might create include Education, Shopping, Entertainment, Building, Exotic Locations, Freebee Locations, Sports and Recreation, Nature, Groups, and Favorites.

quickly teleport to the location just as you would access a bookmark or favorite on your browser toolbar if you wanted to return to that particular website. Landmarks are only as useful as the name you provide to indicate a location. Landmarks that have not been renamed can quickly become unsightly and unusable because you will not remember the purpose of the landmark strictly on the basis of the region name and coordinates. To set a landmark in SL, access the **Menu Bar > World > Set Landmark Here**.

SL is fun, and it is a wonderful place to learn, teach, explore, communicate, shop, and conduct business. However, now that you have learned many of the intricacies of SL, you might be feeling a bit exhausted. When you started SL you never thought you would need the next features presented. But setting your avatar to busy or away will come in handy when you are actually trying to accomplish tasks in world. When setting your avatar to busy/away, SL will automatically decline teleport offers, IMs will receive a "busy mode" response, and your avatar will not hear the local chat.

Wrap-Up

Keywords/Definitions:

Active speakers—a list of all the users who have enabled voice chat; a green dot with waves signifies which avatar is speaking at that current moment

Animation—a series of commands that controls the way an avatar moves for a certain amount of time

Calling card—a virtual business card that can be exchanged between users to share contact information

Camera view—the angle through which a user can view the SL world

Contacts Menu—the list that aggregates all the residents a certain user has befriended and groups to which he or she belongs

Draw distance—the visual range a user can see of the region around him or her from the avatar's position

Friend—a resident who has agreed to be added to a user's list of contacts to facilitate easier communication

Gesture—a short series of movements that controls the way an avatar moves for a short time

Groups—a community of users who share a common interest

Heads-up display (HUD)—an object that attaches to an avatar's screen to provide the user with some added functionality

Instant message (IM)—a private conversation between two or more residents; can be in text or voice chat

Landmark—a virtual bookmark to in world locations

Lip sync—a feature that enables an avatar to move its mouth and hands while the user is voice chatting

Lock talk feature—the ability to press a key or button to enable constant broadcast of voice chat until the user presses the toggle key or button again

Menu bar—the list of options located at the top of the SL client

Popups—message boxes that pop up on the screen to inform a user that a certain action has occurred

Preferences (Ctrl+P)—a menu that controls the settings and controls that help a user adjust the performance of the SL client

Skin—the visual design of the SL client's interface

Snapshot—a screenshot of in world activity that can be taken through the SL client

Sound—a 10-second sound bite that can be uploaded into SL

Text chat—the mode of communication where users can communicate through text

Voice chat—the mode of communication where users can communicate verbally

Chapter 5

Inventory Overload

Every item you pick up in SL™ is stored in your inventory. This inventory is simply a virtual file cabinet that is managed much like the file folders on your computer. It can quickly get out of control, and having 10,000 items or more is not unusual. Without proper organization, you will not be able to locate or use some of the valuable tools you acquire throughout your virtual world experience.

The correlation between your SL inventory and managing your files on your computer hard drive is easy to make. Just as it is difficult to save and manage all the files we store on our computer, it is just as difficult to manage your in-world inventory. When you first enter SL, your avatar is automatically provided with a set of "standard" inventory items, which are contained within the folders. Every item that you possess in your inventory belongs to your avatar. Even teen avatars who start out on the Teen Second Life Grid™ and are aged out to the Main grid can retain all the items they collected. So just as you possess items in RL, when you purchase or are given items in world, you possess them for the life of your avatar. If you have more than one avatar, you can also transfer items from one avatar to another if those items have been set to allow copy and modify properties. However, if you purchased a no-transfer item in world, you will not be able to transfer that object from one avatar to another.

In **Figure 5.1**, you will see the inventory folder hierarchy.

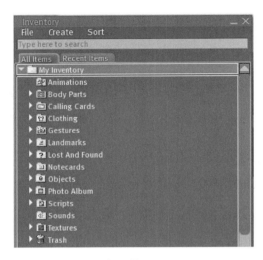

Figure 5.1   Inventory Menu

Second Life inventory is made up of two distinct folders. These folders include "my inventory" and "library." Just as its name implies, "My Inventory" consists of the inventory items you personally collect, whereas the library contains a standard collection of items that is provided to your avatar when you sign up as an SL resident. You may wonder what type of items you will acquire when you are in world. The following is a list of the preset folder headings with a general description of each:

- **Animation**—a set of instructions that manipulates the way an avatar moves. Many animations reside in your library. You can find free animations or purchase complex animations, or you can create your own in world. Animations can be as simple as waving and sitting in a particular position or as complex as a series of animations that you can apply to your avatar to complete a particular task.
- **Body Parts**—when you first enter SL, you are provided with a standard set of body parts. These consist of eyes, skin, shape, or hair, or an object can be created by prims to add enhancement to your avatar's body.
- **Calling Cards**—a simple way to share more information about yourself in world is by giving another resident a calling card. A calling card provides access to an avatar's profile. The profile contains information on Second Life, web, interests, picks, classified, 1st life, and My Notes.

When you get a calling card from someone and "accept it," your calling card is automatically given to the other avatar. Be aware of the residents you accept calling cards from; they will have access to your profile information.

- **Clothing**—SL clothing includes both textures applied to your avatar's body and prims with a texture applied to them. These textures can be any type of color, texture swatch, and image that you can upload in world to become textures in your inventory. Clothing consists of undergarments, shirt, pants, dress, jacket, gloves, socks, and shoes.

- **Gestures**—a gesture can exist either alone or in combination with sound, animation, and chat features. You can either set a pre-defined key to run the gesture or key in the chat area a command that runs the gesture. For example, /wave would make your avatar wave its hand. Aside from finding free gestures and purchasing gestures in world, you can also create your own.

- **Landmarks**—a landmark provides residents in world with specific locations for teleportation. A resident can create a landmark to any in-world location. Once a landmark has been set, it will reside within your My Inventory folder. You must rename your landmarks with unique names, because by default they contain only the general island name and a particular coordinate. Naming your landmark will allow you to quickly find the appropriate landmark and teleport from one location to another easily.

- **Lost and Found**—objects returned to residents can be recovered in the Lost and Found folder. The avatar will receive the following SL message: *"Your 'Name of Object' has been returned to your inventory lost and found."* This will notify you that another resident, more than likely a land owner, has returned an object you may have left on his or her land. This often happens when land owners clean their parcel of unnecessary prims to create more space. The objects will remain in the lost-and-found folder until it is manually cleaned or emptied.

- **Notecards**—a notecard can contain text or embedded items such as objects, snapshots, textures, and more. Notecards provide other residents with information. A notecard has a maximum size of 65,536 bytes.

- **Objects**—objects are a variety of items. Objects are made up of prims. Prims, short for primitives, are the building components to every Second Life object in the virtual world. By combining prims, a resident can create any type of object imaginable. When you "Take" an object in world, it will appear in your object inventory folder.

- **Photo Album**—when using the in-world snapshot feature, you can take snapshots and upload textures in the Photo Album folder.
- **Scripts**—SL scripts are written in the Linden Scripting Language (LSL), which can be thought of as the programming language used in world to create an effect on an object. When a Script is written in world and is applied to an object, it will affect the way an object moves, communicates, or accesses other content. The LSL is an event-oriented programming language, which in layman's terms means the written script causes a direct reaction on the object.
- **Sounds**—sound clips, which can either be found in world or uploaded as .wav files, will be contained in your sound inventory. Sounds must be 16 bit, 44.1 kHz, and only 10 seconds in duration.
- **Textures**—a texture is placed on the surface of a prim to achieve a desired look in world. Textures can be any type of color, texture swatch, or image that you upload in world. Textures allow prims to take form and to become a dynamic 3D World object. For example, in world, a rectangle without a texture is simply a rectangle, but when you add a brick texture it can take the form of a brick wall. This is how you begin the process of building your own in-world SL.
- Several free textures can be found or bought in-world, or you can upload your own images into SL for L$10 per image.
- **Trash**—the forgotten trash folder is where all your deleted items remain until you "empty" your trash.

Inventory Menu

All Items allows you to type in a keyword to search through all your folders to find a particular item with that keyword in its name. This is a good time to mention the importance of naming files. A full discussion of systematic naming and organization of items will be presented later in the chapter.

Recent Items allows you to search for recently obtained items.

Getting Organized

Nothing must be emphasized more than organizing your inventory items in an appropriate hierarchy of folders. We presented the current folder system and a description of the items that are stored within each folder at the beginning of this chapter. The current folder system is effective if you continually update your inventory. However, creating your own system within these specific folders is helpful. You can create folders with a naming system that is associated with particular objects, textures, gestures, etc., that will make it easier for you to retrieve items.

Teleport to SEA[2] at http://slurl.com/secondlife/Teaching%
208/240/114/23 and take a copy of the Hawaiian lei. Next open
your Inventory (Ctrl+I) and click on the Recent Items Tab. When
you begin keying in Hawaiian, you will see that the most recent
items that have *H*, followed by *A*, and so on. Be sure to name
the object something that you will remember and place it in an
appropriate folder, which in this case might be Clothing.

My Inventory contains all the inventory items you collect by purchasing, building your own, or finding for free in world.

Library contains the entire inventory that is provided to you as a
new resident in SL.

In **Figure** 5.2 you will see the File Menu within the Inventory dialog box.

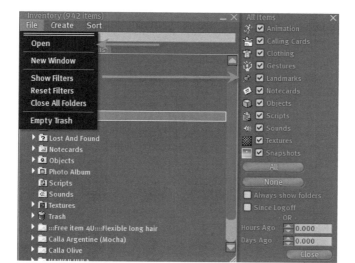

Figure 5.2   Inventory File Menu

To begin, we need to understand all the features available in the inventory
dialog box. The top arrow points to the double line below the File and above
the Open text. When clicked, the double line becomes highlighted and allows

you to peel off the menu as a new window and to place it anywhere within your screen. Below Open is New Window, which will open a new inventory window. The next feature is Show Filters. The lower arrow indicates the menu that appears when you click on the Show Filters option. The filters that are set in SL give you the ability to search the inventory folders smarter and faster. As shown in Figure 5.2, this filter system allows you to filter out folders that are not in use or have not been used within a specific time. The Reset Filter feature allows you to reset the filter to its original features. Close All Folders closes the folder tree and hides all the listed items. You can also do this individually by clicking on the arrow to the left of the folder heading. The last element within the File Menu is the Empty Trash feature. This feature will empty your trash can. You can associate the Trash to the Recycle Bin on your computer. If you do not empty the Recycle Bin on your computer, the files will remain in the Recycle Bin and take up space on your hard drive. Similarly, in SL if you don't "Empty" the Trash folder, the objects will remain in the trash inventory and take up space. Emptying the Trash will help your SL viewer run better.

In **Figure 5.3**, you will see the Create menu within the Inventory dialog box.

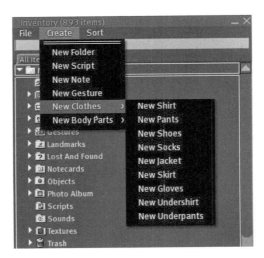

Figure 5.3   Create Inventory

The Create menu has many options for creating more than just a folder system for organizing your inventory. This is also the menu where you will be able to create a script, note (notecard), gestures, clothes, and body parts. If your purpose for the moment is to organize your inventory, then you need concern yourself only with the New Folder feature. To create a new folder, just press Ctrl+I then click on **Create > New Folder**. When the folder is created, you can then name the Folder.

A full discussion on naming and organizing your inventory is presented later in the chapter. However, if you want to create an item listed within the Create menu, the process is simple.

- **Ctrl+I > Click on Create > Choose** the element you want to create. A description of each task is presented in the following.
- **Script**—when you create a New Script, a script asset is automatically created and appears in the script folder. You will first need to name the script (be sure to describe the script action). To create the new script, double-click on it to open the Script Editor. Chapter 8 covers writing scripts.
- **Note (notecard)**—when you create a new note, a note object is automatically created and appears in the Notecard folder. You will first need to name the note with a descriptive name so that you can easily find the notecard later. To create the new note, double-click on it to open the Note Editor. Chapter 6 covers creating a note.

> **Tip**
>
> A note has many uses in SL. A notecard can be shared among users to create a list, provide content, share ideas, or provide a peer evaluation. You can find other uses in Chapter 12.

- **Gesture**—when you create a new gesture, a gesture asset is automatically created and appears in the Gesture folder. You will first need to name the gesture (be sure to use a descriptive name that describes the items associated with the gesture). To create the new gesture, double-click on it to open the Gesture dialog box. Creating a gesture is covered in Chapter 4.
- **Clothes**—when you create new clothing, a clothing object is automatically created and appears in the Clothing folder. You will first need to name the clothing; for example, if you create a t-shirt, you not only want to name it as t-shirt but also add a brief descriptor of what the t-shirt includes, such as "argyle t-shirt." To create new clothing, double-click on it to open the Clothing dialog box.
- **Body Part**—when you create a new body part, a new body part object is automatically created and appears in the Body Part folder. You will first need to name the object. To create a new body part, double-click on it to open the dialog box.

In **Figure 5.4**, you will see the Sort menu within the Inventory dialog box. The Sort menu allows you to sort through the folders within your inventory system. This will sort/place folders in alphabetical order, using all the variables listed within the Sort menu. For example, you may want to sort the folders by date in alphabetical order by name. Or you may want to sort all the System Folders to the top, followed by name. This means that any folder that was created by objects you purchased or were given will drop to the bottom of the folder list.

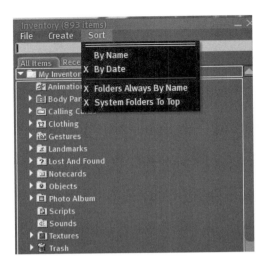

Figure 5.4   Inventory Sort Menu

In **Figure 5.5**, you will see the search feature, the All Items tab, and the Recent Items tab.

Figure 5.5   Inventory Search

In Figure 5.5, the arrow points to the area where you type in key search terms to help you find inventory items. The tab you have selected, All Items or Recent Items, will determine which list the search feature sorts through to produce the results of your query. The search feature incrementally filters the results by each consecutive letter of your key term. This approach helps accommodate search queries where you may uncertain of the exact spelling of the item's name.

Inventory Overload

It has been a few short weeks since you became a resident in SL, and you have enjoyed collecting objects—or so you thought. You open your inventory to retrieve a t-shirt and suddenly find yourself looking at a long list of clothing, with no rhyme or reason to the order. Somehow you neglected to organize and name your inventory items. Now what?

If this scenario just described you, do not quit yet. Several tips are helpful for organizing and controlling your inventory overload. The following section will present suggestions for organization, creating a naming system, cleanup. It will also present and other helpful tips for times when you find that you have let your inventory get out of control.

The most effective way to organize your inventory is to set up a system that works with your specific needs. You can follow several steps to begin the organization process.

Step One—Creating a Folder System

The first step is to decide which folders you currently use the most. Then, determine whether these folders need a subfolder or a series of subfolders to better organize your inventory. Keep in mind that SL provides a set of predetermined folders to help with the sorting process. These folders include animation, accessories, body parts, calling cards, clothing, gestures, landmarks, lost and found, notecards, objects, photo album, scripts, sounds, textures, and trash.

> **Tip**
>
> Realize that sorting can actually flow top-down or bottom-up. Right now, you may be creating folders to start with, but additional needs for new folders may arise after you begin naming and organizing existing inventory objects. Either way works.

Step Two—Creating a Naming System

Once you have properly assessed current folders, names, and objects, the next step is to develop a naming system. Everyone has his or her own preference for naming items. Following are some naming techniques that might help you improve your inventory system process:

- **Date**—include the date of purchase or date that the object was given to you.
- **Name**—include the owner name in description.
- **Type**—include the type of object in the name.
- **Keywords**—include keywords that will help you recall the inventory item.
- **Relevant words**—include words that are relevant or describe the item.
- **Underscore**—include underscore to link key words and dates together.

> **Tip**
>
> Favorites—create a folder called Fav to include all your favorite inventory items. If you want to be more specific/organized, you can create a Fav sub-folder within each folder heading.

Step Three—Cleaning, Weeding, and Trashing Inventory
Deleting Duplicate Items

The first step in the cleaning process is to delete all the duplicate items in your inventory. One of the most common ways that inventory is duplicated is by the many objects that are rezzed when building. These objects are automatically placed back in the folder, often dubbed "object". If you want to quickly delete all these duplicate objects you can complete the following steps.

Press Ctrl+I. In the Search Menu type in the word "Object." All the items in your inventory named Object will appear. Highlight each object (Ctrl+left click) and drag them to the Trash folder.

Do not forget to Empty the Trash by going to **Ctrl+I > File Menu > Empty Trash.**

Tip

If you want to organize folders and clean the inventory within them quickly, follow these simple steps.

Ctrl+I > File > New Window

This will open a new inventory window, making it easy for you to drag and drop inventory items from one folder to another.

Sorting Inventory

Sorting inventory is one of the most time-consuming activities in SL, especially if you have not been mindful and have not kept it up to date. After you have spent a little time in SL, you will find that it is next to impossible to always properly name and store your inventory in the proper folder. However, if you want to be a taskmaster, you can set 15 minutes aside each time you log in to SL to sort, delete, and organize your inventory.

Using the previous tip to open two inventory windows, you can begin the process of cleaning, weeding, and trashing inventory. To take full advantage of the two windows, place them side by side so that you can systematically sort through the folders. To begin, left-click on **Sort > System Folders to Top**. With this setup, you can see the many folders that are added to your inventory when you purchased items in world. These folders are now located at the bottom of your My Inventory list. This set will be the first items that you want to organize, because folders often come bundled with multiple objects, notecards, and landmarks. Determine whether you need every item in the folder. You may find that some can easily be placed in a subfolder you created, whereas others will be easy to trash. Do not feel like you need to keep notecards and landmarks for each object you purchase. A simple right-click on the item will provide you with owner information should you ever want to find the person or the location later. So dump the notecards and landmarks if you do not need them as a resource. As you update one window, the other will follow suit because these windows are mirrors of the same database. So if you take the time to empty the trash, you will see that the objects in the other window have been emptied as well.

To continue the cleaning process, now that you have sorted through the extra folders that have come with purchasing in-world items, you can now move on to organizing your folders. Although this will be a timely process, you can use the filter features in Inventory to narrow your search for unwanted items.

In **Figure** 5.6, you will see two inventory windows with the filter feature set between the two windows.

Figure 5.6   Inventory Filters

The filter feature for Inventory can help you find items quickly in order to weed out the items you do not need. Click on **File > Show Filters**. What appears is the Filter All Items feature, which is wedged between the two invetory windows. The purpose for using the filter feature is to reduce the clutter and the time it takes to open every folder within your inventory. To begin, toggle off every filter by left-clicking the "None" button. Next, choose which filter (inventory item) you want to clean first and toggle (check mark) the item. In Figure 5.6 the Clothing filter was toggled. Next your inventory window on the left shows all elements within the inventory that deal with clothing. In the right pane you see the Clothing inventory folder and subfolders that you can drag the inventory items into. How you have devised your system will determine where you drag the items. Keep in mind that this is also your chance to delete inventory. You can also start using good inventory management practices and naming items properly so that they can be easier to retrieve in the future. Continue through the filters, toggling one on and the others off, to continue the weeding process. Do not forget to reset the filters (**File > Reset Filters**) and empty the trash (**File > Empty Trash**) when you are finished.

Step Four–Storage Ideas

The next step after you have completed the cleaning process is to determine whether you need to store inventory in bulk. The simplest way to store inventory is within a prim. This is known as the storage prim or storage box. Creating a simple storage prim is covered throughout Chapter 7.

To date, I have five avatars. These avatars were not originally created as a means to back up my inventory but rather as a mechanism for controlling the SL environment when I conducted class. As I quickly found out, my alter egos soon became a way to manage my inventory, environment, teaching, business, and entertainment exploration. So aside from suggesting that you create a second avatar for inventory purposes, I would also suggest that you create a second, third, or fourth avatar to help you manage your time in world. I have the following: my first avatar has now been dedicated as inventory backup and "lurker." Although the "lurker" might sound creepy, she merely lurks around my classroom when I am teaching to provide me with an alternate view of students and the classroom. The second avatar I created is the "teacher." She conducts all classroom sessions, workshops, and presentations when I represent my university. My third avatar is my teen grid teacher. She had to complete a background check prior to gaining admittance to our High School College Program. She no longer exists on the SL Grid and can only remain within the confines of our teaching island in the Teen Grid (no exploration capabilities). My fourth and final avatar to date is my book-writing consulting avatar that has been presented in this book. Ekumu is by far the explorer of the group and is more than willing to jump in and get dirty building, scripting, and teaching workshops when needed. So there is more to creating another avatar than SL backup inventory purposes. My suggestion is that you take a bit of time to get comfortable with your first avatar before creating your second. However, when you are ready, jump back in and have fun creating your alter ego. You just might find, as I did, that number two takes on an entirely different life in SL.

Step Five—Inventory Backup

The topic is controversial, albeit timely, in an age where SL backups have become synonymous with theft. For many the need to back up inventory is strictly a legitimate claim to want to save SL inventory items a resident has created. For others inventory backup is a way to steal objects, copy script, and market the products that other residents have created. The solution to this problem is not simple because most residents feel that the backup inventory products infringe upon copyright and open their world up to theft. Aside from the notorious CopyBot, which fueled the in-world demonstration on content theft, to date there are very few ways to back up your inventory. Another program on the scene and available through the Xstreet SL MarketPlace is Second Inventory and can be purchased for L$5999. The program claims to download all items in your SL inventory and replicate them in conjunction with a copyright protection system. This system replicates only items for which the resident has modify, copy, transfer, or original creator permissions. Currently the best way to back up your inventory (that does not cause a revolt among SL residents) is to create another account, ergo, another avatar.

Step Six–Inventory Recovery Steps

A laundry list of steps exists on the Second Life Support Center and on SL Wiki that will help residents recover inventory. Following is a brief list of the most common solutions for lost inventory because at times, although we think we have lost an item, it can actually be caused by friends with special permissions, land owners who delete objects left behind, and computer systems and software programs that at times need debugging.

Lost and Found

Check the Lost and Found folder in your inventory. You may find that the item has been returned to you, and by default, items returned to owners appear in the Lost and Found folder.

Sort and Filter

As previously presented in this chapter, there are many ways to sort and filter your inventory folders to make locating an item easier. Follow the steps presented previously in this chapter to help you filter and define your search for lost inventory items.

Clearing Cache

SL uses your cache to store data on your computer's hard drive. If you find that your inventory is missing items, you can clear the cache and items may reappear in your inventory.

With SL Viewer Open access the **Menu Bar > Edit > Preferences**. Then click on the Network tab. Click Clear Cache button, and exit out of SL.

When you login to SL, open your inventory to see whether your lost items appear.

Internet Connectivity

If you cannot locate inventory items and have tried the preceding solutions, try checking the network connection or changing the type of connection you are using to run the SL viewer.

- **Start > Connect To > Diagnose and Repair**—This approach may repair your current Internet connection. However, if doing so does not solve the issue, you can try connecting with a different network connection if available. Although with Internet connectivity issues, sometimes the best and easiest solution is to log off and then log back on at a later time.
- **Mini-Map**—zooming in to locate your objects (good tip but isn't about inventory...).

Click on the Mini-Map button, right-click the window, and choose Zoom. This allows you to zoom into the map and locate different colors that appear on the map. These different colors represent objects that you own (light blue), objects that belong to a group you are a member of (pink), or objects owned by other residents (gray).

Many other recovery solutions exist to a variety of inventory loss issues. Tips for keeping your inventory tidy include the following:

1. Create an inventory naming system for folders and inventory items.
2. Immediately rename new purchases and creations.
3. Organize inventory and place them in appropriate folders and subfolders.
4. Delete duplicate items.
5. Empty trash.
6. Create storage prims to organize inventory.
7. Back up inventory to another avatar.
8. Clean, weed, and delete.

Wrap-Up

Keywords:

Clothing—assets that an avatar wears on its body

Create (Inventory)—an inventory menu option where a user can create a new folder for inventory management or create a new script, notecard, gesture, clothing, or body part

Filter—a feature in the inventory system designed to help users manage and organize their inventory by type of asset

Library (inventory)—a set of inventory folders with assets every SL resident is given upon joining the SL community

Lost and Found—the folder where returned items are aggregated

My Inventory—the inventory folder that saves all of the assets a user collects during the lifetime of the avatar

Notecard—an asset used to share information between residents

Photo Album—the inventory folder where in-world snapshots are sent upon choosing the Save to Inventory option during photo capture

Script—asset that contains code that instructs an object to behave in a certain manner

Sort (inventory)—an inventory menu feature that changes the cataloging system of an avatar's inventory to assist in inventory management

Textures—images that are uploaded into SL to use for building or sharing information

Trash—the folder where deleted inventory items are sent

Chapter

6

Basic Building Skills

In SL™, everything that you see, touch, and take has been created by someone just like you. This creation process is what is known as building. Building is a rewarding and sometimes even profitable activity that many SL residents love and enjoy. In this chapter we will define the building process and show you how to create your own in-world objects.

All objects in SL are built from virtual assets known as primitives. A primitive is commonly known by its shortened name, "prim."

In **Figure 6.1**, you can see the Create menu of the Build window, where you can see the different types of prims. There are 15 types of standard prims that you may choose to use; however, fundamentally there are only eight different shapes. The seven remaining standard prims are derivatives of the original eight. **Table 6.1** lists the different types of primitives and their relationships to each other.

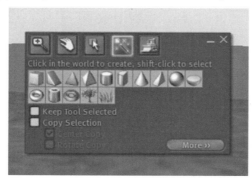

Figure 6.1   Prim Object

Table 6.1   Prim Types

First type	Second type
Cube	Pyramid
Prism	Tetrahedron
Cylinder	Semicylinder Cone Semicone
Sphere	Hemisphere
Torus	
Tube	
Ring	
Sculpted Linden plant	Tree Grass

All objects in SL are composed of one or more of these prims, which may be combined in any configuration to make whatever you can imagine. However, although you are free to build as you see fit, you should recall from Chapter 3 that there is a certain limit to the number of prims that can exist on one space at one time. Much like any other system, SL resides on a server, and everything you do takes up space. You should also remember that building can be done only on land where the owner allows you to do so. To continue the rest of this chapter, you should go to your land or find a sandbox that allows you to practice.

The Build Window

To begin, open your Build window by pressing B on your keyboard. At the top of this window there are five buttons for five different menus. These buttons from left to right open the Focus, Move, Edit, Create, and Land windows.

Focus

Figure 6.2   Focus Menu

The Focus menu (**Figure 6.2**) allows you to edit your camera view. In this menu you can zoom, orbit, or pan. Zoom causes the camera to move closer to your focal

Table 6.2 Camera Options

Camera option	Keystroke
Zoom	Alt+Left-click and hold as you move your mouse forward or backward. If your mouse has a wheel, you can also work the zooming feature by simply pushing the wheel upward to zoom in and downward to zoom out.
Orbit	Alt+Ctrl+Left-click and hold as you push your mouse to the left or right to rotate around your focal point or up or down to rotate above and below your focal point.
Pan	Alt+Ctrl+Shift+directional arrow keys to pan in the corresponding direction.

point so that you can view it in greater detail. Orbit allows the camera to move all around your focal point, which includes positions above or below your object. Pan moves your entire camera view away from your focal point in any direction. This last view is especially useful when you are browsing stores that have products lined up along a wall.

Using keyboard shortcuts, you can access all these camera options. **Table 6.2** explains how to use these shortcuts.

Move

The Move menu (**Figure 6.3**) you allows you to move the prim. To drag a prim, left-click and hold your cursor over the prim and slide it where you want it to go. You can also move it up or down by selecting Lift, or you can spin it with the last option.

Figure 6.3 Move

Figure 6.4   Edit Menu

Edit

The Edit menu (**Figure 6.4**) will become a familiar menu as you experiment with the building process. Although we will explain all these options in greater detail later in the chapter, the following list outlines each Edit setting's purpose.

- The first three options enable you to visually edit the **position**, **size**, and **rotation** of a prim.
- **Select Texture**—allows you to select one or more faces of a given prim so you can apply a texture. Doing so is useful when you only want to apply a different texture to each side.
- **Edit Linked Parts**—allows you to isolate a prim from a linked set so that you can specifically edit its attributes.
- **Ruler Mode**—allows you specify which ruler you would like to use as your grid.
- **Stretch Both Sides**—allows you to stretch or downsize a prim evenly.
- **Stretch Textures**—makes sure that the repeat per face of your texture stays at the same ratio despite an increase or decrease in prim size.
- **Use Grid**—allows you to activate the use of the rulers.

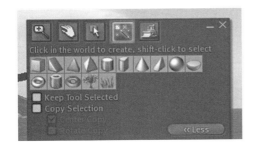

Figure 6.5   Create Menu

Create

The Create menu (**Figure 6.5**) is vital to the building process. As we mentioned earlier, this menu provides you with 15 prim type choices that you may click to select.

The next options are useful for creating seamless copies of an existing prim. The Keep Tool Selected setting ensures that the Create tool will stay active when an object has been created. If you do not have this tool selected, your menu will automatically transition to the Edit menu so that you can modify the prim you just created. Copy Selection copies a highlighted prim. Once selected, the two secondary options become active so that you can specify whether you want the copied prim to have the same center as the original or you want it to rotate from the point of origin. We will show you how to use these settings later in this chapter.

Land

The Land menu (**Figure 6.6**) provides all the tools you need to modify your virtual land. Chapter 9 explains this menu and how the settings work.

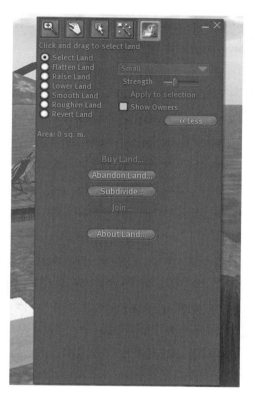

Figure 6.6   Select Land Menu

Making a Storage Box: First Rezz

You are now ready to rezz your first prim. Go back to the Create menu by clicking on the magic wand icon in the top of the Build window. Your cursor will change into a wand, and this is where you should select the prim type you want to rezz.

For this exercise, choose the box by clicking on the box button located to the far left of the Create menu. Doing so will highlight the box button in orange to signify that you have selected that shape. Now click on the ground in front of your avatar, and a small wooden box will materialize.

Tip

When you are editing a single prim, it will appear to have a yellow outline. This highlighting indicator is a visual cue that you are in Edit mode. You will also see a trail of white dots connecting your avatar's hand to the prim. This lets other avatars know that you are currently building.

Objects that contain one or more linked prims will appear outlined in yellow and blue. We will explain linked prims later in this chapter.

Modifying Prims

It may be hard to imagine that this plain box has the potential to become the Empire State building, but it really is possible. Modifying any prim is all done through the Edit menu and the advanced building options.

As you can see in **Figure 6.7**, five modification tabs are located below the Edit menu. These tabs are the General, Object, Features, Texture, and Content tabs. Following is a description of each tab.

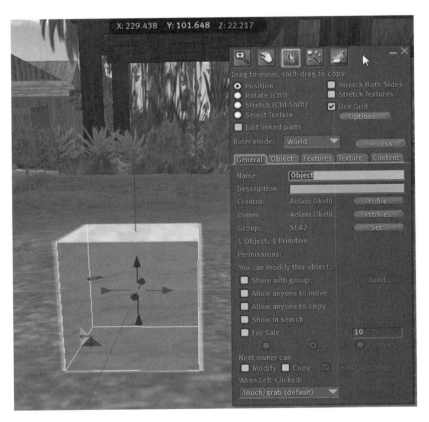

Figure 6.7   Advanced Building Tabs

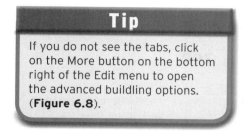

Tip

If you do not see the tabs, click on the More button on the bottom right of the Edit menu to open the advanced buildling options. (**Figure 6.8**).

Figure 6.8   Advanced Building Options

General Tab

The General tab (**Figure 6.9**) is where you label the prim and set its permissions.

The first box allows you to give the prim a new name. "Object" is the default name SL gives to the prim, but we advise you to create a new and unique name that describes what your prim will be. The new name can be up to 63 characters long. This name will be the identifying title that is populated in your inventory should you choose to save a copy for later use.

The second box allows you to enter a description of the object. Although you will not see this description in your inventory, it will be displayed in the tip box that appears when another avatar hovers his or her cursor over your object. The description may be up to 127 characters long. The next three informational fields are automatically created by SL. In this example, the creator and owner are the same, but these names may differ, especially for items that you have bought or received as a gift from another avatar.

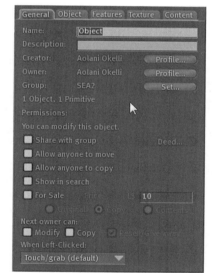

Figure 6.9   General Tab

The group is automatically set to the active group that was enabled when you created the prim. You should be aware of this setting because many islands and spaces are associated with a certain group. This means that anyone not from that group cannot build on that space. For example, on the space for the SEA^2 any object that is not related to group SEA^2 will automatically be returned within 1 minute.

The next line, which reads "1 Object, 1 Primitive," is an informational line to tell you how many objects and prims are in the selected particular build. These numbers can vary depending on the complexity of the build. Because of the ability to link prims, there can be several prims within one object.

sea²

Making a Storage Box: Name Your Prim

Right-click on the box you just created and go to the General tab to rename your prim to "Storage Box #1." In the Description box enter today's date.

Setting permissions for each and every prim is imperative for successful collaborative work. The first five choices set the permissions for **the original object** that is currently highlighted and owned by you. The next three choices set the permissions **for future copies** of this particular object, which will be owned by another person's avatar. Improperly setting these permissions can cause you and your cobuilders to scrap an entire project. For small builds this may not seem important; however, it can be devastating if your project is a building—buildings can easily total 300 prims or more.

Table 6.3 describes the five permissions that you can set for the original object.

Table 6.4 lists and describes the permissions that you can set for the next owner of the object.

The last dropdown menu on the General tab allows you to change the action that is called when an avatar left-clicks on an object. There are seven choices: Touch/Grab (default), Sit on object, Buy object, Pay object, Open, Play parcel media, and Open parcel media. In Chapter 8, we will show you how these options work and explain why you would use the different actions.

sea²

Making a Storage Box: Set Your Permissions

Change the Next Owner permissions of your box to allow modification, copy, and transfer of your prim.

Table 6.3 Object Permissions

Permission	Description
Share with group	Allows you to share the object with the entire group associated with this object. Other group members can edit and modify this object if their role in the group has been granted Object Management abilities.
Allow anyone to move	Allows any SL resident move this object.
Allow anyone to copy	Allows any SL resident to copy this object.
Show in search	Allows the object to show in a search. For example, if you created a prim and labeled it "wooden crate," anyone who searched for "wooden crate" would see this item and its location in the search results.
For Sale	Allows you place this object for sale. After you check this option, the box to the right will become active so that you may set the price of the object. The price defaults at L$10. You may also choose from the following secondary options: 1. **Original**—sells the original of the particular object. The ownership of that exact object will go to whomever buys it. All ownership rights will transfer to the buyer and the owner no longer possess any rights to that object as it exists in world. 2. **Copy**—sells a copy of that object. The original stays in your ownership, but it gives the buyer a copy of your object. You can limit the properties of the copies by selecting (or not selecting) the permissions for next owner. To learn more about these permissions, see Table 6.4. 3. **Contents**—this subsetting gives only the contents of the object to the buyer. You can change the contents by adding or removing items from the Contents tab.

Table 6.4 Next Owner Permissions

Permission	Description
Modify	Allows the next owner to change any of the attributes of the object, which include textures, name, and color.
Copy	Allows the next owner to create an infinite number of copies of the object.
Resell/ Give Away	Allows the next owner to transfer that object to someone else either for free or in exchange for a certain amount of L$.

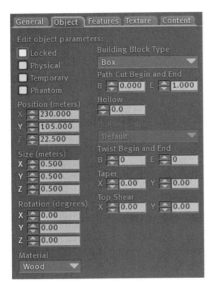

Figure 6.10   Object Tab

Object Tab

The Object tab (**Figure 6.10**) lets you change the parameters and attributes of your prim.

The four options on the top allow you change the state of the prim. **Table 6.5** details the different states of a prim or object.

Unlike real-life states, SL states are not mutually exclusive, and the prim may be in two or more states at the same time.

The next three sets of boxes control the coordinates for the object's position, size, and rotation. We will expand on these traits later in the chapter under Basic Building Techniques.

The Material dropdown menu allows you to change the "substance" of your box. You have seven choices: stone, metal, glass, wood, flesh, plastic, and rubber. Changing the material will change the sound that is played when you or another agent collides with the prim.

At the top of the right side of the Object tab, you may use the next dropdown menu to change the "Building Block Type." With this option you can change the existing prim type to one of the eight fundamental shapes.

Path Cut, Hollow, Twist, Taper, and Top Shear are all intermediate-level building modifications. These settings allow you to change the presentation of the prim by removing or altering the base shape in some form. These settings are particular to the box shape; however, other shapes such as the ring and torus have additional settings that are not applicable in the box shape. For more on these modifications, see Chapter 7.

Table 6.5   Prim States

State	Description
Locked	Renders the object immovable and unmodifiable by all avatars, including the owner. Only the owner of the object may lock or unlock an object.
Physical	Allows the object to be affected by the SL physics. The object is subject to environmental forces such as wind, gravity, and pushing by other objects or avatars.
Temporary	Makes the object temporary and will make the object disappear 1 minute after its initial rezz time.
Phantom	Makes the object a ghost that other objects or avatars can pass through.

Features Tab

The Features tab (**Figure 6.11**) controls the added qualities of light and flexibility. These settings are also considered intermediate skills and will be covered in Chapter 7.

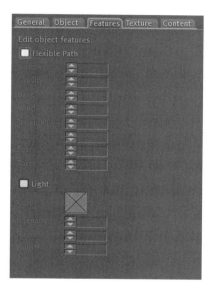

Figure 6.11 Features Tab

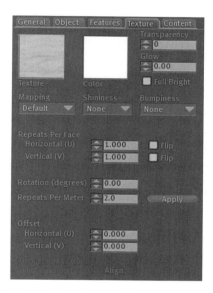

Figure 6.12 Texture Tab

Texture Tab

The Texture tab (**Figure 6.12**) is where you can change the visual look of your prim. Remember texture is an image that you have found, bought, or uploaded and can be overlaid on the surface of a prim.

The first box in this tab allows you to change the texture displayed on one or all sides of the prim. The second box in this tab controls the color tint of one or all sides of the prim. In the Basic Building Techniques section of this chapter, we will show you how to pick and apply a texture from your inventory and how to tint it a different color.

Chapter 7 will discuss all of the other features on this tab; however, **Table 6.6** is an overview of what each of these options affects.

Content Tab

The Content tab (**Figure 6.13**) is where you can manage the inventory of the object. As you learned in Chapter 5, a prim

Figure 6.13 Content Tab

Table 6.6   Texture Features

Effect	Description
Mapping	Controls how the texture is overlaid on the surface of the prim.
Shininess	Controls the reflective quality of the prim. SL does not currently support true mirror reflections; however, you can make it appear to reflect light with this option.
Bumpiness	Controls the graininess of a prim without changing the texture.
Repeats per Face	Controls how many times a texture is repeated on the surface of the prim.
Rotation	Controls the rotation of the texture.
Repeats per Meter	Controls how many times the textures are repeated per meter. This value directly relates to Repeats per Face.
Offset	Controls where the texture begins on the surface of a prim.
Align	Aligns the display of the media texture when creating an object to play parcel media.
Transparency	Controls the transparency of the prim. With this setting you can create up to 95% transparency. For instructions on achieving full transparency, see Chapter 8.
Glow	Controls the illuminating nature of the prim. Chapter 7 will discuss the differences between this setting and light.
Full Bright	Gives an object the illusion of always being lit no matter the time of the SL day.

has an inventory just like your avatar. Although there are some differences in the structure, this tab is where you would add and remove items from an object's inventory. One major difference between an avatar's inventory and the object's inventory is that scripts that are placed in this tab can be active and running. Users create interactive environments with this feature. The next three chapters will discuss this tab and its added dynamics in greater detail.

Making a Storage Box: Add Your Content

Adding items to the Content tab is easy. First, right-click on your Storage Box and select Edit from the pie menu. In the Build window, click on the Content tab. Leaving this window up, open your Inventory (Ctrl+I) and select the items that you want to store in the box.

To select a continuous series of items, press and hold the Select key and then click on the first item of the series. While still holding Select, scroll down to the last item and click it. This will highlight all the items.

To deselect any unwanted item in this series, release the Select key and instead press and hold the Ctrl key. You may then click on the items that you do not wish to include. (You can also use this method to select other items that were not listed in the original series.)

Once you have selected your items, click and hold the selection in your Inventory and drag and drop it into the Content tab of the Build window.

All the select items will now populate the object's Inventory.

Still not sure how to do this function? Check out our SL site at SEA[2], and you will find a video tutorial related to the Content tab.

Now that we have explained the mechanics of the Build window, we are ready to show you some basic building techniques.

Basic Building Techniques

Learning to build is a gradual process. In this section, we will identify key components that you should master before you move into intermediate building.

These components include developing a working and applicable knowledge of the following:

1. Coordinates
2. Positioning
3. Sizing
4. Rotating
5. Grids and rulers
6. Object tab numbers scales
7. Copying prims
8. Linking prims

Coordinates

The coordinates of an object are the numerical values that represent its exact position on a region. In **Figure 6.14**, you can see that a coordinate is represented by three numbers. These numbers reference the object's location on a region's x, y, and z axes. SL uses the object's exact center point to generate these numbers.

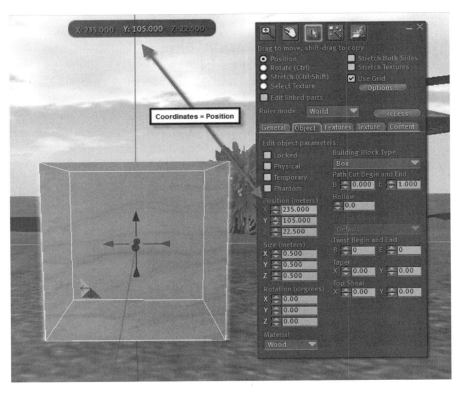

Figure 6.14   Coordinates

As you may recall from Chapter 3, a region is a square virtual space that is 256 meters long by 256 meters wide. This means that any object's x and y coordinates will never be higher than 256 (**Figure 6.15**). The z-axis, however, can reach into the thousands if not more. Many builders take advantage of this seemingly infinite space by building labs, houses, and stores way up in the sky. You can always directly teleport to these spaces, but unless your avatar is wearing a special scripted tool, you will not be able to fly higher than 300 meters, and you will sink if you walk off a platform that is placed above that height. Flight-assisting tools can be found for free all over SL and even at our freebie hut at the SEA[2] space.

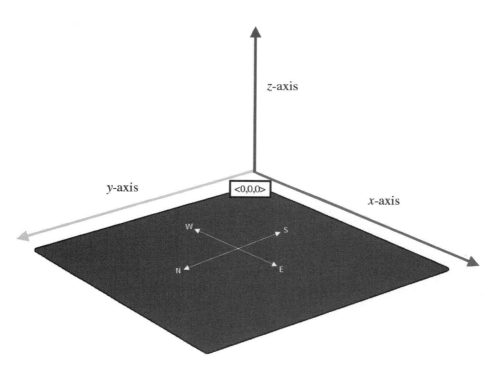

Figure 6.15 Object Location

Positioning

Although the coordinates of the prim give you the exact position, you should know that these are not static values. In fact, you can easily change an object's coordinates by using the position arrows. In **Figure 6.16**, you can see an example of the position arrows.

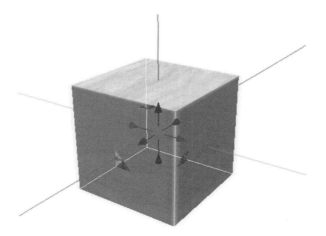

Figure 6.16   Object Position Arrows

The colors of the arrows signify which axis on which you are working. The red arrow will move the prim along the *x*-axis. The green arrow moves the prim along the *y*-axis, and the blue arrow moves the prim along the vertical *z*-axis.

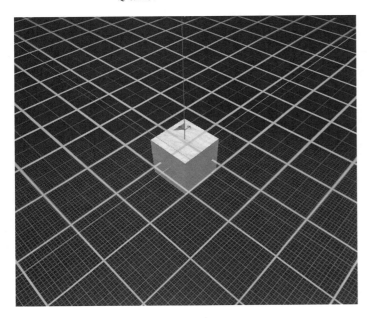

Figure 6.17   Bicolor Arrow Movement

The bicolor arrows are useful for working in two directions simultaneously. For example, in **Figure 6.17**, we are using the green and red bicolor arrow to move the box along both the *x*- and *y*-axes. Because we are working with two different directions, this grid appears to show where your box will appear. We will explain grids in greater detail later in the chapter.

Sizing (Ctrl + Shift)

Similar to the position arrows, sizing a prim is done with its color-coded sizing handles. These handles look like small colored blocks and are located on each face and corner of a prim (**Figure 6.18**).

Figure 6.18 Handles

The following list describes the purpose of each colored handle:

- The red handles will size the prim along its *x*-axis.
- The green handles will size the prim along its *y*-axis.
- The blue handles will size the prim along its vertical *z*-axis.
- The gray handles will size the prim proportionately.

All SL prims are measured in meters. Any prim that you create can stretch to only a maximum of 10 meters long, wide, and tall. To build larger objects you can place two or more maximum-sized prims adjacent to each other until you reach the desired size.

When you are sizing an object with one of the red, green, or blue handles, your object's center point will change. You may recall from earlier discussion that the center point is how SL generates the object coordinates.

Rotation (Ctrl)

Rotation is the third way in which you can manipulate a prim around the different axes. The rotations follow the angles of a unit circle and equal a total of 360°.

As you can see in **Figure 6.19**, rotation uses the same color-coded concept as positioning and

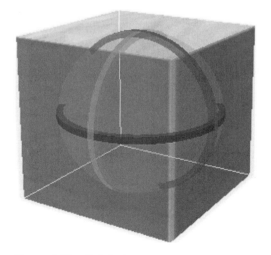

Figure 6.19 Rotate Axes

sizing. However, instead of arrows or handles, rotation uses a ring to surround the corresponding axis. Think of each ring as an individual unit circle. In **Figure 6.20**, you will see a simple unit circle that displays the common degrees that are used for rotation. Remembering these common degrees will be helpful when we cover the Object tab number scales.

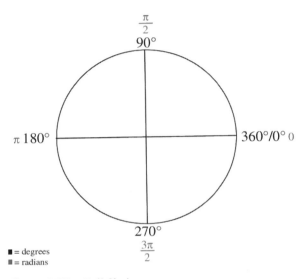

Figure 6.20   Unit Circle

To turn the prim on the *z*-axis, grab the blue ring by clicking on it with your mouse, and then push your cursor around until you have found the desired angle. The red circle turns the prim along the *x*-axis, and the green circle turns the prim along the *y*-axis.

Rulers and Grids

Whenever you use the three previous methods to change a prim's position, rotation, or size, you may have noticed small, white tick marks along the path on which you are working (**Figure 6.21**).

These marks are guide rulers that are quite useful because you can use them for quick, even incremental adjustments.

To use the ruler, click and hold your cursor on the arrow, handle, or rotation circle that you are manipulating. Then, while still holding down your left mouse button, drag your cursor out toward the ruler. This will make the prim jump to the rotation, position, or size that is nearest to your cursor.

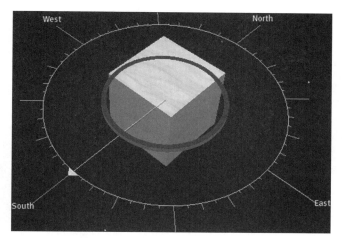

Figure 6.21   Prim Tick Marks

You can change the rubric of the ruler to local position, world position, or reference position (**Figure 6.22**).

Figure 6.22   Ruler Rubric

The local position changes the position of the prim in relation to itself. When using this position, you should realize that the position, differences are always going to be with respect to the last center point of the prim. Every time you move and release the prim to a new location on the ruler, you are also creating a new center.

The world position modifies the prim's attributes in relation to the region's coordinates. This ruler is much more static than the local position because it works with coordinates outside the prim.

The reference position is a useful tool that defines the ruler by the path that you set for it. Torley Linden provides the best explanation in his video tutorial located at http://wiki.secondlife.com/wiki/Video_Tutorial/Reference_ruler_&_grid.

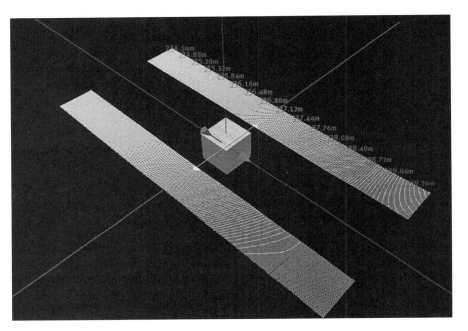

Figure 6.23   Ruler Marks

You can also change the increments between the ruler marks (**Figure 6.23**). This is called the grid. Adjusting this gauge changes how many meters (or fractions of a meter) are set between the tick marks of the ruler. When working with smaller prims you should have this set to a low increment such as 0.1 meters or less. Likewise, when working with large prims you should have these marks set higher, 0.5 meters or more. A good rule of thumb is to increase your grid size if your ruler looks like a solid white line.

To make adjustments to your grid, click the Options button beneath the Use Grid choice in the Edit menu. This will open a dialog box that will allow you to (1) change the increments of your grid and (2) change the length of your grid (**Figure 6.24**).

Figure 6.24   Grid Options

Object Tab Number Scales

Building with precision can be difficult when you are trying to visually estimate the adjustments. Fortunately, all these modifications are actually mirrored with corresponding numbers. These numerical values can be viewed and changed through the Object tab of the Build window.

As you can see in **Figure 6.25**, the corresponding values for the position, size, and rotation are located in the boxes on the left. The top three boxes relate to the position of the prim and are a direct mirror of the object's coordinates. The second set lets you set the size of the prim. And the third set is for the rotation of the prim. To change a value you can use the arrows on the left of each box or just type in the value and press Enter.

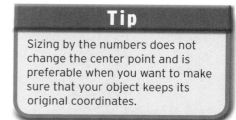

Tip

Sizing by the numbers does not change the center point and is preferable when you want to make sure that your object keeps its original coordinates.

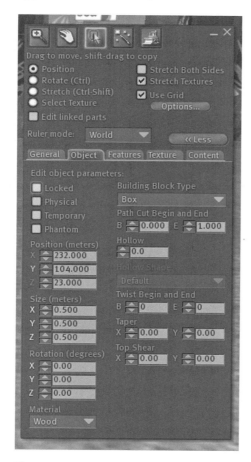

Figure 6.25 Object Tab Number Scales

As you become more familiar with the mechanics of building, you will find that you will use both the visual and numerical techniques interchangeably.

Making a Storage Box: Sizing the Prim

You now have two methods for changing the size of your storage box. These methods are the following:

1. Sizing handles and the grid, and
2. Using the Object tab number scales.

Using one of these methods, change the box to the following sizes:

$x = 1.0$ meters
$y = 0.75$ meters
$z = 0.6$ meters

Figure 6.26   Copy Selection Option

Copying Prims

Building would be a tedious process if the only way to replicate a prim were to rebuild it from scratch. Fortunately, there are two ways to copy a prim without having to set the attributes individually.

The first method is to use the Copy Selection option located in the Create menu (**Figure 6.26**).

To begin, right-click on the item you want to replicate and select Edit from the pie menu. Doing so will highlight the object in yellow (or yellow and blue if it is a linked set of prims).

In the Edit menu check the box entitled Copy Selection. This will activate the two following subsettings.

1. Center Copy will copy the object directly beside your original. This approach is useful when you are creating walls and need your prims to be adjacent to each other.
2. Rotate Copy will copy the prim at an angle from your original object.

Once you have selected one of these options, choose the side of the prim that you want the copy to appear next to and click that side with your magic wand cursor.

Shift, Click, and Drag

You can use the second method to copy a prim quickly because it requires fewer keystrokes. To copy with this method, right-click on your prim and select Edit from the pie menu. Now press and hold Shift as you click, hold, and drag the object away. As you pull the cursor away, a copy of the prim will now sit in the location of the original prim.

> **Tip**
>
> When you use this method, the original will always be the prim that moves with your cursor.
>
> But remember, if you did not set the permissions right, when you copy something there are certain things other individuals may not be able to do, such as change the color/tint or texture.

Both methods are equally effective, but you should choose the method you use by considering the goal of your project. If you are creating a building or a large object that needs to have seamless copies, you should use the first method because this will eliminate the risk of gaps and holes between your prims. Even if you use the ruler and grid with the second method, you still can be a fraction of a meter off and create an overlap. At first the overlapping of prims will seem negligible, but when you or other avatars rotate around the prims, you will see a visual glitch because SL will not know which prim's texture to display first.

My biggest SL pet peeve is overlapping and unaligned seams. It is a waste of time and resources to have to realign prims when SL gives you the tools to make seamless copies. Remember that everything you create has your name all over it, and others can tell if you have tried to take shortcuts when building. Be thorough on the first time around to make the most of everyone's time.

Linking Prims

As we mentioned earlier, several prims can be part of a single object. This is because of a process called linking. Linking two or more prims causes that set to behave as one object. With this approach, the new object can be moved and treated as a single entity.

In **Figure** 6.27, there are two images of the same set of prims. In the left pane, the prims are all unlinked and are highlighted completely in yellow. In the right pane, the prims are linked and are highlighted in both blue and yellow. These colors indicate that the second pane is a set of linked prims, or a "linked set."

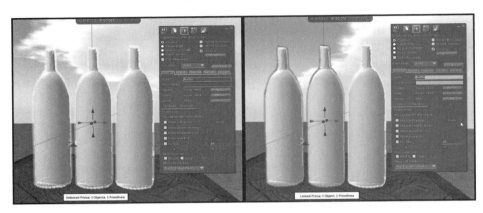

Figure 6.27   Linked Objects

The blue highlight on the first two prims signifies that they are the child prims of the linked set. The yellow outline on the third bottle means that it is the parent prim. In a linked set, the parent prim controls the entire object. It is through this object that SL retrieves the center point for the coordinate, and it is through this object's inventory that all scripts are run. This concept will become important as we move into intermediate building.

Note the informational line that reports the selected object's prim count. The first pane reads, "3 Objects, 3 Primitives," which means that each bottle is an independent parent prim. The second prim reads "1 Object, 3 Primitives," which is further proof that this object is linked.

To link two or more prims together, you should right-click on one of the prims that you want in the linked set and select Edit from the pie menu. Then click the Select key and click on the other prims you wish to include. Once all the prims are highlighted in yellow, press Ctrl+L on your keyboard. The last prim that you selected will become the parent prim of your new linked set. If you wish to unlink them, select the linked set again and press Ctrl+Shift+L.

Tip

Even though an object may be linked, each prim still counts toward a parcel's total prim quota.

Texture Tab Basics

The final technique that you will need to master is picking and applying textures and colors. Textures are important to an immersive environment. Even if you have not gone out and picked up a new texture package, SL provides you with a standard set in your Inventory Library. To texture a prim, right-click on it and select Edit from the pie menu. In the Edit menu choose the Texture tab.

The quickest way to texture an entire object is to double-click on the texture box located on the top left of the Texture tab.

In **Figure 6.28**, the texture box is currently filled with the default plywood texture.

After you have double-clicked on this box, the Pick Texture window (**Figure 6.29**) will appear to the left, where you can either type in a texture name or select one from the generated folders.

Once you have chosen the texture of your choice, click the Select button, and your object will be covered in the new texture.

If you wish to texture only one side of the prim, you should go to the Edit menu and check the Select Texture option. This action will place a circled crosshair on each side of the prim to indicate that all sides are currently selected (**Figure 6.30**).

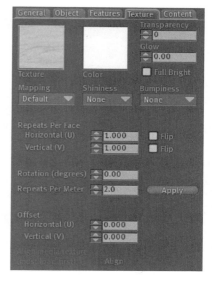

Figure 6.28 Texture Properties

Figure 6.29 Pick Texture Window

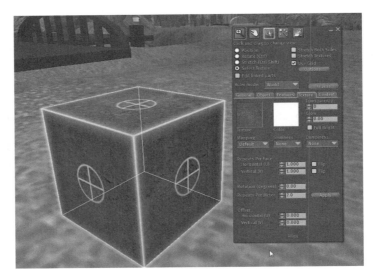

Figure 6.30   Applied Texture

To isolate a side of your choice, click on the ground to deselect the prim. This action will make all the crosshairs disappear. Now click on the side of your choice, and a single crosshair will be displayed. If you have done this correctly, your prim will look similar to the one in **Figure 6.31**.

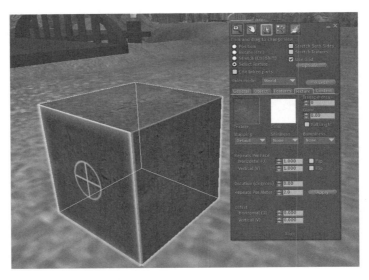

Figure 6.31   Single-Side Selection

Tinting a prim follows the same model. To change the color of a prim, you can double-click on the Color box. In **Figure 6.32**, our Color box is blue. Double-clicking on the box will open the Color Picker, where you can modify the prim's color by either picking from the color box or preset choices or by entering the RGB and HSL values.

Figure 6.32   Object Tint

Once you have chosen your color, click the Select button, and the entire prim will be tinted that color.

By applying a shade of gray to one side of a prim, you can create an effective illusion of depth. In **Figure 6.33** we tinted the right side of the box with dark gray for a dramatic effect.

Creating Notecards

Although notecards are not directly related to the Build window, using them is a basic skill you should learn as soon as possible. As we discussed in Chapter 5, notecards are inventory items that store information. These assets are an effective way

Figure 6.33   Texture Effects

sea²

Making a Storage Box: Adding Texture and Depth

Now that you know how to apply a texture, return to the Edit mode of your Storage box and select the Texture tab.

Double-click on the Texture tab, and search for the "Old wood" texture by either entering the name in the search field or by looking through the Texture folder in the Library folder of your inventory. When you have found it, apply it to the entire box.

Then select the left and right sides of your box (the shorter 1×0.6 sides) and tint them to the following shade of gray:

Gray
R = 191   H = 0
G = 191   S = 0
B = 191   L = 75

Your final product should look like the image in **Figure 6.34**:

Figure 6.34   Completed Storage Box Texture

to disseminate facts, announcements, and reminders because in one notecard you can store text and inventory items such as landmarks, other notecards, and even objects. **Figure 6.35** shows an example of a notecard that includes several of these elements.

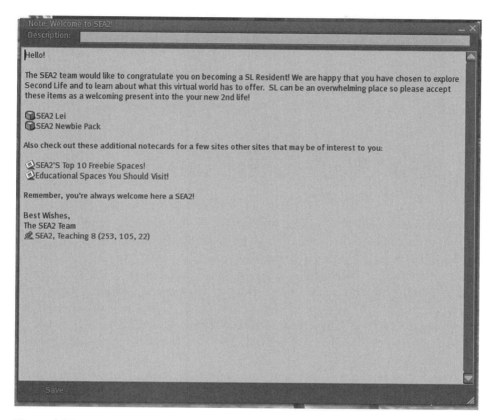

Figure 6.35 Notecard

To create a notecard you must first open your inventory (Ctrl+I). In the menu bar of the Inventory window, go to **Create > New Note**.

As you can see in **Figure 6.36**, doing this will make a new Notecard Editor window appear on your screen. At the same moment, this notecard will also populate in the Notecard folder of your inventory, where SL will automatically default to the renaming mode. You should give this notecard a unique name that describes the contents. When you have chosen a name, press Enter so that the new name will be saved.

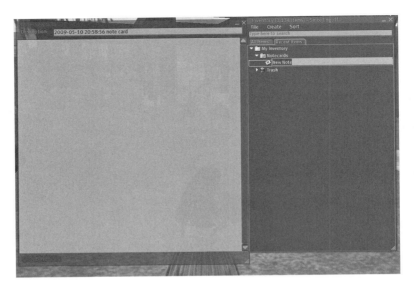

Figure 6.36   New Note

Now you may click on the Notecard Editor and enter your message. Notecards do not support formatting features such as boldface or italics, so you may have to be creative to mark emphasis. You can return to the ASCII techniques of old and use special characters such as underscores and dashes to add visual variance. To add an inventory item to the notecard, drag it from your inventory and drop it into the Notecard Editor. The asset will then become a hyperlink to that item's special ID. Just remember that any item you want to drop into the notecard needs to have full modify, copy, and transfer permissions for the next owner.

Once you have finished editing your notecard, be sure to save it by clicking on the Save button in the bottom-right of the Editor (or press Ctrl+S).

sea²

Making a Storage Box: Create and Add a Descriptive Notecard

As the final touch to the storage box, create a notecard entitled "Storage Box #1" and list all of the contents of the storage box. If the items are too numerous to list, write a detailed paragraph

(Continued)

about the items and their purpose. **Figure 6.37** shows an example of this notecard.

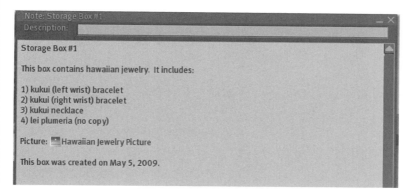

Figure 6.37   Note Content

If possible, take a snapshot of the contents by pressing Ctrl+Shift+S, then save to your inventory (L$10) and save (L$10). Then drag the snapshot from your Photo Album to the notecard, so that when you are reviewing the contents of the box you may refer to the picture.

Finally, add the notecard and the snapshot to the box's inventory. **Figure 6.38** shows the box we created.

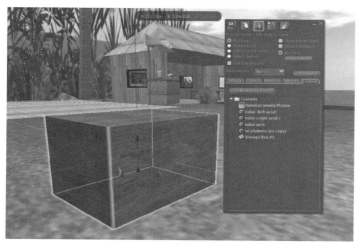

Figure 6.38   Complete Object

Wrap-Up

Keywords:

Advanced building options—the building features that include all tabs that are accessible through the More button of the Build window

Build window (B)—the window that drives the building process through which all building tools may be accessed

Coordinates—the x, y, and z positions of an object or avatar

Create menu—the building menu with which the user may create new primitives

Edit menu—the building menu with which a user may access the advanced building options

Focus menu—the building menu with which a user may manipulate the camera view

Grid (building)—the increments between the building ruler marks

Land menu—the building menu with which a user may terraform land

Link—to combine two or more prims so that they behave as one object

Move menu—the building menu with which a user may visually adjust the position of a prim or object

Positioning—the process of manually changing the coordinates of a prim or object

Rezz—to create or materialize in world

Rotating—the process of moving a prim or object toward a certain desired degree around a specific axis

Ruler—the white guide lines that appear alongside a prim or object when it is being positioned, rotated, or sized

Sizing—the process of changing the length, width, and height of a prim or object

Chapter 7

Intermediate Building Skills

In Chapter 6 we introduced building and all the wonders that SL has to offer you in creating beginning objects. In this chapter we will expand your knowledge of building skills just in case you desire to become a more advanced user and create more of your own tools. These skills will involve making flexiprims and manipulating many intermediate features. These objects will enhance your knowledge and will lead you into Chapter 8, where you will further learn to design advanced builds and be introduced to scripting elements. Get set to learn tips and tricks to make your environments interactive, fun, and engaging. Your students, employees, or clients will all appreciate the effort, and you will feel a great sense of accomplishment. The features you will learn include the following:

Transparency feature	Glow	Repeats per Meter
Path cut Begin and End	Mapping	Offsets
Hollow	Shininess	Flexipath
Shear	Bumpiness	Content
Taper	Repeats per Face	Create a Gesture
Light	Rotation	

Transparency

As you learned in Chapter 6, you can take an object and edit it by using the Build menu. This object can be sized and changed according to the shape you would like it to be or that you need to enhance your land or building.

One way to change an object is to make it transparent. Ever wonder how you can travel through some objects in SL but not others? This section will teach you how that feature works and how to apply it to your own objects.

In **Figure 7.1** you see the property menu of a box that has been created. The box is simply called an "Object" right now, but you should rename it to "Wall" because this is what we will be making.

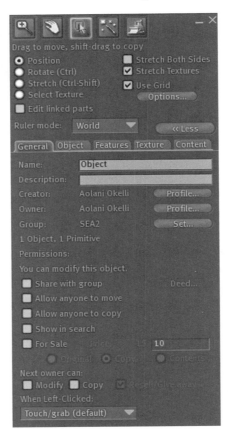

Figure 7.1   Build an Object

After we name it, the wall will be textured and then made into a transparent object so that you can walk through it. You can perform this action with any object you create and any object you pick that grants you modify rights.

Notice the dimensions of the wall (**Figure 7.2**). Especially note that the *x* value and the *y* value are set to 10. As we discussed in Chapter 6, 10 is the largest size you can stretch any side of an object to in SL. You can change these values to match your needs, and always keep in mind that what we show are only examples of the many items you can build and texture. The *y*-axis can be built

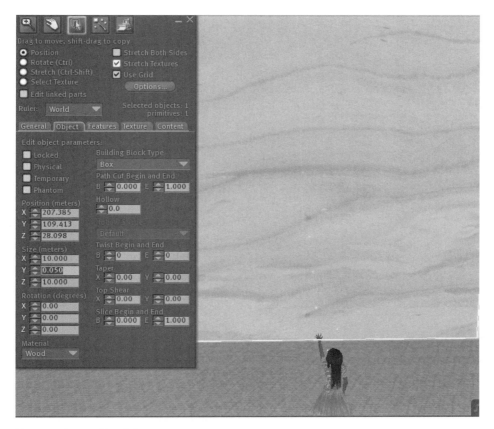

Figure 7.2   Build a Wall

thick or thin, depending on your structure and whether this is an outside wall or an inside wall. Just for effect, go to the Texture tab and make the wall a color with the color picker as you learned in Chapter 6, or give it a texture by choosing a suitable texture through the Texture box.

Under the Object tab, select Phantom (**Figure** 7.3). It is as simple as checking a box to create an object that any resident can walk through. Doing so is useful if you want to distinguish a door from a wall on your space. Using Phantom makes it easier to navigate through SL because you do not always have to find stairs or take elevators to get to a location. It is also a neat trick to use if you are running low on your prim allotment because you can use a single phantom

Figure 7.3   Phantom

prim and overlay an image of a wall and door onto the sides. This will provide the illusion of an entry portal without having to use two or more prims to make the separate pieces. You will learn more about these techniques in Chapter 8.

Figure 7.4 Passing through the Wall

Figure 7.4 is an example of Samia walking through the phantom wall.

Now, some users may not know that this wall is phantom, so an additional step you could take with this object is to make it transparent, as shown in **Figure 7.5**.

To achieve this effect, select the Texture tab and set your texture to Blank; set the Color tab to white or another color or shade of your choice. Then set the Transparency block to 90. You will see the wall almost disappear. This is a useful feature if you need to set up an invisible fence or area around a platform in the sky.

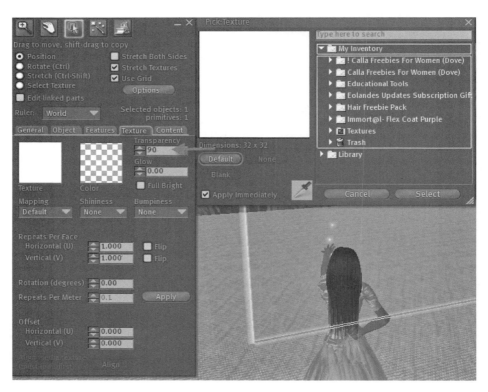

Figure 7.5 Transparent

The maximum transparency you can set through this Build window is 95. At this setting you will still see a faint ghost of your object. For a completely clear transparent setting you will need to apply a fully transparent texture. This texture is often called a 100% alpha texture. Alpha refers to the extra 8-bit channel that is added to a picture to enable the transparency effects. You can find a free copy of this texture on our SEA² space.

In Chapter 6 you learned a great deal about applying textures and how they can immediately change an object.

Importing your own textures for use in SL is also an option. This can be done in a program such as GIMP, Adobe® Photoshop®, Adobe® Fireworks®, or any other image-editing software you are comfortable using. When you are making your textures in an outside program, you should pay attention to the alpha channel. Unless you need a portion of the texture to appear transparent or translucent, you should not use an alpha channel. Eliminating unnecessary alpha channels helps reduce "glitches" in SL where objects appear to sporadically vanish behind other objects.

Path Cut Begin and End

The Path Cut option is located on the Object tab when you right-click on an object. This can cut objects in half, quarters, or other measurements to give you a different variation of the standard shapes. **Figure 7.6** is an example of how a cylinder looks when the Path Cut option has been used. For this object the "B" scale has been set to 0.375, and you can see how the side of the prim path has been cut by that number.

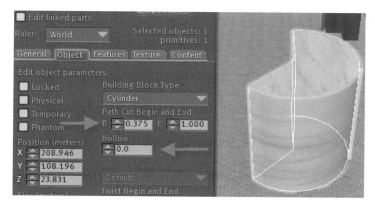

Figure 7.6   Path Cut and Hollow

You can never completely cut the object. No matter which direction you cut from, there will always be a 0.02 sliver of your prim.

Hollow

To make an object hollow, follow the same basic principles as Path Cut. You simply use the Hollow selection you see in Figure 7.6 to change the value.

Figure 7.7 is an example of what happens to the prim when you make it hollow by changing the number in Hollow from 0 to 80. This could be a lower or higher number depending on the shape; however, like Transparency, the maximum value that Hollow can be set to is 95.

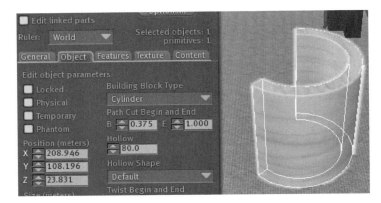

Figure 7.7   Hollow

Light

Using light in a prim on your land can create a wonderful ambiance. It can be done to any object you create. For example, to make this garden light cast a yellow glow, we can set the inner prim to emit light by checking the "Light" box under the Feature tab of the Build window (**Figure 7.8**).

This tab also allows us to add some variations to the new light. We can change the following:

- The color of the light
- The intensity of brightness
- The radius of to how far the prim will cast its light
- The falloff point to where the light will cease to shine

These options are easy adjustments to make; however, to reduce lag many users change their client setting and disable all lights except for the Sun and the Moon. This means that your space will not universally look the same to

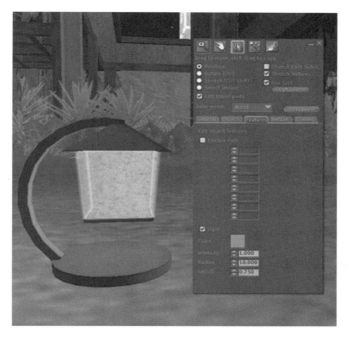

Figure 7.8 Light Feature

every user, so you should not depend on the light feature as a reliable effect to highlight a certain object or area.

If you find that you would like to make an object appear lighted for any user, try using the Full Bright option. Objects with this setting will appear visible and lit up regardless of daylight settings or the individual's client preferences. To set this option, just edit the object, click on the Texture tab, and check the box titled Full Bright (**Figure 7.9**).

Figure 7.9 Full Bright Option

Glow

Adding glow to your object will surround your object with a halo of illumination. The hue of the glow is chosen by the color you set through the Color box in the Texture tab.

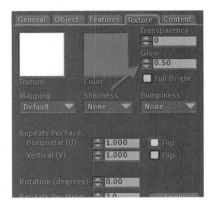

Figure 7.10   Glow Scale

The glow scale (**Figure 7.10**) is located directly beneath the transparency scale and can reach a maximum value of 1.0. Unlike light, glow does not cast light outward.

For example, in **Figure 7.11** you will see a small pink sphere set to a glow of 0.50. Notice how its illumination is completely upon itself and does not reflect upon the surfaces around it.

Contrast this image with **Figure 7.12**.

Figure 7.11   Glow Example

Figure 7.12   Light Feature Example

Figure 7.12 shows this same pink sphere with an active light feature set to 1.0 intensity, 10-meter radius, and a 0.75 falloff. Notice how the light is shed

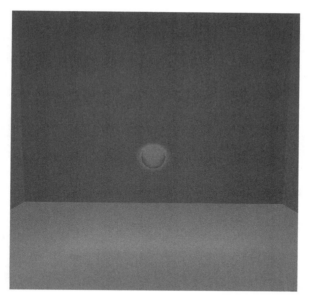

Figure 7.13   Glow and Light Features Combined

on all of the sides of the room but the actual sphere is not illuminated. Thus to make a realistic light, you can combine these features and achieve the look displayed in **Figure 7.13**. Remember that like the lighting feature, the glow feature is client dependent, and users have the option to turn this feature off or on.

Figure 7.14   Texture Enhancements

Mapping

The only two settings for mapping are default and planar. Mapping changes how the texture is displayed upon the side of a prim. The default setting is what SL automatically chooses for any prim, and it displays the texture in relation to its repeats per face. This option can often give certain sides a strange look when you use object manipulation features such as shear and taper (**Figure 7.15**).

> ### Tip
>
> The mapping, shininess, and bumpiness features are listed under the Texture tab and make small or substantial changes to the texture in addition to the application of a texture to your object. This feature can further enhance your environment or can be useful in building some objects for your use. **Figure 7.14** is a screenshot of the three features.

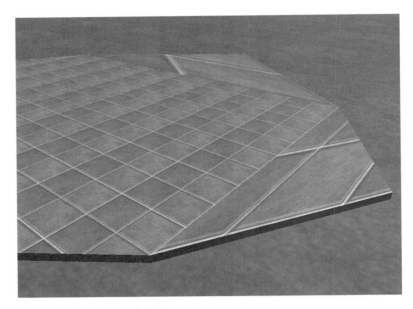

Figure 7.15   Texture Distortion

Planar mapping can help you adapt to these anomalies because it changes how the texture is overlaid on the object's surface. The default mapping tries to fit the entire texture onto the face of the prim, whereas planar mapping applies only the portions of the texture that are relevant (**Figure 7.16**).

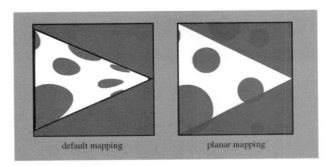

Figure 7.16   Mapping Comparison

To change from default to planar, all you have to do is select the faces of the prim or prims you want to switch over and choose Planar from the drop-down menu in the Texture tab (**Figure 7.17**). After you do this, you will need to

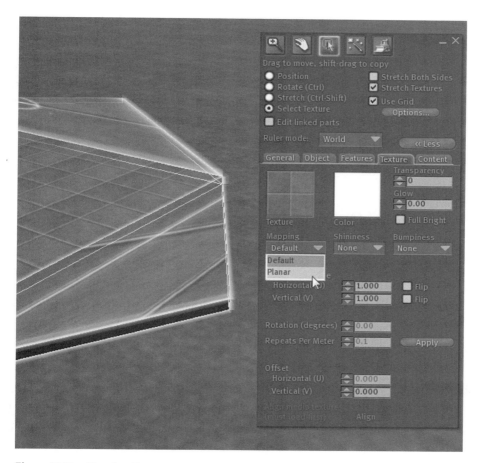

Figure 7.17   Mapping Menu

adjust the number of repeats per face or meter so that it will match the seams of your other textures. This setting will vary for each build.

Shininess

Although no object in SL can have a true reflection, you can make an object appear to reflect light by adjusting its shininess. Like many of the added features discussed in this book, shininess is a client-based feature that users can toggle to improve the Second Life program performance. However, for those that do use

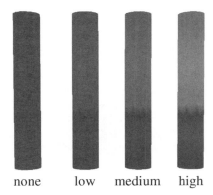

none   low   medium   high

Figure 7.18   Shininess Variations

it, shininess adds a different level of texture to your builds. In **Figure 7.18**, you can see a comparison of the various degrees of shininess, which are none, low, medium, and high.

To produce this effect on any of your builds, you should right-click on your object and choose Edit from the pie menu. Then select the Texture tab and choose the degree of shininess that you would like.

Bumpiness

Bumpiness is an interesting feature that imprints texture images with actual textures such as wood grain, cut stone, and gravel. To add this element, go back to the Edit menu and select from the choices listed under the Bumpiness dropdown menu. The following lists all the variations of bumpiness.

None	Checker	Petridish
Lightness	Concrete	Siding
Darkness	Crustytile	Stonetile
Woodgrain	Cutstone	Stucco
Bark	Discs	Suction
Bricks	Gravel	Weave

Repeats per Face

As we mentioned in Chapter 6, this setting controls how many times a texture is repeated on the face of a prim. These values can be any number between 0 and 100 for both the horizontal and vertical settings. Anything below 1 will give a zooming effect to the prim. In **Figure 7.19** you will see an image of Aolani that was taken on SEA[2].

Figure 7.19   Portrait of Aolani

Figure 7.20 shows you the same picture in SL.

The first picture frame contains Aolani's portrait at a repeat per face of 1 meter by 1 meter. The second picture is the same image of Aolani but with a repeat per face of 0.8 meters by 0.6 meters. Notice that the second image appears to be magnified.

Figure 7.20   Portraits of Aolani In-World

Next to the Horizontal and Vertical scales you will see two boxes titled Flip. When you toggle these boxes on or off it will mirror the texture in its respective direction. This feature is useful when you are matching the seams of textures.

Rotation

Another useful feature for matching seams is the rotation scale. In this box you can change the degree of the rotation of the texture, with the common settings being 0°, 90°, 180°, and 270°.

Repeats per Meter

Repeats per meter is much like the repeats per face except that the textures scales itself to a single SL meter. The maximum value this scale can be is 10 and the lowest it can be is 0.1 meter. This feature is used when you choose use planar mapping.

Offset

The offset scales help you adjust the seams of a texture. The minimum value that both the horizontal and vertical scales can be set to is −1.0 meters, while the maximum is 1.0 meters. This means that the offset can be a whole meter off from its original, default placement of 0. A texture will also default to 0, which is visually indicated by an encircled crosshair.

Flexipath

Have you ever wandered around SL and seen a lot of flags or flexible moving objects? The plants you see moving in the wind of SL as well as other interactive objects such as the skirts that move when you walk are all built with flexiprims. A flexiprim is a prim that responds to wind. Anytime you give a prim a flexible path it will become a phantom object.

To begin using this feature, create a prim and go to the Features tab in the Build window. Click on the flexible-path box, and all the features beneath it will become active as you can see in **Figure 7.21**.

Table 7.1 lists and describes the features related to building a flexiprim.

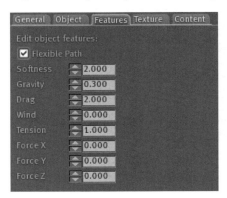

Figure 7.21   Flexible Path

Table 7.1   Flexible Path Options

Feature	Description
Softness	Determines the number of joints a flexible object will have.
Gravity	The downward pull on the prim.
Drag	Affects how fast an object can snap back into place.
Wind	Adjusts how the wind in SL will affect the flexiprim. This feature creates a natural movement in flags, ribbons, skirts, and plants.
Tension	Makes the prim stiff or loose.
Force *x*, Force *y*, Force *z*	These are the directions of the pushing or pulling force on the prim. These are similar to the *x*, *y*, and *z* positional arrows.

Do not be afraid to change each setting just to see the effect on the prim. Trial and error is one of the best ways to learn in SL. In **Figure 7.22**, you see that the cylinder is now leaning over. In **Figure 7.23**, you can check out the various changes in the setting that create this movement.

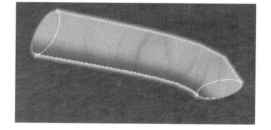

Figure 7.22   Flexiprim Object

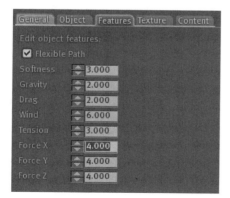

Figure 7.23   Cylinder Flexiprim Settings

The object could also have a texture or a color applied.

Content

The Content tab contains any scripts, textures, notecards, or other items relevant to your prim. If you make a notecard, you can place it in the Content tab so that other avatars can get information about your object, your land, or anything else you would like them to know.

On SEA[2], Aolani has an item known as a Pager. Clicking on the Content tab allows you to see how this object works (**Figure 7.24**).

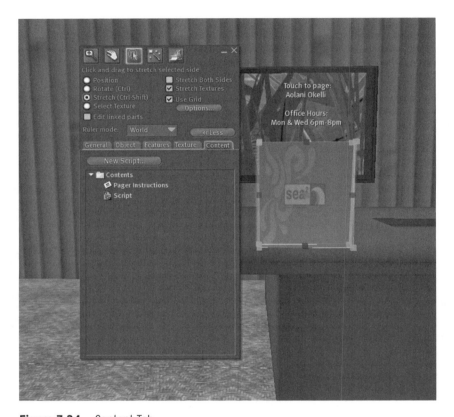

Figure 7.24   Content Tab

There is a notecard of instructions and a script that runs the Pager. This object will summon Aolani when she is in world or send an email to her when she is not in world.

If you wanted to put a notecard in this object, you would simply drag it from your inventory into the Content tab. If you are using a presenter to show PowerPoint, you would drag your images from your inventory into the Content tab, and they would be shown on the screen. If you visit SEA[2], you will see examples of different presentation screens.

Create a Gesture

To personalize your avatar, you can use gestures that your avatar wears. You have some gestures in your inventory, but if you would like to create a custom gesture, you can easily do that. Click on **Inventory > Create > New Gesture** (**Figure 7.25**).

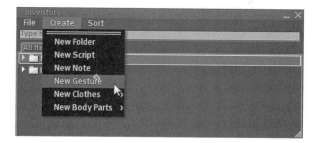

Figure 7.25   New Gesture.

Once you select New Gesture, the following window will appear (**Figure 7.26**).

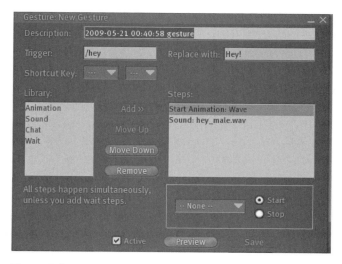

Figure 7.26   New Gesture Window.

Here are several selections such as make a new animation, sound, chat, or wait. You can set the trigger, which is the shortcut that makes the avatar perform the gesture. This is what you would type in the chat area to start the gesture. Type in the description of your new gesture and click Save. This will place the new gesture in your inventory.

sea²

Create a Flag Using Flexiprims by Rezzing a Box Prim with the Following Size:

x = 2.0

y = 0.01

z = 3.0

Rotation

x = 0

y = 90

z = 0

Then make the box a flexiprim by checking Flexipath. The following boxes should have these variations:

Softness = 3

Gravity = 0

Drag = 1

Wind = 10

Tension = 0

Force *x* = 0

Force *y* = 0

Force *z* = 0

Now apply a texture to your flag. If you do not have one that you like, find an image using any search engine and upload to SL. Be sure the image you choose is shared through the fair use act.

Wrap-Up

Keywords:

Flexipath—the building manipulation process that enables a prim to be affected by the variations of SL physics such as wind and gravity

Flexiprim—a prim that has an active flexipath

Glow—a building feature that allows an object to emit a light of its own that does not reflect upon the surfaces around it

Hollow—the building manipulation process that gradually removes the center portions of a prim

Light—the feature that allows a prim to emit light that will reflect upon the surrounding surfaces

Offset—the texturing process of adjusting the center point of an overlaid texture

Path cut—the building manipulation process through which portions of a prim are cut away like pieces of a pie

Repeats per face—a texturing option that allows the user to adjust the number of repeated images that appear on a single side of an object

Repeats per meter—a texturing option that allows the user to adjust the number of repeated images that appear per meter within SL

Shear—the building manipulation process the slants the prim towards either the x- or y-axis

Taper—the building manipulation process that forces the corners of a prim inward to form a point

Transparency—the building feature that changes the opacity of a prim or object

Advanced Building: Design and Interactivity

In the previous two chapters, we introduced you to the immense world of SL building. We showed you how to make and manipulate prims to create several in-world objects that were relevant to your needs. In this chapter you will learn how to design and create advanced builds.

Advanced building may sound like an involved process, but it truly is a gradual progression that you will ease into. However, we should first discuss some key concepts that are often motifs for most advanced builds. First, all the characteristics of advanced objects can be split into the two categories of design and interactivity. **Figure 8.1** shows the breakdown of an advanced build.

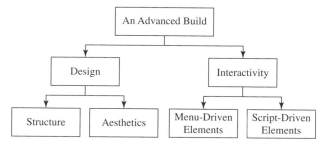

Figure 8.1   Advanced Build Diagram

Design

Design refers to the aesthetics of your project. This includes the composition and visual presentation of your object. You can divide this category into two smaller units, structure and aesthetics.

Structure refers to the components that make up your build. Here you are concerned with the number of prims you use and how you can manipulate these prims to conserve their use. As we mentioned in Chapter 3, each island is allotted enough virtual space for 15,000 primitives to be rezzed at one time (remember, smaller parcels have a fraction of this total). Because of this restriction, the structure of your advanced builds should be as conservative as possible. A creative way to approach this issue is to use object manipulation features such as path cuts and hollows in coordination with huge prims. In **Figure 8.2**, you can see the structural setup of a house's wall.

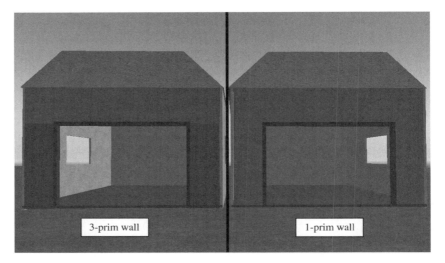

Figure 8.2   House Wall

The left panel displays the house wall set up using three prims. The right pane shows that same wall creatively done with a single prim and a hollow. These methods are useful, but sometimes they can work only so well.

When compositional changes are no longer effective, it is time to "fake it" with the aesthetics. Aesthetics deals with the look of your object. These characteristics are influenced mainly by your textures. Aesthetics may use light and glow, but because these features depend upon conditions of the user's client, we suggest that you use the textures to emulate these effects. For example, you can "bake" light directly onto a textured wall to give the illusion that light is falling upon it. Thus, when you place this texture on a gallery wall in world, it emulates a spotlight without using SL lights.

In **Figure 8.3**, we created this texture, which we then paired with an object created to resemble a track lighting fixture for a truly immersive environment.

Figure 8.3   Gallery Wall

Interactivity

The other major element of an advanced build is the interactivity. All major builds have some form of participatory feature that you or any other avatar can activate.

Under the umbrella of this category are menu-driven elements and script-driven elements. Menu-driven elements are easily set through the Build window's Edit menu. These features include the ability to play and show parcel media and the ability to activate the sales transaction. The following is a list of features that we categorize as menu-driven elements:

- Touch/Grab
- Sit On Object
- Buy Object
- Pay Object
- Open
- Play Parcel Media
- Open Parcel Media

These elements are assigned through the dropdown menu located at the bottom of the Build window in the General tab. When the object is clicked, it calls the action that is set through this menu. To change this element, you just have to change the menu. The following list is an explanation of each action:

- **Touch/Grab** is the default setting that the object calls when an avatar invokes the touch action. If no task is linked to the touch action, then nothing happens.

- The **Sit On Object** action is useful when you are creating chairs or objects for avatars to sit upon. It is also handy when you are creating a teleporter and would like to eliminate an extra step from the process.
- **Buy Object** activates the sales transaction. You cannot set this option if you do not place the item For Sale on the General tab.
- The **Pay Object** choice invokes the Pay dialog. It will not work unless the object contains a script that calls the llSetPayPrice function.
- **Open choice** causes the inventory to display its contents in the Object Content dialog. This dialog gives the user the option to Copy To Inventory or Copy and Wear. This feature is useful for items you are selling in a package. Once the consumer buys and rezzes the package, this option will allow the package to open its inventory to distribute the goods when left-clicked.
- **Play Parcel Media** makes the object a universal play button for the parcel media. With this setting active, left-clicking this object will make all parcel media start playing if the user has parcel media enabled on his or her client. The object that contains the script does not necessarily have to be the object that displays the parcel media.
- The **Open Parcel Media** option opens the media URL.

Script-driven elements involve all the functionalities that can be achieved by adding an active script into the object's inventory. As we mentioned earlier, scripts are assets that make an object do something. "Something" can be anything from displaying floating text to changing a texture on a screen or changing the way your avatar walks. This book will not require you to become a computer programmer. Instead, we will introduce you to the fundamentals of the Linden Scripting Language (LSL) and provide you with resources expand your knowledge or to find a script (or scripter) that can do it for you.

The following section will introduce you to the basics of the language. After we have covered the steps of building an advanced object, we will delve deeper into advanced building.

LSL Basics

LSL is an event-driven language, which means that the written script causes a direct reaction upon the object. Any LSL script is inherently a state machine. A state, much like a human's state of being, is a collection of behaviors that the object associates with a certain task or set of tasks. Each LSL script must have a default state. However, after this state is declared, the object is never required to change states. In the following example, you see the default LSL script. The script opens with "default" to inform the object that it is starting this first state.

Default Script

```
default
{
  state_entry()
  {
    llSay(0, "Hello, Avatar!");
  }
  touch(integer total_number)
  {
    llSay(0, "Touched.");
  }
}
```

A script consists of several coding elements, which include variables, functions, and events. A variable is an element that stores information. It can be any value such as a name, color, or number.

There are seven types of variables. **Table 8.1** lists and defines each variable.

Variables can be user defined, or they may be constants. Constants are useful variables that LSL already stores because they are commonly used. Some examples of constants are PI, INVENTORY_ALL, or TEXTURE_BLANK.

A function is small piece of code that tells the script to perform a task. In the default LSL script, the script uses the function llSay, which causes the object to "speak" a message on the local chat channel.

An event is a special type of function that is defined by the LSL. Examples of an event in the default script are state_entry and touch_start. An event may contain functions within its parameters. In the default script, the function

Table 8.1 Variables

Variable	Description
Float	A fractional number written in decimal form
Integer	A real whole positive or negative number
Vector	Set of three floats to use for coordinates, color, or speed
Rotation	Set of three floats that represent the object's rotation
List	List of values, names, or other variables
String	A variable with letters, numbers, and characters
Key	A unique textual ID that represents an agent or object

Tip

The local chat channel is 0. This is the channel that all avatars see in their regular client. There are several scripted objects that can listen for other chat channels. One such tool is the MystiTool, which that is reviewed in Chapter 12.

llSay is called to say "Touched" when the object is touched in world.

LSL must be written in a certain order or you will get a syntax error. In the in-world script editor you can hover over a function you have written to see its syntactical order. You may also log on to the LSL Wiki (http://wiki.secondlife.com/wiki/Main_Page) for extended help.

The ordering also includes the operators and symbols that inform the script about what or how to perform the next operation.

Table 8.2 lists some common syntactical symbols that we have encountered.

Table 8.2   Common Syntax Symbols and Usage

Type	Symbol	Purpose
Curly brackets	{ }	These symbols open and close an event, state, or function. Each instance must always have an opening bracket and a closing bracket.
Semicolon	;	Each line must be terminated with the semicolon. This tells the script that that line is done.
Parentheses	( )	These symbols work much like the brackets but for elements like functions or state parameters. Each instance must also have an opening and closing parentheses.

Of all the SL activities, scripting is my favorite and what I truly enjoy the most. Unfortunately, I do not always get it right. When I am scripting, I always have a browser open to the LSL Wiki so that I can search for the scripting element that is currently vexing me.

The In-World LSL Editor

Create a new object and name it "Scripting Helper." Edit the object, go to the Content tab, and press New Script. Now double-click on the new script that is generated in the object's inventory.

Figure 8.4 shows you an example of an active script editor. As you can see, the script is written in the white space. You can make changes to the script in this space.

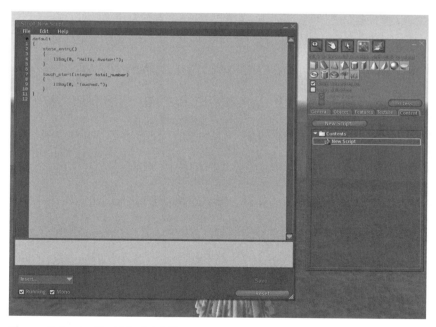

Figure 8.4 In-World Script Editor

The window beneath the editing space is where you will receive messages about errors or successful compilation.

Beneath this space is an informational line that informs you the Line and Column of where your cursor is currently positioned. To the left of the script editing box you will see a numbering structure for the script's lines.

I use the dropdown menu to quickly browse for a function that I usually do not work with but know exists. Then, once I find it, I can insert it by choosing the option, and I can check out the syntactical structure by viewing the mouseover tip. If I still need more help, then I search for that function in the LSL Wiki.

At the bottom left of the script, there is a dropdown menu that lists all the functions, constants, events, and scripting elements.

Helpful Guides

In-world

College of Scripting Music and Science

The College of Scripting Music and Science space is a vast resource for scripting. There are self-paced modules that take you from beginning scripting to advanced scripting. You may also buy the in world book, so you will always have a copy of this space's excellent resources. The sim is maintained by Darwin Recreants, Keystoner March, and Shera Beam and is located at http://slurl.com/secondlife/Horsa/46/243/84.

Bromley College: A Linden Script Tutorial Exhibition

This space is another great walking tutorial in world. As your avatar browses the space, the creators allow you to take free notecards, books, and assignments to help you learn and practice. The space was created by Clive Pro and can be found at http://slurl.com/secondlife/Hyles/124/208/1003.

Online

LSL Wiki

As mentioned, the LSL Wiki is an excellent website for understanding the Linden Scripting Language. The Wiki also has tutorials that users have provided to help you in the learning process. See http://wiki.secondlife.com/wiki/Main_Page.

Script Writing Resources

Scripts can always be copied and pasted into the in-world LSL editor. Following are a few resources that can help you create scripts outside the SL Viewer.

Scratch for SL

Scratch for SL (S4SL) is a great tool for beginning scripters. The program uses a graphic user interface to guide you through the basic scripting process. The program was created by Eric Rosenbaum of MIT Media Labs and can be downloaded for Macs and PCs at http://web.mit.edu/~eric_r/Public/S4SL/.

Stand-alone LSL Editor

The LSL Editor was created as a stand-alone program for writing and editing SL scripts. It can be downloaded at http://www.lsleditor.org/.

Script Me!

This website is an excellent resource to generate a variety of commonly used scripts based on your specifications. All you have to do is go to the web portal and pick an answer for two questions: (1) what you want the scripted object to do and (2) what action you want to happen. The creator, Hilary Mason, hosts the efficient autoscript webpage on her blog at http://www.3greeneggs.com/autoscript/.

Whether you write it, copy it, or buy it from someone else, there are two ways to add a script to an object. With the first method, you may drag and drop it from your inventory just as you would transfer any other asset to an object's inventory. Using the second method, you could create a new script and write or paste the contents directly into the newly made script.

Approaching Your First Advanced Build

Step 1: Make a Blueprint

As you may know by now, approaching your first advanced build should begin with a blueprint. This blueprint does not have to be scaled to exact dimensions or even use any type of metric. Its primary function is to help you organize your thoughts. Questions you should focus on answering are the following:

1. What do I want it to do?
2. What do I want it to look like?
3. What is/are the active element(s) of this build?

For example, **Figure 8.5** is a blueprint for a simple automatic picture viewer. Its purpose is to automatically change the displayed picture after a certain amount of time.

We also decided it should be a simple object in a neutral color because we want the

Purpose: Show different pictures every 5 seconds

Design: Neutral color

Active Element: Front side only

Figure 8.5   Automatic Picture Viewer Blueprint

focus to be on the changing textures. Finally, the only active element should be the single side that displays the pictures. All other faces of the prim should be static.

With this blueprint, we can now proceed to the building process.

Step 2: Define the Structure

This step is where you want to try to think of all the combinations of prims that will comprise your build. Remembering your object manipulations is quite helpful here. Try to imagine how tapering, hollowing, or path cutting can help you use fewer prims.

For our screen projector we have two options.

In the first option, we can use two rectangular box prims placed adjacent to each other (**Figure 8.6**). Our second option is to use one prim with a taper and rotation. With prim conversation in mind, we will use the second single-prim build.

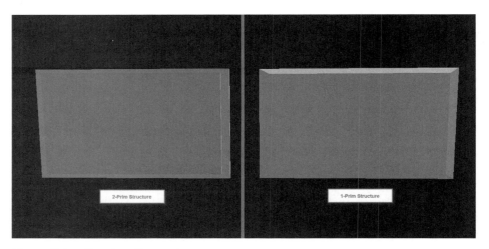

Figure 8.6   Structure Comparison

Step 3: Create and Apply the Textures

Now it is time to create and apply the textures. If you already have a texture you want to use or do not feel comfortable creating your own, you may feel free to skip the first half of this step. To get this texture you may visit our in-world SEA[2] space.

For those of you who do want to learn a little about texturing, read on. As we mentioned in Chapter 7, there are many graphic editing programs that you can use to create textures. These programs include but are not limited to Adobe® Photoshop®, Adobe® Fireworks™, and Corel® Draw™. If you do not have access to one of these programs, a great alternative is the GNU Image Manipulation

sea²

Create the Single Prim Structure with the Following Parameters:

Rotation:	Sizing:	Taper
$x = 2$	$x = 6$ m	$x = -0.10$
$y = 0$	$y = 3.5$ m	$y = -0.10$
$z = 180$	$z = 0.1$ m	

Program, also known as GIMP. GIMP is a free image-editing program that anyone can download from http://www.gimp.org/. In this chapter, we will use GIMP to show you how to make the texture we will use for the static faces of the picture viewer.

First, open GIMP and create a new file by clicking on **File > New**. Under Image Size key in 512 pixels by 512 pixels—the standard SL texture size.

The new window that appears will be automatically filled with an entirely white background. To give the image some texture we are going to add noise by clicking on **Filters > Noise > RGB Noise**.

In the Noise dialog box, change each scale to 0.50 (**Figure 8.7**) and click OK.

Now we are going to add a motion blur by going to **Filters > Blur > Motion Blur**. In the Motion Blur dialog box (**Figure 8.8**) keep the Linear Type and change the Length parameter to 10 and the Angle parameter to 135 and select OK.

As shown in **Figure 8.9**, now we are going to darken the picture by going to **Colors > Brightness-Contrast** and changing the Brightness meter to 6 and the Contrast to –20 and then clicking OK.

To add a nice neutral color, go to **Colors > Colorize** and change the hue to 35, the saturation to 25, and the lightness to –15 (**Figure 8.10**).

sea²

Go to http://www.gimp.org/ and download and install the latest version of GIMP.

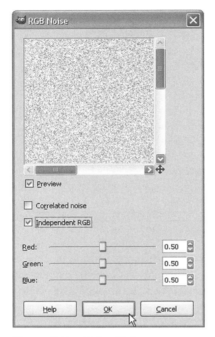

Figure 8.7   Noise Dialog

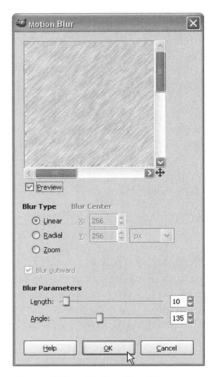

Figure 8.8   Motion Blur Dialog

Now all we have to do is add an inner shadow. You could technically save it as it is now, but a shadow will give the texture a little more depth.

To start, we are going to Show the Grid by clicking on **View > Show Grid**. This helps us keep an even length of shadow on all sides of the square.

Figure 8.9   Brightness-Contrast Dialog

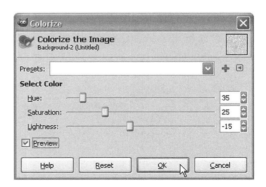

Figure 8.10   Colorize Dialog

Now we need to create a new layer for the shadow. To do so, go to the Layer dialog and right-click on the open space and choose New Layer from the menu (**Figure 8.11**).

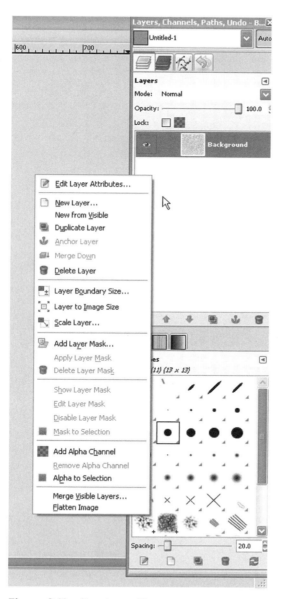

Figure 8.11   New Layer Menu

Figure 8.12   New Layer Dialog

In the New Layer dialog, type "Shadow" into the box for the Layer name and keep the default choices of dimensions of 512 pixels wide by 512 pixels tall and Layer Fill Type of Transparency (**Figure 8.12**).

Now return to your workspace and select the gradient tool from your Toolbox. Change the Opacity to 50, click on the Gradient box, and choose FG to be Transparent. (Your foreground should already be set to black.) Check the reverse box to the right of the Gradient box and enter 30.0 in the Offset setting. Last, choose square from the Shape menu and leave the rest of the settings at the default.

To finally add the shadow, find the center of your image, which is about 250 (half of 512 pixels is 256) on both the vertical and horizontal rulers. Then draw a gradient line from positive 250 to negative 250 on the horizontal ruler (**Figure 8.13**).

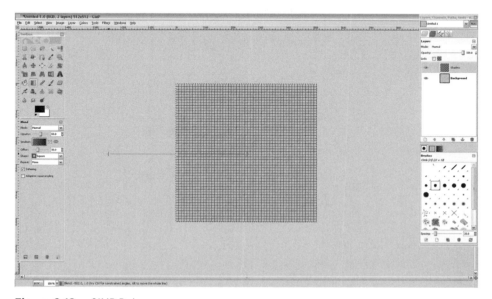

Figure 8.13   GIMP Ruler

After you have applied the shadow, go to **View > Show Grid** to remove the grid. Your image should look like **Figure 8.14**.

Figure 8.14   Applied Shadow Texture

Now you must flatten your Image to combine all the layers. To do this, click **Image > Flatten Image**.

Save your image by clicking on **File > Save As**. Name the texture "picture_viewer_texture," choose a folder location, and select the TarGA file type (**Figure 8.15**).

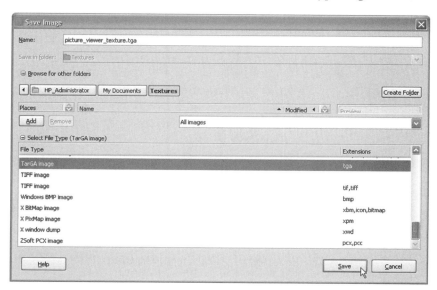

Figure 8.15   Save Image Dialog

Tip

Create a folder where you can save all the textures you make for SL.

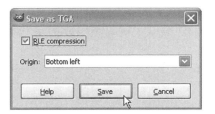

Figure 8.16   Save As TGA Dialog

Figure 8.17   Upload Texture

Then click Save when the Save As TGA dialog appears (**Figure 8.16**).

Now you are ready to upload your texture into SL and use it on your builds.

In SL, go to **File > Upload Image (L$10)** and locate the folder that contains the texture you just made. Once you find the texture, click Open. In the Upload dialog, click the Upload, and the texture will go into your Inventory (**Figure 8.17**).

Step 4: Add the Interactivity

At this point in the advanced building process, you should determine whether your interactive elements are menu driven or script driven. Assigning a menu-driven element was previously explained in this chapter; however, for this picture viewer we must add a script-driven element because none of the menu-driven options allows us to perform the task we need. Thus, with a script, we need to add an asset that gives the object instructions on how to act. The following piece of code is just what we need:

Create the texture from the previous tutorial. Apply this texture to the prim you created in the last assignment.

Automatic Picture Viewer Script

```
integer totalimage = 0;
integer currentimage = 0;
float wait = 5.0;
float counter = 0.0;
integer face = 5;
default
{
    state_entry()
    {
        totalimage = llGetInventoryNumber(INVENTORY_TEXTURE);
        llSetTimerEvent(wait);
    }
  timer()
    {
        counter = counter + wait;
        llSetTexture(llGetInventoryName(INVENTORY_TEXTURE,
        currentimage), face);
        if (currentimage < totalimage- 1)
          currentimage++;
        else
          currentimage = 0;
    }

    changed(integer change)
    {
        if (change & CHANGED_INVENTORY)
          llResetScript();
    }
}
```

This script and its explanation may be found on the accompanying CD found in the back of this book. The script is titled "Automatic Picture Viewer," while its explanation is a document entitled "Automatic Picture Viewer Explanation." An in-text explanation is also available in Appendix D.

By using the resource CD, copy and paste this script into a New Script in your build. Make sure you click Save. Now, if you have not already done so, upload the images you would like to display, and drag and drop them from your Inventory into the Contents tab of the object.

Wrap-Up

Keywords

Constant—a scripting element that has a pre-defined value assigned to it by Linden Lab

Event—a special function that is defined by Linden Lab

Function—a scripting element that instructs a script to perform a task

Linden Scripting Language (LSL)—the event-driven programming language created by Linden Lab that provides functionality and interactivity for all in-world objects

Menu-driven elements (interactivity)—interactive properties that can be added to advanced builds through the use of menu options provided in the Build window

Script-driven elements (interactivity)—interactive elements that can be added to an advanced build only by placing a script in the object's inventory

State (scripting)—a set of behaviors that is declared in a script; every script must have a default state

Statement—a single line of code that ends with a semicolon

Syntax error—an error that occurs during script compilation because of script elements being written in the wrong order

Variable—a scripting element that stores information

Chapter 9

Designing Your Land

Designing Your Land

Whether you are designing an entire campus, or just your office and classroom, this chapter will show you how to use all the objects you have collected to make a space for interactive learning. It is possible to create a replica of a building from your campus, but you can use your imagination and create a room that floats in the sky. You are limited only by what you can imagine. In this chapter we will discuss how to create and decorate your space.

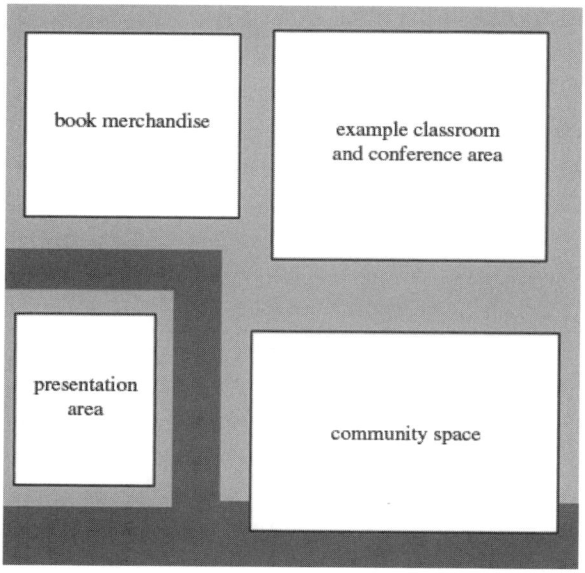

Initially planning your space is quite similar to creating the first draft plan you sketched when you were building advanced objects. To save you time and energy, you will want to begin this project by mapping a layout of your space.

In **Figure 9.1**, you will see our basic sketch for our space. Creating a list of goals for your space will aid you in this first stage because it will help you decide where to place each element.

Figure 9.1 Planning Space

Examples of SEA[2] uses include the following:

- House in-world resources for book purchases
- Display example classroom and conference area
- Create presentation platform
- Designate community space

Remember that nothing is set in stone, so once you have created this list you are free to go back and change these features as your needs change. If you are redesigning your space, you should think about what buildings you can salvage for your next remodel and how you can modify them to evolve as your needs evolve.

> **Tip**
>
> If your current space has a lot of activity going on, an easy fix is to declutter it from miscellaneous plants, decorations, or objects that provide no interactive elements.

While you are planning this space and developing its atmosphere, a key component is the area where you do not have any buildings, plants, or objects. For the optimal immersive experience, you should plan on creating a balance of open space versus developed space. In document design, this is called your white space, or if you are more familiar with the artistic terminology, your negative space. Even though you may have the urge to maximize every meter of your parcel, the proper use of negative space helps the entire parcel feel organized and orderly.

Next, you will want to plan and design the infrastructure on your space, which will include any construction that you expect to remain there for a while. Before you begin rezzing walls and dropping floors, you should answer these three questions:

1. **How will this space or building be used?**

Different uses call for different circumstances. If you are limiting access to a building, you should enclose your space as much as possible to

sea²

Write down your list of goals and create a rough draft of how you want your space to look. Remembering the tips from the advanced building chapter, you will want to consider the different types of users that will be using your space. Remember to think of the functionality you expect from each area.

streamline the flow of visitors. Similarly, if you are creating a resource center, you will want to consider allowing a good amount of vertical space to accommodate the area needed to display the objects you are selling. Many in-world stores are housed in a large building with several floors so the creators can display pictures of each of their products.

2. Who will be using this space?

Thinking of your audience and their skill level is an important consideration when providing any service. By considering potential challenges that your end users may experience, you can make your space more comfortable just by ensuring it is more user friendly.

3. How long will this space be needed?

In the virtual world, it is quite common for a region to be redeveloped quarterly, monthly, and even weekly. Determining how long your structure will be in place helps you plan on how much of your resources you want to devote to building the space. If you are creating a structure for a one-day event, you may not need to be as prim conscious as if you were creating a permanent building to house in-world offices.

An excellent example is our presentation stage and seating. When designing this space we wanted to leave it in the open air so our visitors would be able to come and join the ongoing event even after the speaker had started. Having open spaces is also easier for new users because manipulating an avatar's movements is one of the first challenges they face. We also felt that the presentation space would be fairly static on our island, so we limited our prim use to a single stage, with most of our plants being single-prim decoration. Conscious of our prim limit, the seats at this site are also single prims and are staged in a staggered arrangement. This layout enables each user to see the stage rather than the back of another avatar's head—another consideration for new users who have not mastered the keyboard functions to alter the camera views.

If you are not sure what structures your virtual home may need, here is a list of some common buildings found on active sites:

- **Museums, Art Centers, and Galleries**—These spaces allow you to display curriculum material in a central location. Educators can also use these spaces to feature students' work for assessment or peer reviewing.
- **Social and Community Centers**—Community centers provide your students with an area to meet each other to discuss coursework, talk about projects, or to socialize. It is a good idea to place a code of conduct in these spaces; visitors can review these documents as soon as they enter your space.
- **Classrooms and Labs**—Classrooms and labs can be as traditional or wild as you imagine. Some educators choose to create an environment

that simulates a real classroom to facilitate familiar learning. Others enjoy the dynamic opportunities virtual worlds offer and defy physics with floating orbs, upside-down chairs, and exploding penguins. Whichever you choose, both environments have been proven to contribute to successful course delivery.

- **Offices**—Like classrooms, offices can vary in looks but generally provide students with the who, what, and where of your course, including your virtual office hours, teleport links to your classroom's space, and URLs to outside class material.

- **Conference Rooms or Small Breakout Rooms**—If you plan on using Second Life for collaborative projects, these rooms help you and your students organize meetings. These spaces can also be as impromptu as rezzing a large table on a grassy mall, or they can be static rooms in structured environments.

- **Libraries and Resource Centers**—Libraries and resource centers are excellent hubs for information. Once you have created your curriculum, you can start stockpiling links and objects in these areas for your students to access after class hours. If you are a developer, you can also store commonly used objects for your faculty and students to retrieve when you are unavailable.

- **New User Orientation Halls**—Orientation halls are a great resource for you and your students. If your students are new users, they can explore these self-paced areas to gain a better grasp on working within SL. These spaces are also excellent places to provide freebies for all types of users.

- **Sandboxes**—If your end users will be doing a lot of building, you will want to create a sandbox area for them to use. These areas are usually clearly marked and have an automatic object return, so you will need to warn any students or faculty of the timer you have set.

Prefabs

If you are limited on time and have a few Linden dollars to spend, you may want to consider buying "prefabs," which are ready-made buildings. Many Second Life residents have started virtual businesses that consist solely of creating and

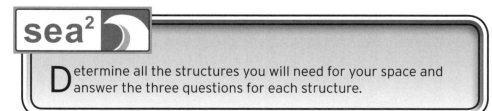

sea² Determine all the structures you will need for your space and answer the three questions for each structure.

selling these buildings for other residents to use. The quickest way to find these buildings is to either search for "prefab" in the in-world Search window or on the Web at the X-Street SL Marketplace (http://www.xstreetsl.com).

Now that we have our buildings, the next step is to work on the other elements that contribute to the ambience of your new space. These elements include terraforming, landscaping, lighting, music, and even wildlife. Even if replicating your First Life is not your plan, adding simple design features such as flowers and trees can give your space a touch of realism that will heighten the sense of virtual immersion.

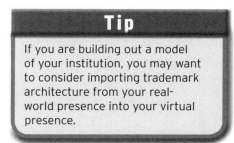

Tip

If you are building out a model of your institution, you may want to consider importing trademark architecture from your real-world presence into your virtual presence.

Terraforming

Terraforming is the act of changing the visual features of your land. In SL you can carve mountains, gorge out canyons, create a lake, or emulate an exotic beach. All this is achieved through either raising or lowering different areas of your land.

To access these tools, right-click on your land and select Edit Terrain from your pie menu (**Figure 9.2**). This window probably looks familiar to you because it is actually the last tab from the Build window that you have been using to create your in-world objects. Before we move on, we will cover what these tools are and how you can use them (**Figure 9.3**).

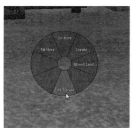

Figure 9.2   Terrain Pie Menu

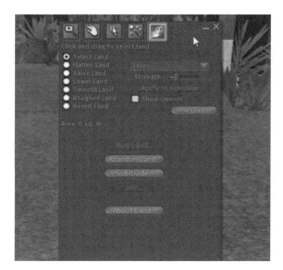

Figure 9.3   Terrain Menu

Table 9.1   Terraforming Options

Options	Description
Select Land	Selects an rectangular area of land
Flatten Land	Levels land to one particular height
Raise Land	Increases height of the land
Lower Land	Decreases height of the land
Smooth Land	Smoothes abrupt height levels
Roughen Land	Increases abrupt height levels
Revert Land	Rolls region back to original terrain of land on last saved by the Estate Owner

Figure 9.4   Select Land Option

Tip

If you raise the land above your buildings, items will be returned to their owners.

Explanation of Edit Terrain Menu

Table 9.1 lists all variations you can use to edit the land. Your default selection will be set to the "Select Land" option.

To select a block of land, click, hold, and drag your cursor over the area that you want to change. The selection you have chosen will now be enclosed in a yellow outline (**Figure 9.4**).

Working with selections of land is useful when you are making large-scale changes. If you use the Raise Land option with a block of land selected, you can create an instant plateau (or the reverse if you use the Lower Land option). To apply these changes to the land, click on your option and select the "Apply to Selection" button beneath the strength slider (**Figure 9.5**).

If you do not need to change a whole section of land, you can also use your cursor to spot-fix areas of your choice. You can change the size of your cursor by using the dropdown menu on the right side of the window to change it to a small, medium, or large size. To control how strongly your adjustments will affect the land, use the strength slider located beneath the dropdown menu.

Flattening land is helpful; however, it is not as intuitive as it may seem. To flatten the land, click and hold your cursor on a space of the ground that has the optimal height. While still holding the left mouse button, drag the cursor over all the areas that you want to match the first height. The leveling of the ground is relative to the location of the first click.

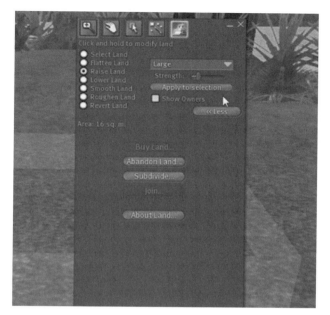

Figure 9.5   Modify Land Menu

For example, in **Figure 9.6**, if we started flattening the land at the top of the small mound on the left, all the surrounding area we touched would rise to meet the apex of the hill. However, if we started on the lower land on the right and dragged the cursor toward the mound, the hill would fade away and level out with the rest of its surroundings.

Figure 9.6   Terrain Example

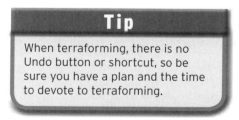

Tip

When terraforming, there is no Undo button or shortcut, so be sure you have a plan and the time to devote to terraforming.

Smoothing the land is also useful because raising and lowering the land can make your space uneven in an exaggerated manner. The smooth land option makes the inclines and rises less steep, whereas roughening the land does the opposite.

Tip

It is best to plan out your land before you place your buildings. Terraforming in world is not a precise art, and it can be difficult to accommodate existing structures.

Reverting the land is a tool you generally will not use. Reverting the land refers to the process of rolling back the shape of the land that your parcel and all the other parcels on that island looked like at the last bake (save) of the raw terrain file. As parcel owners, you may not have been privy to the last save, and it may not look the way you expect it to look.

Lighting

Like real-world settings, placing strategic lights on your virtual space can help set the tone. As a parcel owner, you can add the effect of lighting by creating objects that have an internal light. As you may recall from Chapter 7, these lights are easily made by checking the "Light" box in the Features tab of the Build window.

Landscaping

Once you have terraformed your land, landscaping should be your next step. Plenty of sims sell realistic and affordable trees, flowers, and more. However, you do not have to look any further than your inventory's Library folder for a few default Linden plants to help you get started.

Tip

If your group members receive the message "You cannot create plants on this land" when placing Linden plants, the message is an indication that "Edit Terrain" is disabled on your land.

To turn Edit Terrain on or off, click on the region name at the top of your SL client to open the About Land window. Next, click on the Options tab and look at the box in the top-left corner of the About Land window (**Figure 9.7**).

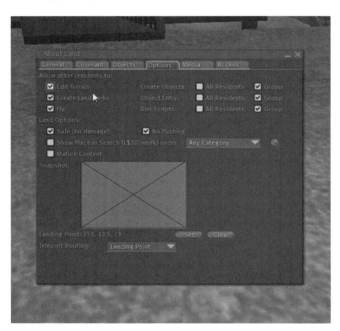

Figure 9.7   Edit Terrain Option

Linden Plants

In your inventory in your **Library > Objects > Landscaping** folder, you have a set of default trees that Linden Lab provides to all users. These plants are great starting points and are really useful if you have a limited number of prims to spend on landscaping because they are special prims and use up the space of only one prim per plant.

As owner of your parcel, you will be able to place Linden plants whether Edit Terrain is on or not. If you do not have a friend to help you, use an alternate avatar to help you test this feature.

You should usually leave this option unchecked, especially if you allow all Residents—meaning all SL users—to create objects on your land. If your students or faculty must use Linden plants, make sure you turn this option off when they are done working so you are not unwittingly inviting unfriendly residents to tamper with your space.

User-Created Plants

In addition to Linden plants, many users have created amazing objects that have the look of real-world plants. These plants generally consist of two or more intersecting flat prims that are textured with images of plants with transparent backgrounds.

> **Tip**
>
> Some creators have used "huge prims" to create large trees that can span beyond the 10-meter prim limit. These huge prims were remnants of the early days of SL when there were no prim length limits. If you do not have a lot of prims to use for a fancy 32-prim golden maple, these huge trees can seriously diminish a low prim count.

With the use of sculpted prims, some users have now made it possible for user-created single-prim plants, too. You can buy your plant base at the X Street SL Exchange. We suggest the Bunny Designs 8-sided version because it comes with a helpful manual to guide you on how to apply a regular plant texture to the sculpted base.

For our space and those that we have designed, we tend to use a combination of these plants. Following is a list we have compiled to help you in your search for your perfect plants. Here are two of our favorite plant sims.

Organica

http://slurl.com/secondlife/Sylvan/187/85/914

Heart Garden Centre

http://slurl.com/secondlife/Heart%201/124/124/28

Wildlife

Plants are great, and with flexiprims they can even sway with the wind, but adding a scampering rabbit or a crying seagull can enhance your environment

sea²

In your design, add at least three plants. These plants can be houseplants, large trees, a tiny flower, or a combination of all three. A designing guideline called the "rule of odds" asserts that objects should be positioned in odd numbers to communicate a sense of balance and comfort. Try this rule when you are staging your plants. In your arrangements, use plants that have various heights to create levels for the eye to follow.

as well. If you are building out a simulation, adding animals can make your underwater scuba trip an exciting adventure. Here are two of our favorite stores for SL wildlife.

Animal Island

http://slurl.com/secondlife/ANIMAL%20ISLAND/128/128/22

Aquatic Friends

http://slurl.com/secondlife/Eydis%20Sands/58/201/26

sea²

Your sketch is now complete, so now it is time to go to your region and build your space. Terraform it first; place your building(s); and then add your lights, plants, and wildlife.

Sounds and Music

Adding audio to your space may be something you thought only entertainment sites do, but adding audio can be useful for you, too. Besides music, you can also bring in other types of audio, such as ambient nature sounds, informative podcasts, or dramatic readings of Dylan Thomas. With that in mind, the first step to adding audio to your space is to decide how adding audio may enhance your space. If your space is the professional face of your company, you may not want to stream a zesty pop station. However, it might be nice to add some soothing music to your welcoming lobby and to keep the rest of the island silent for presentations, conferences, or meetings.

Next, you should decide on the range of the area in which your listeners will be able to hear it. You have a choice to either enable parcelwide audio or to designate a listening station.

Listening stations are smaller parcels within the borders of the land and are a great option when you want different audio on different areas of the same land. In the preceding example, we can create a listening station beneath the landing point of the lobby so that the music plays only in that area.

To create a listening station perform these three steps:

1. Right-click on your land and select Edit Terrain.
2. In the Build window, use the "Select Land" option to highlight the area of land that you want to designate at the new parcel.
3. Select Divide Land, and now you have another miniparcel on your larger space.

You are now ready to set your audio. Second Life supports only mp3 audio files or MPEG streams. If you use an mp3 audio file, SL does not allow you to upload these files, so you will need to host it on an external server. Check with your institution to see if your IT department offers these services; if not, several free and paid web services can help you.

To help you decide which you would like to use, **Table 9.2** compares an mp3 audio file and an MPEG stream.

Table 9.2 Audio Options

mp3	MPEG stream
Plays only once	Streams continuously
User-dependent play mode—will not play at the same time for all users	Plays in real time
Example URL: http://www.domainname.com/possiblefolders/filename.mp3	Example URL: http://71.143.11.100:9000
Common examples: podcasts, single music files, recordings	Common examples: Internet radio stations

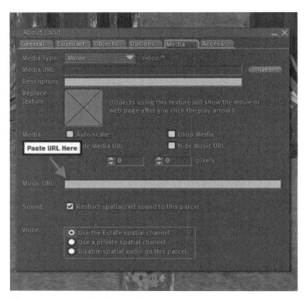

Figure 9.8   About Land Media Tab

To set your audio, perform these steps:

1. Click on the region name at the top of your client to open the About Land window (**Figure 9.8**).

2. Go to the Media tab and paste the audio URL in the Media URL box.

To see some creative ways in which others have used audio, visit these spaces:

Foul Whisperings, Strange Matters
A sim dedicated to Shakespeare's Macbeth that has a creative use of sounds.
http://slurl.com/secondlife/Macbeth/45/48/54

College of DuPage: Tintern Abbey
A creative space based on William Wordsworth, Tintern Abbey
http://slurl.com/secondlife/Eduisland%203/196/72/23

Wrap-Up

Keywords:

Bake (land)—to save the current condition and layout of a region

Huge prims—prims that are larger than the current 10-meter limit that were created and saved before the limitation was imposed

Linden plants—a special plant item created by Linden Lab that takes up the space only of a single prim

Prefabs—prefabricated builds that a user may purchase to develop his or her sim

RAW file—a type of file that an estate owner may upload to redesign the structure of his or her land

Terrain—the actual virtual land that a user can terraform

University and Program Assessment

Need

In an awe-inspiring analogy, Schon (1995), as cited in Burge (2008), presents the complexities associated with navigating a swamp area that consists of the uncertainty, uniqueness, conflict, and difficulty that educators grapple with daily when determining how to balance the use of technology in education. The swamp represents the messy technological foundations that we have created for ourselves as educators, whereas the "high" ground in the passage represents a land that is structured and manageable—a land where student needs, faculty knowledge, administrative support, and technology coexist to present a manageable yet engaging learning environment. In the quest to provide a balance in the use of technology in education, we discovered our own need for virtual environments and became pioneers at our own institution. As pioneers, we dealt with several issues surrounding the ability to integrate virtual environments into our university program. We discuss these issues in the following chapter and hope to provide you with not only the insight on how to gain approval and funding but also the fortitude and thoughtfulness in how to approach the teaching process in world. Therefore, prior to diving into a new technological venue as an educator, you must ask yourself: What is the purpose for integrating virtual environments into my class, program, university, training program, etc? Consider the wisdom of Uli Bernath, former director of the Center for Distance Education, who in an interview states the following:

> *Faculty are important, brains are important, concepts are important, teacher/ learner relations are important. And then if you think technology helps these*

important players in the field to achieve their goals . . . then apply technology; but don't start with 'it' (Burge 2008, p. 9).

As educators we realize that, for today's learner, interaction and social networking have become synonymous. Virtual environments are a phenomenal tool for educators and corporations to use because they allow both teacher and student to share projects, presentations, papers, simulations, and demonstrations within an interactive platform that affords social interactions. Students can work collectively as a team to complete assignments and share experiences in real-time voice communication. Having the ability to see, hear, and work on one another's material creates an online community similar to that which takes place in a library or student center.

Purpose/Rationale

Begin by asking why you want to include Second Life® as a way to engage students in the learning process. As an educator you may see the value in adding a particular method offered by using a virtual environment to teach students. However, your institution may want a strategic technology plan that provides a rationale for implementation. The following section presents the why, who, what, when, where, and how of developing a technology plan along with challenges faced by institutions planning to implement a new technological medium.

Why

1. Why do we need to offer instruction via virtual environments? Asking this question can help guide the rest of your program planning.
   - To reach more students and alumni, retention, recruitment, social networking, community involvement, partnerships, and collaboration.
   - To be more accessible to students, both traditional and online.
   - To keep up with changing technology and changing needs of students.
   - To keep up with current education and economic trends of our global economy.

2. Are there particular programs that we provide that could easily be provided in a virtual environment?

- Education, information technology, computer science
- Support services such as career, technical, or alumni

Who

1. Identify a target population or specific program or service. Is there a certain group that may benefit from virtual environments more than others?

- Major/college
- Class/year—graduating students, incoming students, etc.
- Special population, military, transfer students, online students, teachers, or alumni

2. Who has to buy into or support this product/project?

- Departmental staff
- Academic departments/faculty
- Students/alumni
- Technical support
- Administration
- Corporate executives

3. Who will help operate this program?

- Current staff, or are additional staff needed?
- Student/graduate assistants
- Current technology support systems

What

1. What is the computer literacy level of the student?

2. What is the computer literacy level of the teacher?

3. What is the expected cost?

- Is it necessary to buy software?
  - Costs to students with required hardware needs
  - Hardware requirements
  - Internet connection: cable or DSL
  - Operating system: Windows 2000, XP, or Vista
  - Computer processor: 800-MHz Pentium III or Athlon, or better
  - Computer memory: 512 MB or more

- Video/graphics card for XP/2000: nVidia GeForce 2, GeForce 4 MX, or better; ATI Radeon 8500, 9250, or better; Intel 945GM. Video/Graphics Card for Vista (requires latest drivers): nVidia GeForce 6600 or better; ATI Radeon 9500 or better; Intel 945GM

4. Technical support costs?
5. Training costs?
6. Hire new professional or student staff?

When

1. When to implement the program?
   - Pilot program
   - Scaffold courses in or begin will full implementation

2. When to evaluate it? How often?
   - Survey
   - Focus groups

Where

1. What are other universities doing?
   - What specific programs?
   - Campus offices that could provide technical support?

2. What are your competitors (other colleges/universities/corporations) doing?

How

1. How are we going to evaluate the program?
2. How will we measure its success?
3. How will we market the program or service to our target audience?

Potential Barriers and Hurdles

University Barriers

1. Is upper-level administration favorable toward new technology?
2. What are the media regulations of the institution?
3. Should legal counsel be consulted?

Departmental Barriers

1. Who is responsible?
2. Does this influence job description, work load, etc.?

Generational Barriers

1. Will veterans, boomers, and members of Generation X appreciate and recognize need?
2. Education needed?

The success of any program implementation involves more than simply defining the parameters for integration. It requires a careful, thoughtful process that reviews the aforementioned elements of why, who, what, when, where, and how in combination with a clearly defined road map that will demonstrate a commitment to the program. Creating a program that fosters innovation, collaboration, and evaluation will result in a higher level of adoption that will ultimately provide more positive outcomes.

Tips for program development and implementation include the following:

1. Analyze current program
2. Conduct a needs assessment
3. Evaluate programmatic needs
4. Assess funding needs
5. Create a vision
6. Develop a strategic plan
7. Assess impact
8. Communicate progress
9. Continue to assess the process
10. Review and revise program

Wrap-Up

References

Burge, L. 2008. Crafting the future: Pioneer lessons and concerns for today. *Distance Education* 29(1): 5–17.

Schon, D.A. 1995. Knowing in action: The new scholarship requires a new epistemology. *Change* 27(6): 27–34.

Chapter

Teaching and Training Methods for In-World Engagement

Throughout this textbook, you have learned a variety of basic techniques for learning how to access, maneuver in, and work with SL®. Mastering the SL basics is the first essential step to understanding the vast capabilities available for creating a dynamic environment in SL. At this point, if you do not know how to teleport, fly, and rezz objects, this chapter about understanding and integrating educational tools may seem overwhelming.

Learning the basics is fun, but now it is time to adopt these concepts and create a specialized learning environment. Chapter 12 will outline a variety of educational tools that are available to develop and deliver course material. This chapter will provide you with the methods that have been and can be infused into your courses and training material. These methods make delivering content in virtual environments effective and beneficial. Whether you are part of a business or academic institution, the value of moving content to a virtual environment is important because it can help you can save money and resources.

Purpose/Rationale

Integrating new instructional methods can be a difficult task, but the more complex task is determining the need and purpose for using these new methods.

Whether you are a K–16 teacher, corporate trainer, or military instructor, the instructional methods for the development and delivery of courses should begin with a review of the curriculum and course blueprints of your specific discipline. Start by assessing the material in smaller chunks. Address required

One time I integrated a social networking software program into my online course, hoping that it would create a learning community among students where we would interact within the social space. One student said it was like I was at her house "knocking" on her door, wanting to her come out and play. For that particular student it felt as if I was trying to bring instruction and learning to the confines of her social environment and the student just did not want me there. This leads us to a rather profound discussion about finding the purpose and value of integrating virtual environments in teaching and learning.

textbooks and course content, and then outline goals and objectives for the course. Important to the process is the use of the revised *Bloom's Taxonomy* (Anderson et al. 2001), which helps you determine what type of knowledge is to be learned and what process students use to learn it. Students learn in a variety of ways, and it is important to address the different levels of thinking associated with this learning. The revised *Bloom's Taxonomy* is a multitiered model for classifying thinking. This model is useful for determining the level of value of the materials you create to be used in a virtual world. *Bloom's Taxonomy* classifies student thinking into four distinct areas: factual, conceptual, procedural, and meta-cognitive. These four classifications correspond to the six cognitive levels of thinking complexity: remembering, understanding, applying, analyzing, evaluating, and creating. When this system is used with the content evaluation process, you can determine the cognitive level your lesson or assignment provides. Furthermore, using *Bloom's Taxonomy* allows you to address the level of alignment among standards, educational goals, assignments, and reflective practices with the institution's conceptual framework. As any educator can attest, for teaching certain disciplines some methods are more valuable than others. As educators we have always known that one size does not fit all. For some educators lecture and guided practice might prove to be the most valuable, whereas others might find their content to be delivered more appropriately with small group work.

So we will begin with the planning process. Finding the value in introducing any new technological medium requires forethought, organizational skills, intuitiveness, ambition, evaluation, listening, and the ability to overcome and adapt to challenges. Whatever the method or tool of choice, you must begin with an assessment of your content.

Planning Process

As any instructional technologist will tell you, planning is the first stage in outlining your course or training module. The following outline is a model that can be used for the development of your instructional material. The following model will help you to determine whether you have addressed the appropriate course design methodology:

1. **Plan**—Outline the entire course (Storyboard) content, assignments, interaction, assessment, and evaluation methods. Create a syllabus and pacing guide. By doing so you outline all the specific topics and associated exercises that you will need to cover. Within the planning process you will also need to consider the different types of learning styles associated with your students. This process is usually addressed as you begin to develop the specific lesson plans for your class. Be sure to use and access the material that your institution, state, corporation, business, or education system provides. Pull the standards, blueprints, and pacing guides readily available to help you plan and outline your curriculum. Also be mindful of the resources that are available in world. Depending upon your discipline, you will often be able to connect with other in-world residents who may be willing to collaborate or share documents, presentations, objects, and resources that will help you in the planning process and delivery of your content.

2. **Analyze**—Identify your course objectives, learning outcomes, and deliverables. Analyze how SL tools can improve the delivery of the material to meet objectives. Later in the chapter we provide information on presentations, simulations, special events, interviews/guest speakers, and assessment. This section will give an overview of the various ways in which you can engage students in the immersive learning environment of SL. Feel free to modify the teaching techniques to match your own needs.

3. **Content**—Identify appropriate materials, tutorials, and simulations addressed in the analysis. Determine which elements are appropriate for SL and add value to course content. Not all disciplines are equal. For example: have you ever tried to teach students how to input data in an income statement for an accounting lesson in an asynchronous environment? This is a rather difficult task. However, if you are defining an income statement or discussing a definition, the same

accounting lesson could be delivered in an asynchronous environment. Each discipline is different and requires the professor or trainer to have an in-depth understanding of the content and how it can and should be delivered. Similar concepts have been discussed countless times as educators have made the transition from face-to-face traditional classes to online classes taught via the computer. As noted in Hansen (1993), understanding the curriculum design process is essential for teachers to be able to understand the curriculum development process; to separate "what to teach" from "how to teach"; to connect higher-order learning outcomes; to connect these outcomes to meaningful classroom experiences; and to link these to social, legal, and economic trends taking place in our global economy. By developing a framework for conceptualizing the course and material to be delivered in world, you will be able to focus on what should be learned and how it should be learned. By outlining these areas you will be able to address the content area and the corresponding in-world virtual tool that will provide the most effective way for learning to take place.

4. **Design**—Determine the tools you will need to effectively deliver your content. These tools will include tutorials, objects, textures, and sounds. This is where understanding the first part of the book is essential. Knowing what textures are or how to rezz an object will help you in the design process. Also, understanding how to develop the land on your parcel will help you determine what type of environment you need to create for your students. When you are first entering the virtual environment, it is quite customary to mimic a traditional classroom. Other instructors may choose to maximize on the dynamic features of the virtual environment in SL. SL users are always speculating on the best way to handle this topic, but regardless of which setup you choose, you must make sure it effectively engages *your* students. Be aware that, like most new tools, SL has a learning curve that must be taken into consideration. As you continue to grow and explore new in-world spaces, your space will become more immersive. Within the design phase, it is also important to consider the competency level of the students. What are their computer literacy skills? Are they digital natives? Will they know how to access the course material or will you have to provide explicit directions? When integrating a new tool you truly must be forward thinking. Create tutorials and use available resources to help the students during orientation. It all goes back to basic business concepts of knowing your customer; target market; and, in this case, your students.

Develop a classroom layout of what objects and illustrations/images you might need in SL to deliver course material (textures, objects, tutorials, and audio and video).

5. Integration—Determine an appropriate balance between core content and experiential learning. Be certain that you have found a purpose for integrating SL. We do not proscribe that you jump in with both feet and tell your students that their entire course is in world. Instead, we advise you to outline specific components of the content that can be directly enhanced by the virtual environment. Ask yourself, "What do I want to improve—communication, engagement, experiential hands-on practices?" You may find that you have a lot of uses for SL, or you may find currently SL is best used as a communication tool for you and your students. For example, a virtual space could be a great place to hold office hours or to engage students in simple synchronous dialogue.

Integrate SL through individual or multiple sessions throughout the semester or academic year.

6. Assessment—Record the results and reactions to your course. Assessing your training or course is important as you finalize your sessions. Your assessments should include items that you feel are necessary to enable you to gather useful feedback to improve your program. We all like to think our programs are the best, but assessment gives your students the chance to speak for themselves.

7. Change—On the basis of evaluation, alter the process to improve learning outcomes. Record your changes and why you implemented these changes so you may evaluate the progress of your course.

sea²

Evaluate the effectiveness of environment against learning objectives. Use the revised *Bloom's Taxonomy* grid if you are addressing the cognitive levels of thinking complexity. Evaluate not only your delivery of content and impact on learning but also the environment you wish to create. Determine what types of assessments will be most beneficial. Determine whether subjective or objective assessments will best measure student learning.

The difficult part is over, and now the fun begins. Like all teaching and learning methods, virtual environments can be either an advantage or a disadvantage to the learning process. Technology in and of itself is not the solution to increasing student learning. Technology is a tool to be combined with a teaching method to affect the way in which a student receives, processes, learns, applies, and reflects upon the content. Virtual environments such as SL and Active Worlds are software programs that, when combined with the appropriate content, lesson, and assessment, can influence learning. Furthermore, it is also instrumental to look beyond conventional methods in order to assess what virtual environments can offer your program. As noted previously, learning takes place in a variety of platforms. As educators and technical advisors, we seek not only to teach students about content but also explore ways to engage them in the learning process. For an educator this could mean several things:

- Wanting to provide office hours in world to conduct synchronous chat sessions.
- Placing students in teams to engage them in a synchronous session. Virtual environments also provide a space for creativity, exploration, and peer evaluation.
- Providing your students with exposure to other cultures.

The methods and approaches are limitless, and many of these are addressed in the following section.

Virtual Instructional Teaching Methods

The transition from the real classroom to the virtual classroom is a difficult process. Teaching in virtual environments is a hybrid of traditional techniques that are enhanced with the new methods you have just learned. Following are some of the instructional methods that are effective for teaching SL. Take note of the teaching techniques that are provided to help you determine the purpose for implementing a particular strategy. Try to envision your course material in the context of the scenarios provided. This list has nine different techniques, but within each there are multiple ways to use the method for teaching and learning purposes. The methods include presentations, simulation, special events, interviews and guest speakers, building and scripting, exploration, and assessment.

Teaching Techniques

In a virtual environment a presentation can be a simple lecture with corresponding slides or a dynamic workshop with different objects that can interact with you and your audience. As you will find in Chapter 12, several different types of presentation screens are available for you to use in SL. Determining which approach to take with your students will help you decide which type of presentation area you should create. Consider the following teaching techniques.

Teaching Technique I: Basic Presentation and Simple Seating

Imagine you are teaching a group of students about management and would like to provide a presentation on a particular model. You have created a space that encompasses a basic presentation viewer, and you have uploaded your presentation (which by now has been converted to images and uploaded in world as textures). You have edited the content on the presentation viewer to contain the

textures/slides to be viewed during a presentation that you will relate using a standard lecture format. Be advised that in a virtual environment communication and interaction are key to engagement. So aside from the lecture presentation format, you should include an interactive element to engage the students in the learning process. As shown in **Figure 11.1**, you have arranged the students in a circular pattern by using the simple seating object. This allows students to sit/pose on the floating chairs to

Figure 11.1 Teaching Technique I–Basic Presentation and Simple Seating

view the presentation. Another element you can include is the Soap Box. The Soap Box allows students to interact with one another after your presentation. The Soap Box ensures that a good debate takes place by having the students present the pros and cons of the model presented. Dividing the students into a pro team and a con team is helpful when it is time for them to present their side of the argument.

Teaching Technique II: Community of Learners

Technique two consists of you teaching a design class. As the instructor, you want to include not only the presentation of student work but also a synchronous chat session where student and teacher come together to evaluate the design process. As the instructor, you create a museum filled with presentation viewers or even frame objects that allow students to upload their designs (textures). You hold a synchronous class session where, as a group, you walk through the museum to view and discuss the different designs and the design principles associated with each piece of work. To further increase the learning process, you can include a notecard peer-evaluation system that allows the students to evaluate one another's work.

During my design class, I held a session where I wore a glow ball that said "follow me." This allowed my students to follow me around a design hall that contained both good and bad website designs. The students were able to communicate via voice chat. Throughout the synchronous session we were able to discuss the design principles presented and to apply these concepts to their own website development. The ability to review designs and discuss the principles in a synchronous chat session provided the students with the knowledge and skill to adjust their own websites to improve the quality and focus.

Teaching Technique III: Three-Way Whiteboard

As the instructor, you want to provide a social space where students can congregate in world and review presentations. These can be previous presentations or they could be presentations created by your students. No matter the venue, you could include a multiple presentation viewer that allows you to view the presentations in chronological order. This is often done with help of tutorials that require students to complete one step before moving on to the next. This can be done by using the presenter tool or a three-way whiteboard shown in **Figure** 11.2. In Chapter 12 you will find the location and information to retrieve the tool.

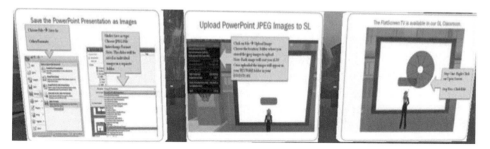

Figure 11.2   Teaching Technique III—Three-Way Whiteboard

Teaching Technique IV: Network of Systems

One of the benefits of SL is that you can interface with many different social networking programs. For example, you can connect to blogs, SLicker® (Flickr®), Twitterbox®, Facebook®, instant messaging to a phone, email, and videos from programs such as YouTube® and Screencasts®. A wide variety of social networking platforms exists to help engage your students. It is easy to develop a presentation area that also connects to a social platform where you can require students to reflect upon the presentation. For example, one connection you can make is to have your students view a video in world and then blog their analysis and reflection. Depending upon the tool of choice, you can incorporate either the blogHUD or the Sloodle Blog tool shown in **Figure** 11.3.

Figure 11.3   Teaching Technique IV—Network of Systems, Sloodle Blog

Once you start to integrate the various methods, you will find that there are helpful tools that will assist you in evaluating your students' level of engagement. Take a look at Ekumu's experience in Second Life.

Simulation

Simulations in SL provide an environment that encourages interaction and socialization among students whose physical location distances them from others. Somewhat like computer simulations, SL simulations provide an interactive environment that encourages student exploration, manipulation, and problem-solving techniques to master course content. However, unlike computer simulations, SL provides a dynamic environment in which students can interact and

As a newbie I started by creating a classroom that resembled a traditional four-wall brick classroom. As I continued to visit other in-world spaces, I realized that I was missing out on a phenomenal opportunity to make my classroom environment more engaging.

Through a rather unconventional thought process, I came upon the idea of creating the seven wonders of the United States. While working with my University's SL support staff, we determined that we would create the Empire State Building, Hoover Dam, Golden Gate Bridge, Grand Canyon, Washington Monument, Niagara Falls, and Cape Hatteras. In developing these in-world spaces, we focused on highlighting a learning component of each location that would correspond to the content of the class.

So for example, at Cape Hatteras, the students were to build an object on the beach outside (sandbox). However, the students were also provided with stairs that allowed them to walk to the top of the lighthouse. At each stage the students would stop and receive a presentation on building concepts. When they reached the top, they not only had a phenomenal view but were also able to receive a quiz through a survey HUD on the concepts they just learned through the presentations. To merge the real-life locations with their SL counterparts, the students also received factual tidbits about the wonder that they were virtually experiencing. Although this lesson was much more developmentally involved than a lecture, the tradeoff was that I was able to develop a truly interactive lesson that retained my students' full attention.

solve problems together. This virtual environment holds students accountable while they are evaluated on their ability to successfully develop solutions and complete tasks in the hands-on environment. SL affords educators and trainers the ability to take abstract ideas and to implement tangible simulations for students to experience and explore. So you may ask, "What does an educational simulation consist of?" In our view, it can consist of any abstract idea that emulates real-world knowledge

What are the key elements for creating effective simulations that provoke critical thinking, problem solving, reflection, and long-term content retention?

The following list outlines strategies for using simulations as a means for teaching and learning in SL:

1. Preparation—The key to any simulation is the amount of preparation that goes into developing the core components of the model. The instructor must address the purpose, content, design, and learning objective of the project.

> **Tip**
>
> Make a simulation meaningful. If you do not, students will lose interest easily and find the simulation tedious.

2. Complexity—Simulations should have various levels of complexity. Every user who becomes an SL resident will not have an extensive gaming background. Therefore, you must address the complexity of the simulation to different skill levels. Usually, the most valuable simulations are those that invoke a higher-order of thinking and require students to solve problems to progress to the next level. When possible and as time permits, integrate simulations where students not only use these higher-order skills independently but also cooperatively. In a synchronous environment such as SL, teamwork is an expectation that infuses characteristics of engagement, networking, and social interaction to achieve common goals. In online environments, teamwork is often a dreaded process because it is often difficult to determine times to meet and collaborate. However, in SL, the synchronous environment and use of simulations fosters teamwork, and students have found its use to be effective in the learning process.

3. Feedback—Feedback allows the resident to reflect on the challenges taught during the simulation and to reflect upon a more tangible outcome. The learner is provided feedback by his or her peers or instructor on the process and mistakes made during the simulation. The learner is, therefore, given the opportunity to address mistakes, solve problems, and use critical thinking and reflection to develop a more sustainable solution to an experiential learning activity. This produces a deeper level of learning as opposed to a lecture and test format.

4. Engaging/Fun—As with any instructional method, creating a balance between fun and effective learning is not easy. However, simulations afford you the creativity to explore new ways to connect with your students. Whether you choose to simulate a technical process or engage in a critique of artwork, SL simulations will provide a game-rich infrastructure that allows your students to formulate solutions and reap the outcomes, whether positive or negative.

The next question must then be, "How can I integrate simulations into my courses or corporate training?"

A wide range of simulations have already been developed and investigated for use in SL. Research has shown that students enrolled in courses that use SL simulations demonstrate a higher level of learning because they are engaged in the learning process and, more importantly, are affected by the outcomes of their decisions. Integrating simulations into your courses is an easy process. The medical community has created many simulations for residents to interact and learn more about the health care field. However, the NOAA has created some great interactive simulations where anyone can have fun. Teaching technique I explains a simulation created by the NOAA.

Teaching Technique I: Simulation

Nothing speaks to students like the interaction (simulation) they will experience in Hurricane Gulf, which was created by the Weather Channel Island. The Weather Channel Island contains a variety of interactive simulations. However, for any scientist, Hurricane Gulf will provide a hands-on experience about how hurricanes form and travel. While you are flying in the observation plane, your avatar will see a reenactment of a hurricane and view the powerful destruction that winds can cause to any building structure. This island is only one of many simulations that are already developed and readily available for instructors to use in their classrooms.

Because many of my students reside in the southeastern portion of the United States, many of them have already experienced the tragedy associated with hurricanes. By participating in the Hurricane Gulf simulation, students are exposed not only to the mass destruction but also to the stories that are shared. This provides them with insight into future emergency planning. Many students have commented on the realistic portrayal the simulation provides. If your class is interested in a fun location where weather meets extreme sports, this simulation is a no-brainer and a great location to visit.

Special Events

Organizing an event in SL is exciting, but at the same time it requires you to address a variety of elements to ensure that your event runs seamlessly.

Just as any RL event planner will tell you, location is the most important element in the planning process. Nothing could be more true than setting up an event in SL because you not only need to determine which location will provide the best return on investment (ROI) but you also need to address the following elements to create a smooth event. The following are strategies for setting up a special event in SL.

1. **Location**—As mentioned before, determining a location that will put both your audience and your speaker at ease is important. Ensure that the setting and ambience of your potential space reflect the tone of your event.

2. **Promotion/Invitation**—An event is not an event if no one attends. In SL it is critical to know your audience. If this is a private function, be sure to send out in-world invitations or an email invitation to an appropriate mailing list. If it is an open event, assess whether you want to post the event in the SL classifieds. Evaluate whether it would be more beneficial to define your target audience and send out promotional material. One thing never changes whether you are in SL or RL: you must analyze the purpose for your event and market it to the appropriate audience.

3. **Technology for Event**—Analyze the purpose and outcome for your event. What type of SL technology will provide the most beneficial, interactive, and immersive environment for participants? Choosing the technology tool to deliver the material will depend upon the content and purpose of your event.

4. **Rezzing Presentation Material**—Determining the technology in the previous step will determine how much building you will need to do prior to the event. Usually you will be able to use many of the predeveloped objects that we have made available through this book and within SEA^2.

5. **Communication**—The communication method you choose will depend upon the number of residents that attend your event. Each element provides a different benefit. Voice chat provides an environment that encourages spontaneous discussions. Text chat provides an ease of communication with more than 15 people in attendance. Instant messages can be valuable when one or more residents wish to discuss a topic further as the main conversation moves forward. Each communication tool provides benefits and each should be evaluated prior to the event date.

6. **Resources**—Special events provide a unique experience for residents to partake in through an interactive environment. However, as a special

event coordinator or speaker you can make the event more valuable if you provide resources for further reading and exploration.

7. **Evaluation**—Nothing could be more valuable than the assessment of your event. Evaluating the successes and failures of an event will prove valuable when developing successive events. This feedback will help you learn the essentials for creating and promoting an event.

Teaching Technique I: Art Exhibit

Holding an art exhibit or gallery is a great example for a special event **Figure 11.4**. Although it takes a lot of planning and practice, it is well worth the effort, as the student from the preceding anecdote can confirm. Areas that need to be addressed include location, space, cost, invitations, communication, rezzing or building the exhibit, and evaluating the event.

Figure 11.4   Technique I–Art Exhibit

Once I taught a student who was an artist. It was interesting to watch her develop throughout the course as she tested and investigated the possibilities of the virtual environment. I was aware that she was a nontraditional student from the baby boomer generation and that she felt that the virtual environment might not be suited for her. Fortunately, I was pleased to find that she was intrigued by SL and ended up purchasing virtual land to open her own art gallery. Today her artwork can be purchased both in RL and SL.

Teaching Technique II: Conference Detail

Not only are they a great way for educators to learn, in-world conferences, workshops, and special events are also a great venue for students to interact and socialize. A great way to learn about the SL environment is to attend or present at an in-world conference. Students can gain a better understanding of the various offerings available through virtual environments when they hear the perspectives of other avatars. Many events exist on a weekly basis. A simple search for a type of business produces several events that showcase industry in SL, while you might also receive information on how to start your own business in workshop events. Type in any topic in the events search panel, and several responses are returned. By exposing your students to the special events, they will not only learn from your course material but they will also learn firsthand by interacting, sharing, and collaborating with other in-world residents.

One of the best experiences my students had was during the semester when they presented at an in-world conference with me on the uses for teaching and learning in an SL classroom. What was exciting was that the students took over the presentation. They provided the audience with accounts of what it was like to be a student taking a course in SL. It provided my students with time to reflect on the methods used and provided the attendees and me with a list of benchmark practices that made a difference in their education.

Interviews or Guest Speakers

Many possibilities exist for wanting to conduct an interview in a virtual environment. You may be trying to provide your students with the opportunity to interact and network with an "expert" in the field, or you might include a casual interview as a way for students to collect qualitative data on in-world interactions, diversity, or culture. Whatever your reason for wanting to have interviews as an element in your course, several strategies exist for creating the right SL interview environment.

1. Address the purpose of the interview.
2. Prepare for the interview—outline the who, what, where, and when:
   - **Who (SL resident)**—Outline appropriate residents to interview. Invite experts to join you in SL for an interview. (If they are new to the environment, be sure to provide them with adequate directions for interacting within the environment.) If it will be a casual interview and you are not sure of the SL resident's background, be sure to address why you are asking questions and to get permission to use his or her answers. Always be sure to cite your interviewee's SL name.

- **What (purpose)**—Before the day of the meeting, determine the purpose for the interview. Develop appropriate questions. If your students are developing the questions, be sure to assess the level and context of the questions. If have notice that the resident will be interviewed, be sure to send a copy of the questions so that the person will be prepared. Keep a copy of the questions close during the interview process so that you can write and respond to answers.
- **Outcomes**—Address the outcomes and deliverables expected from the interview, including for research (an Internal Review Board/consent form), best-practices analysis, or possibly student reflections. Any research conducted on human subjects must be run through an institution's internal review board. Educators must submit an Internal Review Board form and consent form that needs to be approved by the institution prior to collecting information.
- **Where (setting)**—Knowing the layout and location of the interview can be essential to the success of the process. If the interview is with a formally invited speaker, you will want to design the location with objects and textures that will help the interviewee discuss specific elements that he or she is knowledgeable about. For example, if the speaker is an expert in design and has developed a variety of illustrations, be sure to upload the illustrations to be used as a guide during the interview process.
- **When**—Determine a date, time, and location. It is important to address time zones because SL runs on Pacific Time. This is not usually a barrier to interviews, but it should be addressed. Also be sure to provide the exact location within SL. Sending a link for the interviewee to access is the easiest way. However, you can easily teleport the interviewee to the desired location, provided that you have shared friendship. Be sure to address the length of the interview process.

3. Address the best type of interview process for the content to be addressed:

- **Informal interview**—No formal questions, casual meeting and interview with resident.
- **Focused interview**—Question-and-answer interview. Interview is guided by focused questions based on the topic.
- **Open-ended interview**—Question-and-answer interview guided by the resident being interviewed.
- **Closed interview**—Specific questions and answers where respondent must choose from the answers provided. More commonly used for quantitative statistics purposes.

4. Types of topics

- **Behaviors**—about what a person has done or is doing.
- **Opinions/values**—about what a person thinks about a topic.
- **Feelings**—respondents sometimes respond with "I think . . .", so be careful to note that you are looking for feelings.
- **Knowledge**—to get facts about a topic.
- **Sensory**—about what people have seen, touched, heard, tasted, or smelled.
- **Background/demographics**—standard background questions, such as age, and education.

5. Follow-up

- Write down any personal observations—journal reflection.
- Make sure to save text chat as a Word document, or ensure that the recording was saved correctly.
- Send a thank-you note to the interviewee.
- Publish interview recording.

Teaching Technique I: Guest Speaker

A guest speaker provides helping driving home the terminology, models, concepts, and theories that we teach during our classes. Providing a guest speaker in a virtual environment is similar to doing so in a traditional classroom setting. However, SL provides a special environment for the delivery of the message. Guest speakers, if not familiar with the format and program, will need a lot of preparation and guidance. Following the preceding steps will help make your guest speaker event seamless. Be sure to make the topic and connection to what the students are currently learning apparent. Do not incorporate a guest speaker just because you think it will be a fun experience; give your class purpose and meaning. The easiest examples for guest speakers in virtual environments can be as simple as a mentor who will help your students orient themselves to the new environment or as complex as an SL business owner who explains the principles associated with the SL economy and how to make money in world.

Building/Scripting

Building is a means of learning.

As you learned in Chapters 6, 7, and 8, building in SL can provide students with a wide range of activities (**Figure 11.5**). These activities can help in the learning process. As with most 3-D graphic programs, students building or "rezzing" objects in world will use skills to create individual prims that when combined develop one particular object. Building objects in world emphasize

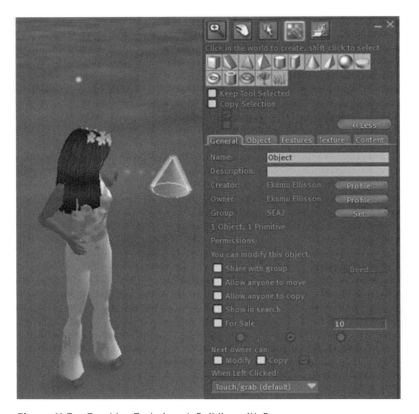

Figure 11.5   Teaching Technique I–Building with Purpose

exploration, creativity, visualization, and critical-thinking skills to help students rezz 3-D graphic designs. While building in world, students will learn about design theory, storyboarding, photo/texture manipulation/editing, and 3-D modeling. Throughout the building process, several programs can be used for editing photos and/or texture development. These programs are used outside the SL environment. As discussed in Chapter 7, some of these programs are Adobe® Photoshop®, Adobe® Fireworks®, Adobe® Illustrator, PhotoSEAM, Filter Forge, and Microsoft® Office® PowerPoint® Adobe®, Paint®, or GIMP.

In the production process, students plan, analyze, and develop visual objects by using mathematical calculations and design techniques for rezzing unique in-world objects. The dynamic environment lets students build these objects and incorporate scripts that can induce the object to move, run a process, interact, communicate, or animate. This encourages students to collaborate to solve problems and master course content. The following are strategies for using building as a means for teaching and learning in SL.

Teaching Technique I: Creating an Object

Hands-on activities are one of the elements that students enjoy most about SL. The environment allows students to explore ways to plan, create, edit, and manipulate objects to create a 3-D representation. Many different ways exist to incorporate building and scripting into courses. As you begin to address the ways in which you feel building and scripting can be included in your classes, be mindful of the skill level, the need for hands-on help, and the direction that is required. Conducting a class that includes your personal direction on rezzing and manipulating an object will surely be a highlight of your course.

When I first began teaching in-world, we had a limited amount of land. As our university expanded, we formulated new ideas for designing our in-world campus land and for involving the students in the creation of the campus. The assignment became more meaningful because I quickly learned that many of my students had never physically stepped onto our campus. By asking for real-world informative facts, you require the students to build the object and research its history. This provides the students with an assignment that not only challenges their building, mathematical, and design skills but also has them completing research that strengthens their critical-thinking and analytical skills. The student reflections indicated that they not only enjoyed the building process, but the activity also strengthened their ties and connections to the university community.

Exploration

As discussed in Chapter 1, there are many different types of virtual environment programs. Some can be described as fully contained on a server. This means that the environment is available only to those within the community that uses it. Other virtual environments are available to several users by simply creating an account. Both programs provide different benefits. For example, a self-contained virtual environment on a server will protect the users involved, meaning that only those with permission can use it. An example of this would be Active Worlds®.

Active Worlds was specifically designed to enable the creation and low-cost deployment of large-scale metaverses that run within your own environment (server). SL can be considered a multiverse user-friendly platform that allows users from anywhere to create an account and access the environment. As mentioned, there are both positive and negative aspects to having an open virtual interface. The negative aspect is that it allows griefers to interfere with you and your space. As mentioned in Chapter 4, these individuals can irritate residents by bumping them or by attaching things to avatars. The positive aspect of having an open environment is that it allows residents to explore the many different islands that have been developed. New users may often think that they must create everything within their environment, but in reality many lands are fully developed and require only that we visit them to find new ways to interact and learn.

As a business person, you could teleport to IBM to learn more about products that are available in world. As a doctor or hospital administrator, you could travel to Palomar West Hospital, which is opening in 2011 and will provide simulations of the latest advances in robotic medical technology. If you are an educator, you could travel to the NMC Island to learn more about teaching and learning in SL. If you want to explore recreations of RL in SL, you may want to take your students to explore the Sistine Chapel or Long Beach Carnival Amusement Park. SL is an environment that allows you to teleport from one location to another, making visiting and exploring these other lands simple and easy.

The following are strategies for encouraging exploration in SL as a teaching method:

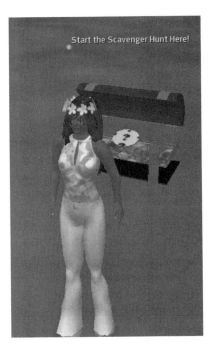

Figure 11.6 Teaching Technique I–Scavenger Hunt with HUD

Teaching Techingue I: Scavenger Hunt

All different types of scavenger hunts exist in SL (**Figure 11.6**). As an educator you may want to create a scavenger hunt for your students. The scavenger hunt could consist of a hunt for objects and clues across your own parcel of land, or you can broaden it to include all islands in SL. You can create your own scavenger hunt by creating notecards, objects to locate, and locations to which to teleport in world, or if you want to make it a bit more intriguing you can include clues that students must figure out before they can move on to the next location.

My classes have incorporated a scavenger hunt across my campus land. It includes clues that students must figure out before they can explore a new area on our campus. The scavenger hunt has students explore in-world locations looking for particular types of objects that will help them throughout the semester. They are also required during the scavenger hunt to take snapshots to be posted in their reflective blogs (an assessment piece). What has been instrumental is that many of the residents my students come in contact with through their travels have actually become guest speakers in our class. It has been an extremely valuable exercise.

Teaching Technique II: Resident Exploration and Research

Research can be conducted on any topic in SL. Depending upon the discipline you teach, it is easy to develop a project that includes students exploring and interacting with other residents in world. The side piece to the exploration activity is that the students can create a survey to be completed by residents they come in contact with in SL. The survey becomes a part of a larger-scale research paper or presentation. Students are learning a variety of skills through the use of this activity. First, students formulate a hypothesis that they must investigate for their research project. Second, the students learn how to create an in-world survey object or HUD for other residents to complete. Third, students are gathering data by interacting with residents in SL, exploring new locations, and tabulating the data for completing a statistical analysis. Fourth, students are researching a particular topic and are developing a paper or presentation that can be presented both in RL and SL. The teaching technique adds value to any discipline and helps students to be engaged during the research process.

Evaluation, Assessment, and Testing

What would learning be without a means to assess and evaluate the level of student learning and performance taking place? Assessment is the process of quantifying, describing, judging, gathering data, and giving feedback about performance (Bush and Lambrecht 2008). However, assessment and evaluation take on new meaning when adapting the processes to virtual environments. As with any in-world activity, you must be a visionary. It takes forethought into how to develop and provide material within the virtual environment, and the assessment and evaluation process is no different. Determining what type of assessment to include is always a challenge and will be based upon the curriculum, course objectives, instructional goals, and alignment to state standards.

In a virtual environment the process becomes more complex because other elements are factors in what type of assessment and what type of document the student must produce, but the teacher will also need to determine the delivery method. Especially now, it is critical that teachers are explicit in the directions they provide to students. For example, a student is given an assignment to write a paper on the foundations of education. Originally it could be assumed that the student was to submit a paper document to the teacher on the stated deadline during class. With the onset of online education, this assumption cannot be made because many other factors come into play. Should the paper be a Word document? In what format should the paper be saved? What is the delivery method of the paper (email, dropbox, blog)? Is the paper even a Word document or is it to be developed as a presentation? So many options for developing course material have complicated online instruction. The following are strategies for determining the types of assessments, the development process, in world assessments, and the submission methods that can be used within virtual environments.

Types of Assessments

Formative vs. Summative

Formative assessment is generally a term used to describe an assessment that guides the learning process, whereas summative assessment is used to measure the learning outcome. Whether formative or summative, assessments can be classified as objective or subjective, and many "layers" of assessments exist within these parameters.

- **Objective assessments**—based on the premise that there are right and wrong answers and that all students should learn the same facts. Objective assessments fall into three main groups: multiple choice, true/false, and matching-type questions.
- **Subjective assessments**—based upon judgment. Subjective assessments (essays or extended-answer questions) have been thought to contain biases based on subject matter and content, as well as cultural biases. If you are developing a subjective assessment it is suggested that a rubric accompany the assessment.
- **Performance-based assessment**—similar to subjective assessment in that it measures student achievement.

- **Self-assessment**—can also be categorized with subjective assessments because it allows the students to evaluate their own performance and level of achievement.
- **Peer assessment**—also subjective because it allows student peers within the class to evaluate and judge the level of knowledge, skill, and achievement.
- **Criterion-referenced or standard-based assessments**—measure student achievement against a specific objective or standard.

Process for Developing Assessment

Evaluate the effectiveness of environment against learning objectives. Use the revised *Bloom's Taxonomy* grid to assess whether you are addressing the cognitive levels of thinking complexity. Evaluate not only your delivery of content and effect on learning but also the environment you wish to create. Determine what types of assessments will be most beneficial. Determine how you plan to assess the methods. Ask the following questions:

- What are your course objectives?
- What is it you want your students to learn?
- Are there specific state standards that must be met?
- Which assessment method will best lend itself to the student achieving the intended goal?
- What assessment method will best measure what your student has learned?
- Will the virtual environment delivery methods affect the type of assessment you develop?
- How will students be able to submit assessment within virtual environment?

Similar to any assessment development, these questions will help you address some of the design considerations associated with virtual environments.

Types of In-World Assessments

Objective Assessment
- Tests
- Survey HUDs

Subjective Assessment
- Presentations
- Papers
- Objects
- Objectives with scripting

- Blogs
- Peer evaluation
- Demonstrations
- Simulations
- Team/group work
- Case studies
- Projects
- Portfolios
- Machinima

In RL, developing appropriate assessments is a difficult process that requires development, evaluation, and a continuous improvement process. As educators, we attempt to assess student learning and are therefore interested in two separate, but closely related, matters: Are we asking the right questions? And are we asking the questions in the right way to measure learning? The first question is a conceptual inquiry that deals with aligning the assessment with the curriculum. The second matter is technical and deals with how the assessment is developed. Assessment of student learning can vary from informal assessments of whether students are "getting it" to formal assessments of student learning that contribute to their grades in the course. SL provides a different environment for learning to take place and therefore as the instructor you must evaluate not only the assessment and delivery of assessment but also the method for obtaining the student results. In SL this can be a difficult task. We mentioned cubes earlier and they can contain the student artifacts that they created in world for the instructor to evaluate. The Student Cube can contain many of the items included within the following list.

- **Notecard**—A notecard can be used as a form of peer evaluation from one student to another to evaluate projects, presentations, or papers. A notecard can also be used in world to pass on helpful information from one resident to another. This approach allows other residents to drop notecards into an object that belongs to you. These items are great for giving feedback or leaving messages.
- **Object**—An object is a great assessment tool that can be used for evaluative purposes in SL. The SL object could be the artifact you evaluate based on the design, level of building skill, or scripting skills, whereas the object might be simply an object that contains material to link to an artifact such as sound, video, web page, or blog.
- **Blog**—A blog is a journal that is available on the Web. Individuals update the blog on a daily/weekly basis by adding content, such as text, images, video, or sound. Blogs are an excellent tool for evaluative and reflective purposes. Dependent upon the software platform you are using, Sloodle® now combines a blog feature that allows

students to send images from their in-world explorations directly to their blog, making the process fast and convenient.

- **Twitterbox™**—Just as a student might blog his SL experiences, another tool available is Twitterbox. Twitterbox is an object in SL that allows residents to post and receive updates of Twitter messages. For an instructor the tool could be used to track in-world experiences as they happen with students.
- **Presentation Viewer**—The presentation tool provides students with the ability to upload a variety of presentations for assessment purposes. These might include a tutorial, a presentation on a topic in class, or a display recording various events that have taken place in world.
- **Machinima**—The combination of filmmaking, animation, and sound. Machinima combines these elements to create a video. The Machinima can be captured using Fraps™ or Camtasia™ software. These tools capture the desktop and thereby capture the events taking place in SL as they happen.
- **Survey HUD**—The survey HUD is a tool that was created to perform real-time, in-world data gathering. However, as an assessment tool for students, the survey can be used as a means of test taking. The survey HUD provides the students with options for answering multiple choice questions. The answers from each student are gathered, and a grade can be given just as it would be in a traditional classroom setting.

Teaching Technique I: Blog

A blog is a website that contains regular updates and entries about different subjects deemed important by the individual maintaining the blog (**Figure 11.7**). The subjects of blogs vary depending upon the user's interests or what he or she is trying to share or express. As a teaching tool, a blog is an extremely effective way for students in world to share their experiences and to report their use, travels, locations, and even their interactions with other residents. As SL has progressed and the use of interactive tools continues to grow, many different types of blog tools have been developed for use with SL. The blogHud, Sloodle Blog toolbar, or even the blogHut are ways to communicate and share information about an SL experience. However, the blog tool can be used for more than evaluating student knowledge; it can also be a means of research assessment. Provided that appropriate IRB forms have been approved, a blog can be used as a means for documenting trends and themes that appear in blogs consecutively with your students. For investigating a new method of instruction, active research is a valuable method for evaluating the effect on student learning.

Figure 11.7 Teaching Technique I–Blog

The use of the Sloodle Blog toolbar in combination with Moodle Blog has been a valuable means of reflection for my students. The students have been able to document their first experiences, travels, interactions with residents, and most important, obstacles for communicating and interacting within a virtual environment. The blogs have provided me with the ability to change and adapt my instruction each semester to better serve the students with a rich and engaging learning community environment.

As an educator, I understand the value of tests and assessments. However, I am not a firm believer that students' education can be summed up by the score they receive on an objective multiple-choice test. I have come to realize over time that assignments, projects, papers, reflections, application, critical thinking and is more important to the learning process than a student's ability to regurgitate definitions for 30 minutes. The ability to authenticate learning through critical thinking, application, and reflection produces students who are far more educated to enter the global workforce. Therefore, my quizzes in SL are not a definition, theory, or model regurgitation. In fact, the quizzes I present my students in world are engaging and interactive, which is what this environment is all about. The quizzes I incorporate are based on tutorials, presentations, simulations, and interactions that take place in world. They require the students to recall an event or experience that took place and to provide an answer (**Figure 11.8**). The quizzes are not meant to

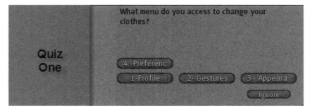

Figure 11.8   Teaching Technique II–Quiz

produce failure but rather to engage the student in the learning process. Students in my courses receive quizzes after they climb the steps of Big Ben or take a boat ride through the Hoover Dam or even walk across the glass bridge in the Grand Canyon. The quiz feature combines simulation with critical thinking and content knowledge and therefore helps the student apply concepts learned during the simulation process.

Teaching Technique II: Quiz

With the emergence of multiuser virtual environments and the increased use of Web 2.0 technologies, today's classroom has changed greatly. Increased online collaborations and the formation of learning communities, coupled with new software platforms, are shaping the way we educate our students. The paradigm shift that is taking shape has been brought about by the way students access, learn, and collaborate the online environment As teaching and learning continues to develop within virtual environments, educators must be cognizant of assessing student artifacts that are produced within the SL environment as opposed to traditional assessment processes.

Wrap-Up

References

Anderson, L.W. (Ed.), Krathwohl, D.R. (Ed.), Airasian, P.W., Cruikshank, K.A., Mayer, R.E., Pintrich, P.R., Raths, J., & Wittrock, M.C. 2001. *A Taxonomy for Learning, Teaching, and Assessing: A Revision of* Bloom's Taxonomy of Educational Objectives (Complete edition). New York: Longman.

Hansen, R.E. 1993. A Technological Teacher Education Program Planning Model. *Journal of Technology Education* 5(1): 21–28.

Chapter 12

Teaching and Training Tools

Virtual environments are a phenomenal tool for educators and corporations because they allow both professor and student to share projects, presentations, papers, simulations, and demonstrations within a platform while still accounting for social interactions. Students can work collectively as a team to complete assignments and share experiences with real-time voice communication. As we stated in previous chapters, the ability to see, hear, and work on one another's designs creates an online community, just as you would see occurring in a library or student center.

Communication and interaction is the key to teaching and engaging students in the learning process. Notably, the inclusion of synchronous technology tools alleviates the barriers traditionally associated with the distance that exists in online courses. By fostering virtual communication and interaction through collaboration, teamwork, feedback, engagement, and constructivists learning activities, educators can alleviate students' and instructors' feelings of isolation. SL, in combination with social presence tools, is a viable way to reach the new generation of game-oriented students.

Although virtual worlds are often thought of in the context of a game, sometimes educators can turn this stigma into a positive asset. Within this chapter, gaming will be covered as a beneficial instructional strategy that educators and trainers may use in the virtual classroom.

We believe that virtual classrooms create a learning environment that promotes social activity. These social spaces ensure that each participant has a strong social presence. Virtual classrooms enrich the learning community with interactive tools that help students interact with one another and their instructor.

By now you have learned that building social spaces in SL is truly right at your fingertips. Whether you use an object from our backpack of tools or create it on your own within SL, you can easily create a virtual classroom of your own.

Virtual environments provide limitless opportunities to create a fluid community that easily connects the course material to your class. For example, in an era where electronic books are becoming the norm, virtual reality environments allow you to create bookshelves with books that literally link to the text material. This aggregation allows you to bring the focus onto the material while using the advantages of technology. You have learned how to create these objects in previous chapters, but this chapter will introduce you to tools that others residents have developed to help you satisfy your classroom needs. Although understanding how these items work is extraordinarily helpful, this chapter provides you with alternative options that will save you the time and effort in creating them.

The following is a list of tools that can be used in conjunction with virtual environments to communicate, interact, learn, and explore.

Presentation

The use of presentations for delivery of material is prevalent today. Although SL is an experience that may not need the same tools as our face-to-face environment, we feel that presentations are a valuable resource in SL. This section outlines presentation screens, whiteboards, television screens, and other objects that display written material captured as an image (**Figure 12.1**).

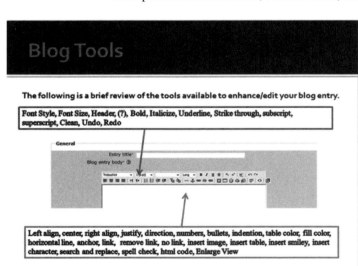

Figure 12.1   Presentation

Preso-Matic Turbo Presentation Tool

The Preso-Matic Turbo Presentation Tool is a user-friendly slide viewer that provides preloaded instructions on how to upload material that was created by Doctor Patridge Allen. To use this object, you will need to convert PowerPoint slides to images and upload the images in world as textures. The Preso-Matic offers push buttons to control the direction of your presentation without the use of menu controls. The permissions allow you to modify, copy, and rezz multiple copies. The tool is free and can be found at http://slurl.com/secondlife/Adobe/143/156/51 as well as in the Xstreet Marketplace. The Preso-Matic is one of the easiest tools to use and incorporate for giving in-world presentations.

VComm Presenter

The VComm Presenter (**Figure 12.2**) is a presentation tool that imports a PowerPoint presentation or a PDF file through a space's parcel media. Because this system eliminates the need to upload textures, the presentations load much faster. The VComm Presenter also allows you to upload a video to the presenter and has a set of easy-to-use buttons to switch between the interfaces.

Figure 12.2 VComm Presenter

To get a free copy of the beta version (educators only), send an email to support@vcommpresenter.com with the following information:

Subject: beta test subscription

- Avatar first and last name
- In what area will you use the presenter?

This feature will be available on SL Exchange and in world soon.

- URL: http://www.vcommpresenter.com/
- SLURL: http://slurl.com/secondlife/Aresch/39/73/25

Pointer Tool

The pointer tool allows you to place a prim over your slideshow presentation to be able to point to specific elements within your presentation. It also contains a feature that allows it to glow so that each participant can view the element. The slide pointer was created by AntonioGPS Zapatero and is available at http://slurl.com/secondlife/Aresch/39/73/25 free for educators.

Chalkboard

The chalkboard allows you to type in the chat area text material that will be posted on the chalkboard by using a notecard feature. The creator of the free chalkboard tool is Salahzar Stenvaag and this tool can be found at http://slurl.com/secondlife/Pergola/106/32/22.

The three-way whiteboard (**Figure 12.3**) allows you to place a series of textures on the three-way whiteboard and, provided that you label the textures appropriately (1, 2, 3 or a, b, c), the whiteboard will present them in that order. As you move to the next slide, the whiteboard will update the series of textures. The creator of the three-way whiteboard is Simon Kline, and the tool can be found at https://www.xstreetsl.com/modules.php?name=Marketplace&file=item&ItemID=1106570&random=17216 for L$50.

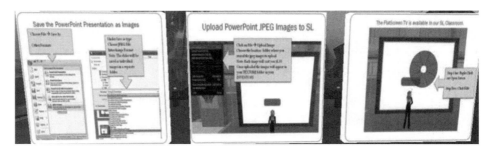

Figure 12.3   Three-Way Whiteboard Tool

Information Sharing

Thinc Book and Thinc Book Copier

The Thinc Book and Thinc Book Copier are two of our favorite tools (**Figure 12.4**). The Thinc Book is an object that allows you to input textures into a book that when clicked will turn the page. The Thinc Book offers a vast array of ways to assess student work. One use of the Thinc Book is the creation of a portfolio

Figure 12.4   Thinc Book

for students. It is a great way for students to keep track of their material and to produce it for sharing with others. In conjunction with the Thinc Book is the Thinc Book copier, which, of course, allows you to make copies of your book to share with others. Both these objects, as well as many others, can be purchased at THiNC SL (created by Toneless Tomba and the THiNC staff), an in-world virtual business for L$75. It is located at http://slurl.com/secondlife/THINC/128/105/71.

Figure 12.5   Photo Display Board

Photo Display Board

The Photo Display Board (**Figure 12.5**) allows you to easily drag snapshots (textures) from your inventory to the display board. This is a simple process that will help you form a community online. The Photo Display Board was developed by Ewan Mureaux and can be found on Xstreet SL Market for L$100 at https://www.xstreetsl.com/modules.php?name=Marketplace&file=item&ItemID=943456&random=70232.

BrainBoard

Nothing creates an outline, storyboard, or mind mapping like the BrainBoard (**Figure 12.6**). This phenomenal tool created by Jeff Lowe allows you to collaborate in world. It is a collaboration tool used for brainstorming or notetaking in a virtual environment. Users can create short text

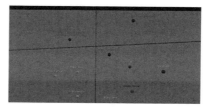

Figure 12.6   BrainBoard

notes, edit existing notes, differentiate notes by text color, and rearrange the position of notes on the board. To get more information about the tools Jeff Lowe has created, access http://theimmersivelife.wordpress.com/.

As a professor, I am always after new ways to get my students to work together. Is the biggest complaint, finding time to communicate with different schedules? The BrainBoard is the answer. It allows users to create text, edit text notes, and rearrange the positioning of the notes independently. What makes the tool even more helpful is that you can import and export information.

Spidergram

The spidergram, created by Eloise Pasteur, is a specialized tool that allows you to entitle and connect planning balls (**Figure 12.7**). The tool lets you not only link ideas but also add script for accessing notecards or websites. The Spidergram can be found at http://www.apez.biz/modules. php?name=Shop&op=product&id=144720 or the Xstreet Marketplace for L$150.

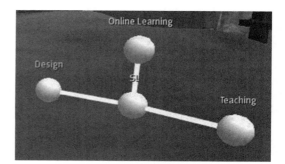

Figure 12.7   Spidergram

Notecards

Notecards are a great way to provide information you want to share with other residents. A notecard dispenser will also provide a good way to give out landmarks, and they can easily be created. And a free version is available in the SEA[2] freebie hut.

Nametag

A nametag is a great way to display your avatar name, company, or school affiliation. It is simple to edit and wear. And a free version is available in the SEA[2] freebie hut.

Communication

Teacher's Leash

The Teacher's Leash (**Figure 12.8**) allows a resident to touch the "object" to summon you. The leash enables you to provide information about your in-world office hours and classes and will immediately contact you. Nothing summons a person better than the Teacher's Leash. It is a great way to let students know you have been viewing their projects while also summoning them if they do happen to be in world. The Teacher's Leash allows you to be summoned both in world via instant message

Figure 12.8   Teacher's Leash

or by sending you a personal email message if you have set up the association. It is fabulous for a variety of reasons but provides a venue for quick and easy communication. The Teacher's Leash was created by Dagmar Kojishi and can be found for free at http://slurl.com/secondlife/WindingRiver%20Campus2/216/214/498.

Speaker Buddy

Figure 12.9   Speaker Buddy

If you want to provide a realistic presentation, with the ability to recall your notes quickly, Speaker Buddy is a phenomenal tool (**Figure 12.9**). The Speaker Buddy object comes in different styles—cushion, podium, or others. The Speaker Buddy allows you to review your notes as you are presenting. A neat side feature is that it will put you in various poses throughout your speech while secretly giving you cues on what hand gestures you could use to make your presentation look more realistic. The Speaker Buddy can be found at http://slurl.com/secondlife/Info%20Island/45/209/39 for L$300 and was created by Dagmar Kojishi.

Simple Seating

If you are holding an event or providing a presentation, Simple Seating (**Figure 12.10**) is the easiest way to set up chairs to offer your attendees a comfortable

Figure 12.10 Simple Seating

seat along with an appropriate pose. Simple Seating offers two different choices, circle seating small and large. The seats provide a fast and easy way to make any location presentation ready. The tool was created by Dagmar Kojishi and can be found at http://slurl.com/secondlife/Info%20Island/49/237/34 for L$50.

Soap Box

Nothing screams opinionated like the Soap Box. If you plan on conducting an in-world session that includes speech making and debates, the Soap Box will help residents have the floor without inter-ruption. The Soap Box gives a resident speaking rights while allowing each event attendee to register to get in line for speak-ing privileges. The soap box was developed by Eloise Pasteur and can be purchased as Apez.biz for L$150.

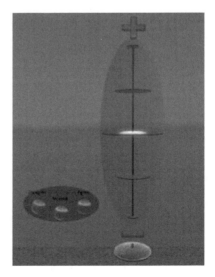

Assessment

Attitudometer is a tool that allows you to gauge the opinion of your participants (**Figure 12.11**). The use of the tool is simple, it uses either a HUD or voting sta-tion to capture participants' votes. They will cast their vote of Agree, Disagree, or Neutral on your question. All that is left is to watch the 3-D gauge move to the level of

Figure 12.11 Attitudometer

agreement or disagreement to your question. Created by Jeff Lowe, the tool and more information are available at http://theimmersivelife.wordpress.com/facilitatortoolbox/attitudometer/. You can purchase the attitudometer at the Xstreet Market Place at https://www.xstreetsl.com/modules.php?name=Marketplace&file=item&ItemID=1366655 for L$4,500 or US$20.

Visitor Counter

Counters provide an easy way to keep track of the number of residents that visit your parcel of land in SL. The counter can be as basic as tracking the number or as thorough as tracking statistics about the residents who visit your land. Several counters exist in world. You can access one at http://slurl.com/secondlife/Sanggae/205/9/922

Survey HUD

The Survey HUD has multiple purposes in that it can be used to survey in-world residents as well as a means for providing quizzes. A great strength of SL is that it allows you to communicate with residents from all over the world. The Survey HUD will allow you to formulate a questionnaire to gather data about in-world immersive activities. It is also helpful for evaluating residents' knowledge on a particular subject. Either use is beneficial for assessment and research purposes. The free Survey HUD was developed by Stella Costello and can be retrieved at http://slurl.com/secondlife/Teaching%208/179/110/24.

Video

Video is a powerful tool, and within SL and you can show videos from other websites such as YouTube. You can also create videos called Machinimas. Following are some tools that help you with this feature.

Filming Path

Filming Path is the premier machinima camera in Second Life. Filming Path allows you to track movement, place target locations for camera position, and edit your track. You can access Filming Path Studio in SL at http://slurl.com/secondlife/Mortons%20Gully/205/27/35. You will find many different types of products located at Geuis Dassin and Nand Nerds Filming studio that will help you with the filming process.

MachinimaCam

MachinimaCam HUD is a camera system that will allow users to track avatars by changing the angle and position of the camera. It is truly an interactive interface and easy to use with HotKeys as your controls. This tool was created by CodeBastard Redgrave and can be purchased in multiple locations: Xstreet Market Place for L$2,000, OnRez, or in world at http://slurl.com/secondlife/Strata/40/30/.

Fraps

Fraps is a screen-capturing tool that automatically captures audio and video on your desktop. The user can customize settings and frame rates. You can download a free, restricted version at http://www.fraps.com/download.php.

VidMon Poster

VidMon is a useful, open-source, and free tool that allows multiple people to watch different videos at the same time and place. The tool holds 30–40 URLs and is customizable. It was created by Bucky Barkley and is available in world for free at http://slurl.com/secondlife/Sunpixels/44/177/26.

You can read more about the tool at http://buckybarkley.wordpress.com/vidmon-3x-documentation/.

Learning Management Systems

Sloodle is a mashup between two open-source systems, Second Life and Moodle™. Moodle is a learning course management system that offers several tools for helping educators provide web-based material. "Moodle is a Course Management System (CMS), also known as a Learning Management System (LMS) or a Virtual Learning Environment (VLE). It is a Free web application that educators can use to create effective online learning sites."(moodle.org)

The combination of Second Life with Moodle brings SL educators options for engaging students in the learning process while also offering tools for delivery of course material, evaluation of content knowledge, and engaging with the use of interactive tools for critical thinking and reflection. A list of tools available through Sloodle follows.

The registration booth allows users to register their avatar with Moodle, thereby linking their SL avatar with their Moodle account (**Figure 12.12**).

Figure 12.12 Sloodle Registration Booth

Web-intercom is a tool that makes the local chat log available in Moodle. Students can chat live while in Moodle, log the session, and archive the chat for future reference.

Sloodle Toolbar (**Figure 12.13**) provides gestures, a list of avatars, and the blog feature to quickly add text into your Moodle blog.

Figure 12.13   Sloodle Toolbar

Vending Machine (**Figure 12.14**) is a great feature that allows users to click on a vending machine to access objects. Once you add the objects or notecards that you want to distribute, a dialog menu lists these items so the students can pick the items they wish to retrieve. It is truly an interactive and fun tool.

Figure 12.14   Sloodle Vending Machine

Assignment Drop Box

Assignment Drop Box (Prim Drop) is a tool that allows students to submit their objects (assignments) within SL for grading purposes.

Other Sloodle tools exist and are currently in the beta-testing phase. Please check http://www.sloodle.org/moodle/ to receive the latest listing of features available.

Between-World Communications

Twitterbox

Twitterbox is a mashup between Second Life and Twitter®. Twitter is a way to communicate, interact, and stay connected with people who also "Tweet" (communicate) using the application. Twitterbox is an object in SL that allows you to receive Twitter feeds in world. Twitterbox can be retrieved in world at http://slurl.com/secondlife/caledron/89/46/26 or at the Xstreet Market Place for L$0 at https://www.xstreetsl.com/modules.php ?name=Marketplace&file=item&ItemID=1433029.

SlickrView

SlickrView (Flickr) is the creation of Matt Biddulph's that brings Flickr® photos into SL. A frame posted in SL encompasses a tag that looks up your avatar name and brings up one of your pictures in Flickr. You can view Matt's video tutorial at http://www.hackdiary.com/2006/05/29/alas-second-life-web-20-in-a-virtual-world/.

Second LifeLink–Facebook®

Second LifeLink® for Facebook is the latest mashup to hit the Second Life scene. The Second LifeLink application integrates Facebook and Second Life but with only minimal features in its current beta format. Second LifeLink's current integrated applications include seeing who of your Facebook friends are in SL, what their avatars look like, SL online status with the ability to teleport to their current in-world location, and sharing favorite SL locations. You can retrieve more information about the program at http://www.facebook.com/apps/application.php?id=1042435556.

Blog HUD

Blog HUD is a tool that will let you blog from within SL and post it in your own blog or photo-sharing account such as Flickr. A blog is a website that contains regular updates and entries about different subjects deemed important by the individual maintaining the blog. Subjects can range from emerging technology to how the individual enjoyed her dining experience at a particular restaurant. The tool was created by Koz Farina, and you can retrieve it at http://bloghud.com/.

Multiple-Tool Applications

MystiTool

The MystiTool was created by Mystical Cookie and combines a variety of phenomenal features within one HUD. Some of the features include the following:

- Stores up to 45 of your favorite locations.
- The object rezzer will allow you to quickly rezz your favorite objects without having to search your inventory.
- Quickly rezz a sky platform for on-the-spot meetings. Or rezz it high in the sky above the clouds to reduce your prim use.

- **Flight Assist**—allows you to fly to any elevation in world. You will find that many residents build above the clouds, and the flight assistant will help you reach those areas.
- **URL Catcher**—gives you a popup of any URLs placed in the chat, making it easy to quickly teleport to new locations.
- **MystiTable**—provides a table that will add a chair every time a seat is taken.

The MystiTool provides many other features such as creating your own plugins and automatic updates. The MystiTool can be obtained at the Xstreet Market Place at https://www.xstreetsl.com/modules.php?ItemID=120285&file=item&name=Marketplace for L$423.

Teacher's KitBag

The Teacher's KitBag provides several tools for use in world. The following provides a list of the tools, brief description, and creator's copyright. You may retrieve a copy of the teacher's toolkit at http://slurl.com/secondlife/UoP%20Island/240/19/5 for L$0.

This tool was developed by Uliana Richez on behalf of the Technology Supported Learning Group, University of Portsmouth for the Higher Education Academy Subject Network for Information and Computer Sciences.

- **Alert Rug**—lets the land owner know if someone has entered their location.
- **Chatbox** by Jeffrey Gomez—displays one line of text chat at a time above the avatar's head in a transparent cloud.
- **Cubist Scarborough's Action Point Board** tool—places a numbered tile above your head taking notes, sharing agendas, or listing tasks to be completed.
- **Cubist Scarborough's Chat Hat**—displays the text chat above your head.
- **Feedback Survey**—sends you the resident's responses via an email message. This survey works with multiple-choice questions.
- **Freebie Giver** into a Folder when touched by a resident in world will provide all the contents to the resident touching it.
- **GPL Chat Logger**—turns all your chat sessions into HTML documents that can be shared for review of the conversation.
- **ICT Library: Education Tour 01**—takes residents on a tour of educational places available in world.
- **TreasureHUD**—can be used if you want to tour different location and want to add a quiz into the tour, or to stop someone from going to the next location until he or she has something while there.

- **Media Player**—streams videos to a screen player in world.
- **Nerd Gadgets Emailer 100**—allows you to send email from Second Life to real-life email accounts.
- **Online Status Indicator**—lets residents and visitors know you are in world.
- **Pie-chart-maker**—displays a simple pie chart.
- **People Sorter**—allows you to sort people on the basis of the response they give to your question.
- **Notecard Dropbox**—allows other residents to drop notecards into an object that belongs to you. Great for giving feedback or leaving messages.
- **Security Pictureboard**—displays a series of pictures/textures and enables you to lock the permission. This way other residents cannot change the pictureboard without permission.
- **Scrolling Display Board**—displays a series of images/textures and has it set to continuous loop.
- **SpeakEasy HUD**—reads the notecard text and place it line by line in the chat window.
- **Starjunky's Note Projector**—floats the notecard content in midair.
- **TreasureHUD**—allows you to build a quiz-based treasure hunt in world.
- **Visitor List Maker**—compiles information on who has visited your classroom and land.
- **Website Loader**—opens a website by using the SL web browser.
- **Website Dynamic Display**—displays a website on a board for viewing purposes.

In conjunction with the textbook, the authors made a variety of instructional tools available to the reader at our in-world location SEA[2]. This provides you with the quickest and simplest way to integrate SL objects into your classes or any SL environment. The SLURL location is http://slurl.com/secondlife/Teaching%208/227/114/23.

Chapter 13

Your Moodle/Sloodle Connection

Moodle

Moodle is an open-source course management system (CMS) developed by Martin Dougiamas in the social constructionist tradition. It contains activity modules (such as assignments, forums, and wikis) to build richly collaborative communities of learning and deliver content to students.

> *The word Moodle was originally an acronym for Modular Object-Oriented Dynamic Learning Environment, which is mostly useful to programmers and education theorists. It's also a verb that describes the process of lazily meandering through something, doing things as it occurs to you to do them, an enjoyable tinkering that often leads to insight and creativity. As such it applies both to the way Moodle was developed, and to the way a student or teacher might approach studying or teaching an online course. Anyone who uses Moodle is a Moodler (Moodle 2009).*

A CMS is an interactive website that can hold course content and is used instead of personal websites to securely hold student content. With many state and federal regulations in place to be sure individual information is not passed into the wrong hands, it is important to secure information such as grades, names, and personal information. A CMS can also be a method of communicating within the system through use of email and other modes such as messaging.

Moodle is used by many community colleges, public school systems, and universities to deliver course material as a supplement for face-to-face classes or for courses delivered completely online. It differs from other CMSs because of the interface and the open environment. Instructors and trainers using Moodle take advantage of all the features, creating a rich social environment. This rich environment is the result of an entire community of developers. It is also easy to use and manage simply by going to http://moodle.org, where you will find support and a community willing to share ideas and their talents.

Moodle can be downloaded to a desktop or to a server and can be managed by one person or more. As with any system, it requires maintenance, upgrades, and troubleshooting. It can be run off a single desktop or laptop, though, by an instructor or trainer willing to take on that responsibility. There are also other modules that can be downloaded and placed into Moodle to customize your course.

Moodle also has other features that make it a compelling CMS to use, such as blogs, chats, quizzes, grade book, and RSS feeds. Another feature used consistently is the ability to have a profile with your information as well as a photo. Social presence abounds in education and training, and being able to see a name and picture of someone begins to make you feel that you know the person a little better. Using a CMS to deliver course material or training is important because it becomes a one-stop place for your course content and is available 24/7 by your students as long as they have an Internet connection.

Other course management systems are Blackboard, Angel, and E-College, just to name a few of the most popular ones. These are used in many educational institutions with great success and offer features that are compelling to use. However, they are not open source, and thus they do not have the flexibility for development that Moodle and other open-source systems have.

Because of the structure of Moodle, it was a perfect candidate to incorporate into a virtual world. That virtual world is Second Life, and the result is "Sloodle."

Sloodle

Sloodle began because individuals need additional tool sets for supporting learning and teaching in a virtual world. Sloodle is a combination of Moodle and Sloodle and was developed for use within SL®. It is actually a plug-in for Moodle with easy installation. The application is integrated into Moodle so you can be in world and receive material and be looking directly at course material in Moodle. Sloodle provides a range of tools to use in world to enhance learning in SL. Development is funded and supported by EduServ, and the original work was done in Scotland. Sloodle is also an open-source system, and the developers saw a need to incorporate the use of SL. You can find out how to download Sloodle at http://slisweb.jsu.edu/sl/index.php/Download_Sloodle.

The creators of Sloodle keep the software open source, and the application programming interface can be edited if you are good at programming. You will find different versions of the software, as well as extensions, add-ons, and plugins.

There are classes in world on Tuesdays, and you can also find the objects in world at http://slurl.com/secondlife/Sloodle/132/132/2.

These classes are led by an avatar, Fire Centaur, who is one of the creators who is constantly updating and improving the plugin.

You must join the Sloodle group to get the latest information about update availability. Some of the items are still in development, such as the Quiz Chair. Others may not work with your version of Moodle. The current version of Moodle is 1.9.5, and you should check each Sloodle tool to see what version it is compatible with. You can check the versions of Moodle at http://moodle.org.

Joining the Sloodle group and visiting the island will keep you in the loop with individuals who can provide support for you. That is one of the nicest things about Sloodle and other open-source platforms: the constant support and open sharing environment.

You learned a great deal about Sloodle in Chapter 12 and about the tools for teaching and learning.

Teaching and Learning with Sloodle

Sloodle makes teaching and learning more interactive and gives educators a valuable tool to use. By recording chats and other activities from in world to real time, this tool has opened the door to move from different environments.

Other Uses for Second Life

Throughout this book we have detailed tips, techniques, and guides on how to incorporate SL into your classes and training. In this chapter we would like to recognize some other uses for this platform for both in and out of the educational sector. As we have mentioned before, in SL you are limited only to what you can imagine. Appendix A will provide you with an extensive list of businesses, schools, and organizations that are using Second Life in new and interesting ways. In the coming sections of this chapter, you can read about some general practices these organizations have followed which may be adaptable for your own institution.

Other SL Uses

Nonclass Educational Uses

Jumping straight into the commitment of fully virtual, synchronous classes may not be the best first step for everyone. If the thought of modified curricula makes you tremble, try scaling back your big goals to a shorter, more manageable adaptations. Following are some ways in which other instructors have used SL.

Office Hours

Offering virtual office hours can be a good way to help both you and your students adjust to the dynamics of a virtual world. By removing the stress of deadlines and assessment, you and your students can explore more without feeling the pressure of being on task. Although this approach does limit you to being near an Internet connection, it frees you from the constraints of your real office. Creating a virtual office and holding office hours for advising and one-on-one help in SL is an excellent way to connect with your distance education students. By placing a face (albeit a virtual face) to the name, both you and your students can to reach beyond the impersonality of emails.

Both the Teacher Leash and Pager from Chapter 10 are excellent tools to manage these virtual meetings. With each tool you can display your hours in your virtual office and be on call for pages that come from in world even when you are not.

Workshops and Conferences

Virtual workshops and conferences are on the rise as travel budgets are being reduced or cut completely. Hosting a virtual workshop requires more planning and involvement than establishing office hours, but it can be a rewarding experience if done correctly. The following section lists questions you should consider before hosting your own conference.

1. **Where will your conference be?**

   Even a virtual conference needs real estate. If your institution, company, or business does not have its own space in SL, you should begin by canvassing virtual spaces that would be willing to donate virtual space, partner with your group, or rent you some space for the time you need it.

   You should begin by asking for help from others like you on listserves or mailing lists such as the Second Life Educators List, Non-Profits Mailing List, Businesses, or Healthcare Support and Education lists. A complete list of Linden Lab–hosted listervers can be found at https://lists.secondlife.com/cgi-bin/mailman/listinfo. If you cannot find someone on these lists, try visiting in-world spaces similar to your institution and inquire about the possibility of hosting or partnerships. If all else fails, you can rent land from other residents or through Linden Lab. For more information on LL land rentals, go to http://secondlife.com/land/rentals.php.

2. **When will your conference be?**

   Give yourself ample time to prepare documentation, build your environment, and market your conference. If you will be inviting guest speakers you should be sure to give them enough time to prepare. You should develop a timeline that will outline what tasks you need to complete.

   Develop contingency plans to implement if important personnel do not appear or if technical issues occur, such as the failure of voice chat functionality. For example, some conferences use other programs such as Skype or Centra as a backchannel to SL voice.

You should also remember to consider the different time zones and find the optimal time span for your audience. Some conferences span days, whereas others hold repeat sessions for all interested parties to visit.

3. How will you manage avatar traffic?

No matter how long your conference lasts, you should prepare for the influx of avatars. The default number of avatars that can be on one region is 40. You can increase this number in the Region/Estate tab; however, you risk increasing lag, which could detract from your users' overall experience. If this menu is unavailable to you as a parcel owner, consider setting time blocks for your event or broadcasting the event on other sims or through other media, such as uStream.

You should also decide if you will be using landing points or direct teleportation, as discussed in Chapter 3. Direct teleporting allows avatars to come to your space at any coordinate. They may look you up on the map and select any coordinate on your region to teleport. Landing points and teleport hubs lead all avatars to one entry point. Telehubs can be set only through the Estate/Region tab and only by an Estate Manager. If you are not an Estate Manager, then you will need to use a landing point, which serves the same function but is set up through the About Land window. For instructions on how to set a telehub or landing point, refer to Chapter 3.

4. Who will manage your conference?

We advise that you decide how much of a policing force you want to be present at your site. Having many congregated avatars may attract some unwanted visitors. It is impossible to control all variables, but you should create a team to help facilitate the event. We suggest you have the following:

- **Greeters**—Greeters help attendees find where they need to go and where to get information. You should have signs with directions and instructions, but live contact is often quicker and more effective. Greeters can use both text and voice chat to communicate. You can even have your greeter use a SpeakEasy tool to handle any standard message so he or she can juggle IMs too.

- **A Grief Manager**—A grief manager should be there to provide security. He or she should have the capability to eject and ban a user from the parcel and to restrict public access should you need to lock down the site during the event. Estate manager permissions are a great bonus because they can control the use of Voice Chat on the island in case a griefer begins to voice unwanted comments.

- **Technical Support Staff**—In our experience, you can never have too much technical support. We advise that you have at least one technical support staff member per 10 attendees. These helpers will generally communicate via IM with users who are experiencing issues connecting, viewing, or interacting with content. Some common technical support problems that your helpers should know how to fix are:
  - Trouble hearing and viewing parcel media (videos)
  - Installing Voice Chat equipment
  - Enabling and using the Voice Chat feature
  - Adjusting the volume of Voice Chat from other avatars
  - Controlling reverberation from open mic and Talk lock combination
  - Muting distracting music or avatars
  - Changing draw distance to improve viewing range
  - Checking transaction history to confirm sending and receiving of payments (if applicable)

5. **What type of users will be in your audience?**

   As a conference coordinator you should try to consider all types of users. Decide who your audience will be and try to anticipate their range of experience. We understand that this can be a difficult task and suggest that you try to balance and inform your audience as much as you can prior to the event. If you believe your event has advanced tasks that new users may have difficulty performing, you should include this information in your marketing strategies. This message does not need to be elaborate and can be as simple as sending out a greeting notecard that lists the necessary skill level. Other conferences may cater directly to beginning users and should be noted as such so that more experienced users will know what to expect. If you choose to serve both ends of the spectrum, be sure that your agenda reflects this balance. Nothing is worse than attending an event that pointedly leaves you out.

Uses in Other Industries

Technical Support

Second Life can be a creative way to provide tech support. Live contact is easier and quicker than exchanging tickets and emails. In fact, in 2007, Best Buy's Geek Squad agents used to do just that. From 6 p.m. to 3 a.m., the Geek Squad was in world to offer SL residents free computer advice (AP 2007). Although we do not think it is quite that necessary for all-night support, using Second Life to host a weekly support event would provide a useful and informal way to manage routine support.

Corporate Training and Uses

If you are a corporation, you are always looking for ways to improve how you do business. SL allows corporations to provide various methods of training and to change the way business is done with online meetings.

Instead of travelling to a location, the avatars can meet in world, sharing PowerPoints and interactive objects that lead you through a training exercise. Also, by using the pager, instant communication is always available, creating a community within your far-reaching corporate branches. Remember, lectures are only somewhat effective in SL and you need to keep everything interactive. Have small tests or quizzes to see what the participants have learned. Create small groups and give leadership to other avatars to give them a chance to expand and grow.

You can also perform interviews through SL. There are so many people; you need to find out only if the potential employee has an avatar or if he or she would consider joining SL. If it is a technical position, what better way to find out if the person has good technical skills? Again, use your imagination for everyday tasks that can be done in a not-so-everyday manner.

Another way corporations could use virtual worlds is to provide simulations of their product line or of new things related to what they do for business. For instance, if you are in the computer business, you can build out an environment that is interactive and has objects that represent the new computer system. The interactive object can then link out to information about the product. An even better functionality would be to make these objects interact with your avatar. You could also work through support issues by clicking on an interactive design that took you through a step-by-step process of how to solve a problem. Can this be done on a regular web-site? Sure. But in SL you can make it much more interactive and visual and provide users with a notecard so they do not have to search websites again. A simple search in someone's inventory would bring up your company name and a solution to the problem.

Using surveys is a good way to determine whether the online sessions were of value. You could also do a survey of your product through SL and collect data that can be beneficial for future use.

Military Training

Using a 3-D environment for training military pesonnel is not new, but using a virtual world is a bit different from past environments used by the government for training. Gaming has been a popular choice for using interaction within the game to simulate a war environment.

Many groups are coming together now to "toot the virtual world horn" for uses of worlds such as SL and Active Worlds. Through the Federal Consortium for Virtual Worlds, military agencies are seeking ways to simulate or enhance military training for exercises in the field. To find out more, visit http://www.ndu.edu/irmc/fedconsortium.html.

Medical Training

Hospitals and medical facilities are prominent in SL, using it for simulations, offering information about the medical community and providing training. Many institutions that provide a degree in a medical curriculum contain a broad population and offer online courses. Simulations in SL can assist with training the medical community of the future. The Ann Myers Clinic is one such space that is exploring that opportunities of virtual training through Second Life. To learn more, visit their in-world space at http://slurl.com/secondlife/Hospital/143/194/22.

Interior Design

SL is an excellent way to bridge the distance between users from different geographical areas, and for interior design, this concept is no different. For aspiring design students, SL provides a free and user-friendly interface for professional critique. SL provides a medium for the student to create a portfolio of work and to build 3-D models to represent their designs. It is also an excellent way to reach potential clients because of its cost-effective nature. Interior designers can create virtual showrooms for clients to actually walk through and explore as opposed to images on a display board. The designer can also use this virtual space as a front for his business should he or she choose to start his own company.

Wrap-Up

Reference

Associated Press. "Best Buy to Open 'Geek Squad Island' in 'Second Life' Online Game". Fox News. http://www.foxnews.com/story/0,2933,264325,00.html.

Chapter 15

Tying It All Together

Virtual environments provide a fascinating 3-D platform where residents design the physical world in which they interact. As a new SL® resident, you may have encountered, in your travels, several unique ways for incorporating SL into your business, training, or educational courses. This book covered several different features for creating and maintaining your SL viewer. We have also contributed several personal reflections and perspectives on tools that can be incorporated into a variety of venues for in-world interaction and collaboration. In closing out this adventure, we would like to present a few more items to help you prepare for your next SL adventure.

Types of Lag

Throughout the book we touched on various topics that dealt with the performance of the SL Viewer. In staying with the theme of this chapter, we wanted to be sure to provide insight into the performance of your computer and its ability to run SL. One issue often associated with SL is lag. SL lag can be defined a few different ways. Client lag occurs when you have a low frame-per-second (FPS) rate and means that your computer is having difficulty processing everything the SL viewer is trying to complete or view in your avatar's case. Network lag is the ability of the network to move data from Linden Lab servers to your computer, whereas server lag refers to how long it takes your computer to communicate with the Linden Lab server. To determine which lag issue you are encountering, you can access the Statistics bar. Doing so will provide a clear indication

Figure 15.1   Statistics Bar–Client Lag

Figure 15.2   Statistics Bar-Network Lag

of what lag issues you may have with your computer (client), network (computer connection), and server connection (**Figure 15.1**).

Ctrl+Shift+1 will pull up the Statistics bar.

FPS should average around 30, and if it drops below 15 you will begin to experience problems.

Bandwidth (**Figure 15.2**) readings are also available in the Statistics bar.

Packet Loss should be at 0.0%, but if it does specify a number, you are likely to have lag issues, disconnect, or crash.

Ping Sim number is best when it is low. The ping sim number represents the amount of time the data take to travel from Linden Lab server to your computer.

Sim FPS and Physics FPS maximum is 45 and is not the cause of your lag. Any time these drop below 43 FPS, you may experience server lag.

The next question after residents learn about the different types of lag is always "How can I fix lag issues?"

The first step in improving the performance of your SL viewer is determining whether client, network, or server lag is causing the problem. Once you determine which area, you can try a few of these solutions to help you improve performance.

Client Lag Solutions

1. Change the graphics quality
   - **Ctrl+P > Graphic Tab > Window Size**
   - You can change the size of your window to 1024 × 768 or 800 × 600 to help increase performance.
   - **Ctrl+P > Graphic Tab > Quality and Performance**
   - You can lower the quality to Mild or High if you are experiencing problems set at Ultra.
   - **Ctrl+P > Graphic Tab > Draw Distance**
   - You can lower your draw distance to 64 m; however, this will minimize what you see, so if you are flying, you will have difficulty finding your location. If you are taking a photograph you might want to adjust the slider higher so that you can obtain a better snapshot.

- Ctrl+P > Graphic Tab > Object Mesh Detail > Drag Slider to Mid
- Ctrl+P > Graphic Tab > Flexiprim Mesh Detail > Drag Slider to Mid
- Ctrl+P > Graphic Tab > Tree Mesh Detail > Drag Slider to Mid
- Ctrl+P > Graphic Tab > Avatar Mesh Detail > Drag Slider to Mid
- Ctrl+P > Graphic Tab > Terrain Mesh Detail > Drag Slider to Mid
- Ctrl+P > Graphic Tab > Sky Mesh Detail > Drag Slider to Mid

In fact at this stage it might be good to uncheck all the graphic boxes to reduce the amount of processing your computer has to complete to display certain objects in the SL environment.

2. Deselect Property Lines

- Ctrl+P > **Property Lines** (make sure there is no X next to it)

3. Deselect Land Owner

- Ctrl+P > **Land Owner** (make sure there is no X next to it)

4. Lower your ARC (Avatar Rendering Cost)

- Ctrl+Alt+D > **Advanced Menu** > **Rendering** > **Info Displays** > **Avatar Rendering Cost**
   - This will display your ARC. The lower the ARC number, the less taxing it is on your client to display your avatar.

5. Decrease the number of objects you have within your land. There is no simple process for this other than taking the time to clean house.

6. Check Video Graphics Card; it might be time for an upgrade.

Network Lag Solutions

1. Increase disk cache size to 1,000 MB

- Ctrl+P > **Network Tab** > **Drag** the slider all the way to the right.

2. Decrease Maximum Bandwidth to 500 Kbps or the default of 300 Kbps

- Ctrl+P > **Network Tab** > **Drag** the slider to the center or until it reads 500.

Server Lag Solutions

1. Remove large prim items you might be wearing (hair, clothes, objects). This may help reduce the number of prims within your location.

2. There are also objects you place on your avatar such as glowing jewelry that can lag a space. Sometimes your hair can also cause lag if it is prim heavy. Usually, the jewelry that glitters and glows will be the culprit and you may have to remove those during the lag period.

3. HUDs can create a lot of lag, and when you arrive on some islands, you are immediately asked to remove them. You will usually be given a

few seconds to remove it before you will automatically be teleported out. One such HUD is one we have already mentioned, the Mysti-Tool. Because of the depth of this tool, it can create a lag. It is something that continuously runs, requesting and delivering information.

Different Types of SL Viewers

To increase your SL experience, there are also other viewers you can use instead of the regular SL Viewer. The following is a list of these viewers and their differences.

SL Release Candidate

The SL Release Candidate viewers are optional viewers you can download and install from http://secondlife.com/support/downloads.php. These viewers are updated continually because they are the clients that programmers work on. These viewers also have the latest bug fixes and the features that Linden Lab will release to the public shortly. If you like to stay abreast of the newest client, this is the one you want to install. For instance, lip-syncing is in this client, which is a wonderful feature for your avatar when you are making Machinimas.

You can also give feedback to Linden Lab about these clients and help them fix anything you see wrong in the new clients before they release them. Once perfected, these are the new clients that are released as updates on the SL Viewer site when you launch the software.

Any of the Release Candidate viewers set up to be downloaded all connect to the main Second Life Grid so that you are not using an alternate client. Thus, any information you place within your avatar's inventory, all your transactions, and any changes made to your avatar are still being downloaded in real time.

Dazzle

Dazzle is another viewer made by Linden Lab that improves the aesthetics of SL and creates an environment you can use that is accessible and visually more appealing. The user interface is important to Linden Lab because it improves your sense of being in real time and interacting with avatars that are closer to a real-life look. That is why they are constantly working on other viewers that improve that experience for you.

Dazzle can be downloaded from https://blogs.secondlife.com/community/features/blog/2008/02/20/dazzle-is-here-to-improve-your-interface.

Once you download these viewers you still have access to the regular client on your computer system. It does not affect these in any way, and you can run two viewers at once if you have a system with good processing power.

Although the SL Client, the Release client, and the Dazzle client are some of the most popular, there are other clients you can experiment with if you so desire. You can find a list of these at http://wiki.secondlife.com/wiki/Alternate_viewers.

Keep in mind that we are not experienced users of all these clients and do not know what they will do to the performance of your machine. They are just suggestions to consider if you are a bit brave and want to expand your knowledge and views of SL. Also, we have no control over these client's being available for download or how often they change.

Code of Conduct

Important to the functionality of SL is the ability of residents to interact and communicate appropriately. Although SL is an open-source program, a set of standards known as the code of conduct was introduced by Linden Lab to keep in-world disturbances at bay. Linden Lab created "The Big Six," and a resident who violates these can be suspended or even banned from using SL. The Big Six include the following:

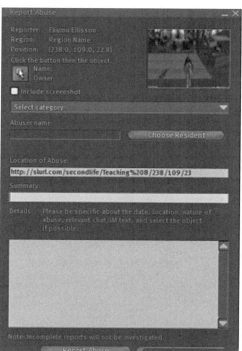

- Intolerance
- Harassment
- Assault
- Disclosure
- Indecency
- Disturbing the peace

Residents who abuse their SL privileges can be reported by other residents. All abuse reports are investigated. To report abuse, click Help on the **Menu Bar > Report Abuse (Figure 15.3)**.

As shown in Figure 15.3, before sending the report you will need to select the abuse category, enter the abuser name, and input the details of the abuse that occurred.

Aside from Linden Lab's having a code of conduct, many subcultures have created their own codes that are enforced within their parcels of land. For example, the New Media Consortium created their own rules of conduct that are based on their overarching goal, which is to encourage exploration. Visitors

Figure 15.3   Report Abuse Form

> **Tip**
>
> If you want to safeguard your land, we advise that you create a way for residents to report abuse. In the SEA^2 area we have a mailbox where residents can submit abuse reports. This allows us to track the behavior of avatars on our land. We can then eject avatars from our land, and although they can remain on the outskirts (border) of our land, they will not be able to mistreat residents trying to learn and interact collaboratively.

to their island are to observe appropriate conduct, language, and behavior as one would expect to find in a model 21st century workplace. Also they should limit building and rezzing activity in the Sandbox, which has been created expressly for that purpose, and to return your items to your inventory before you leave.

You will find that many in-world communities contain their own code of ethics, rules of conduct, and suggested behavior. If you are creating an environment where several residents will be interacting, we suggest that you create a code of conduct or set of rules that avatars must follow within your parcel of land.

Culture

There are many cultures in SL, and they are all represented in various regions, lands, and parcels. Exploring SL is one of the ways to discover a new culture, learn a new language, find a new hobby, or expand your knowledge.

You will find artists, creative individuals, architects, shows, educators, and even politicians in SL. During the 2008 presidential elections, Barack Obama and Hillary Clinton both had campaigns in SL. You could attend a political rally, watch as the election results were tallied, and even attend the inaugural ball.

We have all experienced discussion with individuals we would never have without SL. Often you are in SL and you are approached by avatars who are thousands of miles away from you. There is much to learn from all these individuals, and if you are outgoing enough to text or chat, there is a wealth of knowledge available. With various HUDS you can wear, which translate text from 21 or more different languages, you can easily converse with them and visit their regions by simply teleporting.

Etiquette

Just like RL, SL contains many different types of cultures. To understand how to act appropriately in SL, new residents must become familiar with the various cultures that exist in SL. Just as you will find in RL, SL residents should be cognizant of the beliefs and value systems that stem from interacting in a

As a teacher, mentor, and friend in SL, I often have many different things I am working on when I am in world. At times I go in world to rez objects for my class, whereas at other times I go in to provide support to new residents. At other times I am conducting class and do not have time to chat for fun. As a noob, keep in mind that many residents you come in contact with are not being rude but rather are taking care of business.

virtual environment. Residents who are new to the SL environment must also recognize that different parcels of land may contain different cultures and therefore different etiquette rules. For example, within an island you can easily move between different cultures (American to French) within a couple of meters. You could also move from one subculture to another and therefore find your avatar compromised by those you come in contact with. The first, most basic rule when interacting with residents, just as you would in RL, is "Do unto others as you would have them do unto you." Be respectful of other avatars and do not presume that everyone in world wants to be your friend. First try starting a discussion with a simple chat. The other resident, if interested, will follow suit and chat with you in world. Keep in mind that often the residents you come in contact with in world might not respond to your "hello" because they might be working, building, or communicating with another avatar.

Should you find another resident intriguing, you can start a conversation with a simple hello. If he or she responds, you can continue the conversation by asking general questions about if the person leases or owns land, where he or she likes to visit, objects the person would suggest that you buy, locations where you can obtain helpful objects, and what he or she spends time doing in world. All this information will help you learn about the various cultures in SL.

Another etiquette rule is to ask another resident before you offer friendship. Do not assume that all residents want to be friends. When you become friends with other residents it lets that person track your in-world status, location, and even share and manipulate objects. Offering friendship without asking can be

> ### Tip
>
> A great way to learn more about the resident you are chatting with is by accessing the person's profile.
>
> **Right-Click > Select Profile > Review 2nd life, Picks, Interests, 1st Life, and Notes**
>
> All these elements may provide you with further information about the avatar you are chatting with and give you some topics to discuss.

considered rude by some and you might end up scaring off a possible friend and mentor.

This brings us to the rules of behavior. It is important to understand the culture behind SL. The difficult element is that SL contains so many subcultures that there is no simple way to learn every subculture etiquette rule. With that said, there are many "standard behaviors" that can be applied across RL, SL, and every other Internet environment.

This takes us back to the "do unto others" statement, which can be applied to any environment.

- Think about what you write before you press Enter; written words can often be misconstrued with particular tones associated with a simple innocent comment you may have made. (Think before you act or, in this case, chat.)
- Just like email, chat logs can be saved and archived. Be careful what you put in writing.
- Listen to what other avatars have to say before you comment.
- You can be anonymous. Although your avatar has a different name from your RL name, it does not mean that other residents are not keeping track of your SL avatar's behavior.
- SL residents can be evicted from parcels of land by the owners. So misbehavior does have consequences.
- Subcultures may have rules; be respectful of other cultures.
- Being an avatar's friend gives you the opportunity (when selected) to locate them in world. IM your friend to ask permission before you teleport to their location. They may be conducting business or working on a project.
- Do not disturb other events, classes, or conversations. If another resident tells you that she is busy, move along and find someone else to interact with in world.
- Do not offer objects to other residents before asking if they would like the item. (Sometimes objects come with scripts that are harmful.)
- When appropriate, use SL names even if you know the resident's RL name. It may be that other residents in world do not know the avatar's RL name and you are jeopardizing the person's anonymity.
- Be patient with newbies. Remember that at one time you were just as inquisitive and curious about the SL environment. Should a resident bump into you, it could just be that the person is just learning to walk/fly.
- Be patient. Learning the vast array of SL etiquette is time consuming. Should you find that you made an etiquette mistake, simply apologize.

Griefers

We discussed griefers in our previous chapters and made you aware that there are individuals in SL that like to have fun by causing others grief. In essence this is not much different from RL, and you must remember that if you are ever approached by anyone you do not wish to talk to or who makes you feel uncomfortable, the keystroke Ctrl+Shift+H will return you to your safe zone.

Griefers cause discomfort and annoyance on large scales at times, creating havoc on lands by building objects that can interact with other avatars and place unwanted scripts in your territory. We have also covered ways to control your regions so you can control or minimize being "griefed." Do not let these individuals interrupt or even stop you from using SL.

Future Impact

The impact of Second Life is evident from the number of users currently in SL and the daily growth. This actually applies to other virtual worlds as well; they have all grown in use—not to the extent that SL has grown, but it seems virtual worlds are becoming more popular as a way to meet, train, and educate.

With different economic times and other things that affect your business, virtual reality is a great way to have meetings with workers from around the country. It is also an alternative to web conferencing because it is a bit more interactive and can be seen as more productive. With offices all over the globe and individuals teleworking more these days, it is also a way to keep your business or institution components involved with each other. You can have offices

In one region where I was an estate manager, I accidently left on Edit Terrain in the options. This certainly was a mistake and one I would not forget. When I returned to my region the next morning, I could not see any of my buildings and I had an inventory report that my objects had been returned. What happened? The land was raised over all the buildings and they were below where I was standing. I was devastated. But Linden Lab is dedicated to helping you make SL a good experience. The Region owners contacted Linden Lab, they did a rollback of the server, and I was able to recover most of the environment.

for workers, let them personalize those offices, and put information in the spaces relevant to current projects. What a great way for others to get to know one another by seeing likes and dislikes and personal spaces they may never see.

As with the growth of the Internet, it is hard for anyone to project where virtual worlds will go from here. However, their use cannot be denied.

Economics—Making Money

The economy in SL is alive and growing. Virtual worlds are becoming a good business and it is quite evident as you look around and see all the items that can be purchased. Although the fees seem minimal, with thousands of avatars in SL, it requires only a few to purchase items from your store, business, or your educational tools to make you an entrepreneur. The prospects of making money in SL are exciting because it is a budding marketplace for virtual goods and services. "In 2008, virtual goods entrepreneurs, landowners, in-world builders and service providers generated user-to-user transactions totaling US $350 Million" (Linden 2009).

If you look around in SL you will see many items that are free for your use because of the common theme of open source and sharing. However, you also have to pay Linden$ for items that are for sale, such as the following:

- Furniture
- Hair
- Skins
- Custom skins
- Land
- RL real estate

- Plants
- Scripts
- Presenters
- Buildings
- Boats
- Exercise equipment

Selling is only one option in SL for making money. You can also get a job. Some of the jobs you can get in SL include the following:

- Builders
- Dancing
- Host
- Greeter
- Programming (scripting)

- Camping
- Designer
- Security guard
- Graphic artist
- Creating textures

Many possibilities exist for making a few dollars to making several thousand per month. There are also individuals who pay you to take part in their research.

Although this may not seem like much, again it is the multitude of activities that can produce an income for you. If you would like to learn more about the economy in SL, visit http://wiki.secondlife.com/wiki/How_to_make_money.

Education

The question of what level of impact SL will have on the education arena remains undecided. However, teachers and instructional designers are flocking to workshops, seminars, and conferences to find out how to use virtual environments for teaching and learning. More than 250 universities are participating in SL, showing that the level of interest in virtual environments and education is high. Eventually the use of virtual environments will be synonymous with the delivery of education both at a distance and within a traditional classroom.

Currently, only a few elementary and middle schools are using SL. However, Ramapo Central School District in 2006 began using the SL Teen Grid. The students involved in the Teen Grid project are engaged in content mastery through the use of simulation, role playing, content creation, problem solving, critical thinking, and collaboration in the SL virtual environment. Furthermore, the Horizon Project reports that both high schools and colleges are using virtual worlds to collaborate with other schools to study different cultures that would traditionally be impossible because of location. The list of universities that are creating campuses in SL is long, and they are continuing to explore new

John Kirriemuir wrote an article to measure the impact of SL for educational purposes. What struck me as I read through the personal reflections of so many educators teaching in SL is that just as with any technology tool, using traditional teaching methods (90-minute lecture) in a virtual environment will be as effective as a 90-minute lecture in a traditional classroom setting. Virtual environments provide the rare opportunity to think creatively and dynamically, as well as establish new ways to deliver content. If you are not going to use the environment creatively, then SL will not be an effective learning tool for your students.

ways for which SL can affect teaching and learning. We have presented several resources for educators to access; none is more important than the list of groups available to join. We would be remiss if we did not mention the support that the NMC (New Media Consortium) provided us during our own efforts to develop a virtual campus. The NMC has provided training and support for more than 125 institutions. If your school is interested in becoming further involved in virtual environments, we suggest that you access the group resources and review the current virtual projects taking place.

Since its origination in 2003, Second Life has grown to more than 18 million registered residents. The single most important aspect to be aware of as virtual environments become more prevalent in education is that the use of SL should not be for power or prestige, but rather for finding a purpose for using SL as an instructional method that might not be present in today's traditional classroom setting. When you, the educator, find the value in the instructional delivery method, you have found a reason to use Second Life.

Wrap-Up

References

Kirriemuir, J. (March 2008). "Measuring the Impact of Second Life for Educational Purposes." Eduserv Foundation. Retrieved from the World Wide Web on May 25, 2009, at http://www.eduserv.org.uk/~/media/foundation/sl/impactreport032008/impactreport%20pdf.ashx.

Linden, M. (April 2009). "State of the Economy." Retrieved from The World Wide Web on May 25, 2009, at https://blogs.secondlife.com/community/features/blog/2009/04/09/state-of-the-economy.

New Media Consortium and Educause Learning Initiative. *The Horizon Report*. 2007 ed. Austin: The New Media Consortium, 2007. Retrieved from the World Wide Web on May 25, 2009, at http://horizonproject.wikispaces.com/Virtual+Worlds+-+Impact+on+Education#toc20.

Wong, G. 2006. "Educators explore 'Second Life' online." CNN.com. Retrieved from the World Wide Web on May 25, 2009, at http://www.cnn.com/2006/TECH/11/13/second.life.university/index.html.

Appendix A

In-World Educational Spaces and Virtual Hot Spots

Name	Link
Second Life Business and Industry	
Avon	http://slurl.com/secondlife/Pruni/221/24/56
Dell	http://slurl.com/secondlife/Dell%20Island%204/3/162/24
Marzipan's Closet Businesswear	http://slurl.com/secondlife/Shubelik/17/21/22
SL Business Listing	http://slurl.com/secondlife/Waterton%20Way/188/110/22
Sun Microsystems, Sun Pavilion	http://slurl.com/secondlife/Sun%20Microsystems%201/128/128/71
Second Life Colleges and Universities	
Bradley University	http://slurl.com/secondlife/Bradley%20University/98/207/24
Bowling Green State University Virtual Campus	http://slurl.com/secondlife/bowling%20green%20state/140/140/140/
Campus: Second Life	http://slurl.com/secondlife/Campus/150/100
Democracy Island (NYLS)	http://slurl.com/secondlife/Democracy%20Island/116/220/
Gateway Technical College	http://slurl.com/secondlife/Gateway%20Technical%20College/128/128/17
Harvard Law School's Austin Hall	http://slurl.com/secondlife/Berkman/69/54/24/
Hong Kong Polytechnic University	http://slurl.com/secondlife/Polyusotel/114/158/26/
ISTE Island	http://slurl.com/secondlife/ISTE%20Island/92/83/30
Montclair State	http://slurl.com/secondlife/Montclair%20State%20CHSSSouth/125/154/23
North Carolina Virtual Public Schools	http://slurl.com/secondlife/North%20Carolina%20Virtual/139/157/32
Northern Illinois University	http://slurl.com/secondlife/Glidden/88/166/30/
Ohio University Second Life Campus	http://slurl.com/secondlife/ohio%20university/20/36/24/
PSG Academy Campus	http://slurl.com/secondlife/Kings%20Bishop/38/227/23

Name	Link
Saint Leo University Virtual Campus	http://slurl.com/secondlife/Saint%20Leo%20University/128/128/41/
Science Center	http://slurl.com/secondlife/Bradley%20University/99/129/25
Tulane SCS Island	http://slurl.com/secondlife/Tulane%20SCS/128/125/23
Virtual University of Edinburgh	http://slurl.com/secondlife/Vue/205/53/30
VSTE Island	http://slurl.com/secondlife/VSTE%20Island/53/87/24
Second Life Entertainment	
Abbotts Aerodrome	http://slurl.com/secondlife/Abbotts/116/170/65/?title=Abbotts%20Aerodrome
Amusement Park	http://slurl.com/secondlife/Salpaus%20Nature/125/110/23
Clovers Docks	http://slurl.com/secondlife/clyde/94/23/21/?title=Clovers%20Docks
Hollywood Complex	http://slurl.com/secondlife/Hollywood/141/53/26/?title=Hollywood
Neo-Realms Fishing Camp	http://slurl.com/secondlife/Alston/41/87/22/?title=Alston
Numbakulla	http://slurl.com/secondlife/Numbakulla/216/19/22/?title=Numbakulla
Samurai Island	http://slurl.com/secondlife/Samurai%20Island/154/98/23/?title=Samurai%20Island
Sapphire Moon Casino	http://slurl.com/secondlife/ritch/33/138/37/?title=Sapphire%20Moon%20Casino
Second Life Travel Guide	http://landmarkisland.ning.com/
SL Things to Do: Where do you want to go today?	http://www.slthingstodo.com/main/AllThingsToDo
SLTrip Tips	http://www.sltriptips.com/
The Edge	http://slurl.com/secondlife/edge/126/127/101/?title=The%20Edge
The Pencil Factory	http://slurl.com/secondlife/The%20Port/31/66/26
The Sistine Chapel	http://slurl.com/secondlife/vassar/165/91/24

Name	Link
Traveling Avatar	http://travelingavatar.quickanddirtytips.com/flying-in-second-life.aspx
Tringo	http://slurl.com/secondlife/IceDragons%20Playpen/128/127/24/?title=Ice%20Dragon%27s%20Playpen
Wengen	http://slurl.com/secondlife/Wengen/98/232/93/?title=Wengen%20Chairlift
Museums and Art Galleries	
Research Park Red Rock Theater	http://slurl.com/secondlife/Research%20Park/191/32/45 http://tinyurl.com/cg5fxa
Linden Gallery of Resident Art	http://slurl.com/secondlife/Kirkby/225/184/33
Paris 1900	http://slurl.com/secondlife/Paris%201900/128/128/2
Space Flight Museum Spaceport Alpha	http://slurl.com/secondlife/Spaceport%20Alpha/141/128/451
Second Life Government/Military	
Army Information Center	http://slurl.com/secondlife/Army%20Information%20Center/128/128/2
U.S. Military Veterans Center	http://slurl.com/secondlife/Patriot%20Island/73/239/29
U.S. Military Veterans Center (2)	http://slurl.com/secondlife/Asha/25/46/40
USS Nautilus (U.S. Navy)	http://slurl.com/secondlife/USS%20Nautilus/123/81/26
USS Seawolf (U.S. Navy)	http://slurl.com/secondlife/USS%20Seawolf/128/128/2
Virtual NUWC (U.S. Navy)	http://slurl.com/secondlife/USS%20Nautilus/122/76/26
Second Life Groups	
Education Island	http://slurl.com/secondlife/Education%20Island/136/82/27
Academy of Second Learning	http://slurl.com/secondlife/eson/32/162//
ARISENet Teacher's Group, Eduisland	http://slurl.com/secondlife/Eduisland/231/29/23
Campus Second Life	http://slurl.com/secondlife/Campus/153/144/28
EduIsland Commons	http://slurl.com/secondlife/EduIsland/122/127/23
Insight Virtual College	http://slurl.com/secondlife/Insight%20Virtual%20College/128/128/32

Name	Link
Institute For Cooperative Education (ICE Headquarters)	http://slurl.com/secondlife/Creative%20Learning/128/128/26
NMC Conference Center	http://slurl.com/secondlife/NMC%20Conference%20Center/12/28/23/
Orientation Island	http://slurl.com/secondlife/Orientation%20Island%20Public/97/155
The Photo Institute	http://slurl.com/secondlife/The%20Photo%20Institute/171/73/25
Second Life Medical and Health	
Second Life Health Education (Navid Tomlinson)	http://healtheducationsl.pbwiki.com/
A Sexual Health SIM in Second Life (University of Plymouth)	http://slurl.com/secondlife/Education%20UK/33/63/22
Ann Myers Medical Center	http://slurl.com/secondlife/Hospital/143/194/22
Biomedicine Research Organization, Biomedicine Research Labs	http://slurl.com/secondlife/Biomedicine%20Research%20Labs/54/169/22
Genome (Biology, Genetics)	http://slurl.com/secondlife/Genome/130/130/48
Health Behavior Research Center	http://slurl.com/secondlife/Montclair%20State%20CHSSSouth/176/210/2
Heart Murmur Sim (medical assessment experiment, built 3/06)	http://slurl.com/secondlife/waterhead/130/37
NOAA's Virtual Island	http://slurl.com/secondlife/Meteroa/177/161/27/
Second Life Medical Library	http://slurl.com/secondlife/Info%20Island/112/8/33
Solar Eclipse Planetarium	http://slurl.com/secondlife/Midnight%20City/94/76/27/
Spaceport Alpha	http://slurl.com/secondlife/Spaceport%20Alpha/23/51/22/
Svarga	http://slurl.com/secondlife/Svarga/128.0/128.0
The U.S. Centers for Disease Control and Prevention (CDC) in Second Life	http://slurl.com/secondlife/Juwangsan/218/223
UC Davis' Virtual Hallucinations	http://slurl.com/secondlife/sedig/27/45/22/

Name	Link
Second Life Shopping	
Armord Tower	http://slurl.com/secondlife/Miramare/192/38/33/?title=Armord
Buckaroo Educational Tools	http://slurl.com/secondlife/Sunpixels/44/177/26
Couture	http://slurl.com/secondlife/Couture%20Isle/112/128/55/?title=CoutureIsle
Gnubie Store	http://slurl.com/secondlife/Powder%20Mill/121/142/34
Italy Island Resort	http://slurl.com/secondlife/ITALY%20ISLAND%20RESORT/129/194/26
Luskwood Creatures	http://slurl.com/secondlife/Lusk/211/120/52/?title=Luskwood
Midnight City	http://slurl.com/secondlife/Midnight%20City/114/141/28/?title=Midnight%20City
Mystical Cookie Designs	http://slurl.com/secondlife/Blumfield/24/148/297
Penrith Greenpeace	http://slurl.com/secondlife/Penrith/230/120/43
Rafalee's Store	http://slurl.com/secondlife/Juree/16/120/65
Tableau	http://slurl.com/secondlife/Midnight%20City/114/141/28/?title=Midnight%20City
The Bazaar	http://slurl.com/secondlife/Stillman/148/87/23
The Free Dove	http://slurl.com/secondlife/Gallii/113/53/33
YadNi's Junkyard	http://slurl.com/secondlife/Gallii/113/53/33
Second Life Teaching and Training	
Info Island (Incorporating SL and ICT Libraries, TechSoup)	http://slurl.com/secondlife/Info%20Island/52/193/
InfoIsland—the Second Life Library	http://slurl.com/secondlife/Info%20Island/67/70/33
NMC Orientation	http://slurl.com/secondlife/NMC%20Orientation/69/107/32/
Building	
Crystal Gadgets	http://slurl.com/secondlife/Babeli/127/108/24
Interactive Linden Script Tutorial	http://slurl.com/secondlife/Daydream%20SE%20Islands/206/40

Name	Link
Ivory Tower of Prims	http://slurl.com/secodnlife/Natoma/210/164/27
Harbinger's Haven Builder's Sandbox	http://slurl.com/secondlife/Lozi/225/71/25/
Builder's Paradise	http://slurl.com/secondlife/Moore/205/147/21/
Prim Docker	http://slurl.com/secondlife/Jeolla/247/205/86
Textures	
1700 Free Textures	http://slurl.com/secondlife/Sakaw/15/251/89
PRO Textures	http://slurl.com/secondlife/Rock/148/60/25/
Texture Paradise	http://slurl.com/secondlife/Swordfish%20Island/128/128/23
Twisted Thorn Textures	http://slurl.com/secondlife/THE%20TWISTED%20THORN/128/178/26
Textures Unlimited	http://slurl.com/secondlife/Clyde/128/159/32
Texture Store No. 1	http://slurl.com/secondlife/Terra%20Nautica/91/80/22
Textures by Torley	http://slurl.com/secondlife/Here/35/44/26
Scripting	
Bromley College's A Linden Script Tutorial Exhibition	http://slurl.com/secondlife/Hyles/122/202/1003/
College of Scripting Music and Science	http://slurl.com/secondlife/Horsa/46/243/85
The Particle Laboratory, Teal	http://slurl.com/secondlife/Teal/180/74/21

Appendix B

Web Resources

Name	Link
Basic Introductory Support	
Second Edition	http://secondedition.wordpress.com/sl-glossary/
Second Life Handbook	http://slhandbook.com/
Second Life Lexicon	http://slisweb.sjsu.edu/sl/index.php/Second_Life_Lexicon
Second Life Support	http://secondlife.com/support/
SimTeach	http://www.simteach.com/
SLTutorials.net	http://www.sltutorials.net/
Blog	
CoolCat Teacher Blog	http://coolcatteacher.blogspot.com/
In The Grid is a blog about Second Life	http://www.jasonpettus.com/inthegrid/index.html
Kronos personal narrative SL story.	http://slambling.blogspot.com/
MUVE Forward provides information on emerging technology.	http://muveforward.blogspot.com/
Second Life Art News	http://sl-art-news.blogspot.com/
Second Life Blog	https://blogs.secondlife.com/index.jspa
Second Life Education Blog	https://blogs.secondlife.com/community/community/education
Second Life Research Blog	http://secondliferesearch.blogspot.com/
SL Presence Blogspot	http://slpresence.blogspot.com/
SLED Blog	http://www.sl-educationblog.org/
SLED Picayune	http://sledpicayune.blogspot.com/
Suffern Middle School Blog	http://ramapoislands.edublogs.org/
Ubernoggin (Intelligirl)	http://ubernoggin.com/
Conferences	
Immersive Education Events	http://immersiveeducation.org/events/
Second Life Community Convention	http://www.slconvention.org/

Name	Link
SLanguage conference on language education in virtual worlds.	http://www.slanguages.net/home.php
Corporate Information	
SL Corporate Use	https://lists.secondlife.com/cgi-bin/mailman/listinfo/slcorporateuse
AHG Inc.	http://www.ahg.com/courses/second_life_courses.htm
Virtual Aloft	http://www.virtualaloft.com/
Fashion and Shopping	
Second Style—the best SL clothing, hair, skins, accessories and more.	http://www.secondstyle.com/
Fabulously Free in SL	http://fabfree.wordpress.com/
Second Life Pros	http://www.secondlifepros.com/free-stuff-in-second-life/
Groups and Listservers	
New Media Consortium	http://www.nmc.org/
Google Gaming and Learning in SL Group	http://groups.google.com/group/gaming-and-learning-in-sl?&hl=en
Healthcare Support and Education with SL	https://lists.secondlife.com/cgi-bin/mailman/listinfo/healthcare
HybridLife.net	http://hybridlife.mypacis.com/
MediaGrid's Immersive Education	http://immersiveeducation.org/
SaLamander Project	http://eduisland.net/salamanderwiki/index.php?title=Main_Page
Second Life Profiles	http://slprofiles.com/
SIMTEACH	http://simteach.com/sled/db/
SimTeach Second Life Grad Colony	http://www.simteach.com/wiki/index.php?title=Second_Life_Grad_Student_Colony
SL Nonprofits	https://lists.secondlife.com/cgi-bin/mailman/listinfo/nonprofits
Mixoom	http://mixoom.com/

Name	Link
SLED List	https://lists.secondlife.com/cgi-bin/mailman/listinfo/educators
Slrl—Second Life Research Listserv	http://list.academ-x.com/listinfo.cgi/slrl-academ-x.com
SLUniverse	http://www.sluniverse.com/php/
The ACHUB Sharing Immersive Experience	http://audiocourses.pbworks.com/
Government Information	
Government (GuSL)	https://lists.secondlife.com/cgi-bin/mailman/listinfo/government
Health Care and Medicine	
SL Healthy	http://slhealthy.wetpaint.com/
News, Magazines, and TV	
3PointD—Mitch Kapor on the Power of Second Life	http://www.3pointd.com/20060820/mitch-kapor-on-the-power-of-second-life/
Metaverse Messenger	http://www.metaversemessenger.com/
Second Life Community Newsletter	http://secondlife.com/community/newsletter.php
Second Seeker provides SL reviews.	http://secondseeker.com/
SL Boxxet	http://www.boxxet.com/Second_Life/best.box
SL Herald	http://www.secondlifeherald.com/
SL Insider	http://www.secondlifeinsider.com/
SLCN.TV	http://archive.treet.tv/
Virtual World News	http://www.virtualworldsnews.com/
Virtual World News Network	http://www.ivinnie.com/
Wired Article on Second Life—Travel Guide	http://www.wired.com/wired/archive/14.10/sloverview.html
Research	
LibOpenMetaverse	http://www.openmetaverse.org/projects/libopenmetaverse
Learning Circuits Blog—Second Life is Not a Teaching Tool by Tony Karrer	http://learningcircuits.blogspot.com/2006/11/second-life-is-not-teaching-tool.html

Name	Link
Second Life Research Blog	http://secondliferesearch.blogspot.com/
Teaching Methods	
Alliance Library System	http://alliancelibraries.info/secondlife.htm
Good Practices for Teaching and Learning in Virtual Worlds (NMC Wiki)	http://sl.nmc.org/wiki/Good_Practices_for_Teaching_and_Learning_in_Virtual_Worlds
Paul Andrews Teaching Video Resources	http://trainingvideos.hscs.wmin.ac.uk/second1/index.html
Second Life Video Tutorials	http://wiki.secondlife.com/wiki/Video_Tutorials
Videos	
Machinima.com Second Life Channel provides a variety of video resources.	http://www.machinima.com/channel/view&id=10
Second Life Podcasts and videoblogs	http://www.mefeedia.com/channels/secondlife
Seriously Engaging: The Story of the NMC Campus	http://sl.nmc.org/2006/06/12/seriously-engaging-movie/
SLGuide	http://www.slguide.com/
YouTube—Molotov's SL Story	http://www.youtube.com/watch?v=wa7u0a9pUSs
YouTube—NOAA's Virtual Island for scientific investigation	http://www.youtube.com/watch?v=is8YX32GAyQ
YouTube—Texas State Campus Tour	http://www.youtube.com/watch?v=iRNP6IJwY90
YouTube SL	http://www.youtube.com/watch?v=UFrMPXnQY8o
YouTube video—PR perspective on SL.	http://www.youtube.com/watch?v=synxFmQJ_0A
Tool Resource	
Avimator	http://www.avimator.com/
DAZ3D free trial software	http://www.daz3d.com/i/software/studio/?cjref=1
Eloise Pasteur Educational Designs	http://educationaldesigns.eloisepasteur.net/
GIMP is an image editing software program	http://www.gimp.org/
Giving a PowerPoint Presentation in SL	http://oreilly.com/pub/h/5239
getPAINT.net	http://getpaint.net/

Name	Link
Second Life list of Tools	http://secondlifer.wikispaces.com/tools?f=print
Second Life Tool Ranking	http://second-life-tool-ranking.ning.com/
Second Life's Texture Tool Wiki	http://wiki.secondlife.com/wiki/Texture_Tools
Second Life's Travel Hub	http://landmarkisland.ning.com/
SL Trip Tips	http://www.sltriptips.com/
SL Wiki on Animation	http://wiki.secondlife.com/wiki/Animation
SLMaps	http://www.slmaps.com/
SLNameWatch	http://slnamewatch.com/
Sloog	www.sloog.org
Wiki	
Second Life Wikia	http://secondlife.wikia.com/wiki/Main_Page
SL Experiments Wiki	http://slexperiments.pbworks.com/
Salamandar Wiki	http://eduisland.net/salamanderwiki/index.php?title=Main_Page
Second Life in Education	http://sleducation.wikispaces.com/
SimTeach Wiki	http://simteach.com/wiki/index.php?title=Main_Page

Appendix C

Shortcut Keys

Shortcut	Action
F1	Second Life Help
Ctrl+A	Select All
Ctrl+B	Build
Ctrl+C	Copy
Ctrl+D	Duplicate
Ctrl+E	Deselect
Ctrl+F	Search
Ctrl+G	Gestures
Ctrl+H	Chat History
Ctrl+I	Inventory
Ctrl+L	Link (selected objects in edit)
Ctrl+M	World Map
Ctrl+Shift+M	World Map
Ctrl+P	Preferences
Ctrl+Alt+Shift+P	Show Property Lines
Ctrl+Q	Quit the Second Life Viewer
Ctrl+R	Run Mode (toggle switch)
Ctrl+Shift+S	Take Snapshot
Ctrl+T	Instant Message open/close
Ctrl+U	Upload Image
Ctrl+V	Paste

Shortcut	Action
Ctrl+W	Close Current Window
Ctrl+Shift+W	Close all Windows
Ctrl+X	Upload Image
Ctrl+Y	Redo
Ctrl+Z	Undo (once while in edit—chat window off)
W+↑	Move Forward
S+↓	Move Backward
A+←	Turn Left
D+→	Turn Right
Shift+←	Move Left
Shift+→	Move Right
Arrow+Double-Tap	Run
Ctrl+R	Always Run
Hold Down E or Page Up	Fly Up
Hold Down C or Page Down	Fly Down
Arrow+E (Tap)	Jump
Ctrl+Shift+H	Teleport Home
/	Show Chat Bar
Esc	Hide Chat Bar
Ctrl+H	Open Local Chat
Ctrl+T	Open Contacts
Ctrl+Shift+F	Open Friends

Shortcut	Action
Ctrl+G	Open Gestures
Ctrl+|	Open Last Chatter
Ctrl+0	Zoom In
Ctrl+9	Zoom Default
Ctrl+8	Zoom Out
Hold Alt+Mouse to navigate view	Zoom
M	Mouselook
Esc	Reset View (double-tap if necessary)
Alt+Shift+F	Joystick
Alt+Enter	Toggle Fullscreen
Ctrl+Shift+Y	Midday View
Ctrl+Shift+N	Force Sunset
Ctrl+Alt+M	Mouse Moves Sun
Ctrl+Alt+6	Turns Fog Off
Ctrl+Alt+Shift+=	Turns Particle Effects On/Off
Ctrl+Alt+Shift+3	Remove Linden Trees On/Off
Ctrl+Alt+Shift+5	Remove Ground Cover On/Off
Ctrl+1	Focus
Ctrl+2	Move
Ctrl+3	Edit
Ctrl+4	Create
Ctrl+5	Land

Shortcut	Action
Ctrl+Alt+D	Open/Close Debug Menu
Ctrl+Shift+G	Grid Selection Pull down
Shift+G	Use Selection for Grid
Ctrl+L	Link (object edit mode)
Ctrl+Shift+L	Unlink (selected objects in edit mode)
Shift and Drag	Duplicates Object (when object is in edit mode)
Ctrl+Shift+1	Statistics Bar
F2	TOS Window

Appendix D

Glossary

Active Speakers—a list that displays all the users who have enabled voice chat; a green dot with waves signifies which avatar is speaking

Active Worlds—A 3-D virtual world created by Active Worlds Inc.

Advanced Building Options—the building features that include all the tabs that are accessible through the More button of the Build window

Animation—a series of commands that control the way an avatar moves for a certain amount of time

Appearance—the process through which a user may edit the visual attributes of an avatar's body to include height, weight, pigmentation, hair, clothing, etc.

Avatar—the virtual entity that represents a user in a virtual world
Synonym: agent

Bake (land)—to save the current condition and layout of a region

Build Window (B)—the window that drives the building process through which all building tools may be accessed

Building—the act of constructing an object or primitive or item by manipulating size, texture, or other object manipulation features

Buy—the initial action an avatar must initiate to enter a buying transaction; this action may be accessed through the pie menu

Calling Card—a virtual business card that can be exchanged between users to exchange contact information

Camera View—the angle through which a user can view the SL world

Camping Out—a generic phrase used to describe the newbie practice of playing out an action to receive a minimal payment of Linden$; camp sites are a business gimmick used to attract users to a sim

Chat—the method of communication that avatars use to converse; can be either text or voice

Client—the SL program that is installed on the end user's account upon account verification; it is the portal through which a resident will log in to the SL virtual world

Closed Estate—a private sim that is available only to the owner and the residents he or she selects

Clothing—assets that an avatar wears on its body

Communities—special-interest sims that new users can choose to begin their journey in SL

Constant—a scripting element that has a predefined value assigned to it by Linden Lab

Contacts Menu—the list that aggregates all the residents a certain user has befriended and groups to which he or she belongs

Coordinates—the x, y, and z positions of an object or avatar

Create (inventory)—an inventory menu option where a user can create a new folder for inventory management or create a new script, notecard, gesture, clothing, or body part

Create Menu—the building menu that the user may use to create new primitives

Default Avatar—one of the 12 generic avatars that a user may choose from during account creation

Draw Distance—the visual range a user can see of the region around him or her from the avatar's position

Ecosystem—habitats where a population lives and functions together as a unit

Edit Menu—the building menu that a user may use to access the advanced building options

Estate—the entire virtual space that an avatar owns; may be one or more regions

Estate Manager—resident who can set land permissions through the Region/Estate menu

Event—a special function that is defined by Linden Lab

Filter—a feature in the inventory system designed to help users manage and organize their inventory by type of asset

Flexipath—the building manipulation process that enables a prim to be affected by the variations of SL® physics such as wind and gravity

Flexiprim—a prim that has an active flexipath

Fly—the action that an avatar performs when a user presses the Page Up/Page Down or ESC keys on the keyboard

Focus Menu—the building menu that a user may use to manipulate the camera view

Freebies—objects such as clothing, furniture, or cars that any user may pick up for a minimal price ranging from L$0 to L$10

Friend—a resident who has agreed to be added to a user's list of contacts to facilitate easier communication

Function—a scripting element that instructs a script to perform a task

Gesture—a short series of movements that controls the way an avatar moves for a short time

Glow—a building feature that allows an object to emit a light of its own that does not reflect upon the surfaces around it

Grid (building)—the increments between the building ruler marks

Griefer—an individual who intends to cause harm or discomfort toward other avatars and their property

Groups—a community of users who share a common interest

Heads-Up Display (HUD)—an object that attaches to an avatar's screen to provide the user with some added functionality

Hollow—the building manipulation process that gradually removes the center portions of a prim

Home (Ctrl+Shift+H)—the location that your avatar remembers as its origin; the default is the first island the user rezzed into upon coming to the Main grid but can be changed by going to World → Set Home to Here

Huge Prims—prims that are larger than the current 10-meter limit that were created and saved before the limitation was imposed

Instant Message (IM)—a private conversation between two or more residents; can be in text or voice chat

Inventory (Ctrl+I)—a system that saves and stores an avatar's property, which includes all assets such as landmarks, notecards, calling cards, objects, and clothing

In-world—the term used to describe the act of being logged in to SL

Land—a generic term to refer to the virtual real estate of a business, institution, or store within SL
Synonyms: space, area, sim

Land Menu—the building menu that a user may use to terraform land

Landmark—a virtual bookmark to in-world locations

Library (inventory)—a set of inventory folders with assets every SL resident is given upon joining the SL community

Light—the feature that allows a prim to emit light that will reflect upon the surrounding surfaces

Linden Dollar Exchange—the system through which an avatar can trade Linden dollars in exchange for real-life currency

Linden dollars (L$, Linden$)—the SL currency used in world

Linden Lab—the company that created Second Life®

Linden plants—a special plant item created by Linden Lab that takes up the space of only a single prim

Linden Scripting Language (LSL)—the event-driven programming language created by Linden Lab that provides functionality and interactivity for all in-world objects

Link—to combine two or more prims so that they behave as one object

Lip Sync—a feature that enables an avatar to move its mouth and hands while the user is voice chatting

Lock Talk Feature—the ability to press a key or button to enable constant broadcast of voice chat until the user presses the toggle key or button again

Lost and Found—the folder where returned items are aggregated

Main Grid—the system that serves and caters to all adult users of the Second Life® virtual world

Menu Bar—the list of options located at the top of the SL client

Menu-driven elements (interactivity)—interactive properties that can be added to advanced builds through the use of menu options provided in the Build window

Move Menu—the building menu that a user may use to visually adjust the position of a prim or object

My Inventory—the inventory folder that saves all the assets a user collects during the lifetime of the avatar

Newbie—an inexperienced new user
Synonym: noob

Notecard—an asset used to share information between residents

Object—a term commonly used to refer to SL items that have been built out of one or more primitives

Offset—the texturing process of adjusting the center point of an overlaid texture

Open Estate—a sim that is open to all SL residents

Parcel—a portion of a region that can vary in size

Parcel Media—audio, images, video, or web content that an owner may link to a certain space

Parcel Music—an mp3 or live stream of music that a parcel owner may add to his or her space

Path Cut—the building manipulation process through which portions of a prim are cut away like pieces of a pie

Permissions—settings that can restrict or allow other users to copy, modify, or transfer SL assets

Photo Album—the inventory folder where in-world snapshots are sent upon choosing the Save to Inventory option during photo capture

Picks—a tab on the SL profile where the user may list sites that the user believes is noteworthy to visit; a common business strategy for stores and businesses is to offer rewards to users who display the store's site in the user's Profile picks

Pie Menu—the circular wheel menu that is accessed when an avatar right-clicks on an object, land, or another avatar

Popups—message boxes that pop up on the screen to inform a user that a certain action has occurred

Positioning—the process of manually changing the coordinates of a prim or object

Prefabs—prefabricated builds that a user may purchase to develop his or her sim

Preferences (Ctrl+P)—a menu that controls the settings and controls that help a user adjust the performance of the SL client

Prim—a fundamental shape used and manipulated in the building process to create objects
Synonym: primitive

Profile—a listing that describes information about a particular user and his or her avatar such as rezz date, groups to which that avatar belongs, and information about the user's 1st life

Project Wonderland—a virtual environment created by Sun Microsystems® Laboratories

RAW file—a type of file that an estate owner may upload to redesign the structure of his or her land

Region—a piece of virtual real estate that is 256 meters by 256 meters

Repeats Per Face—a texturing option that allows the user to adjust the number of repeated images that appear on one side of an object

Repeats Per Meter—a texturing option that allows the user to adjust the number of repeated images that appear per meter within SL

Resident—the generic name for a Second Life user

Rezz—to create or materialize in world

Rezz day—the actual date that a user created a certain avatar; this information is automatically generated on the user's profile under the 2nd life tab

RL—real life

Rotating—the process of moving a prim or object toward a certain desired degree around a specific axis

Ruler—the white guide lines that appear alongside a prim or object when it is being positioned, rotated, or sized

Sandbox—a designated space set aside for building; these spaces usually reset after a certain amount of time

Script-driven elements (interactivity)—interactive elements that can be added to an advanced build only by placing a script in the object's inventory

Script—asset that contains code that instructs an object to behave in a certain manner

Search (Ctrl+F)—the process of looking for sims, objects, or other SL elements by entering keywords into a query system

Second Life® (SL)—a 3-D virtual world created by Philip Rosedale of Linden Lab in June 2003

Sell—to offer an object or asset for sale in exchange for a certain amount of Linden dollars

Shear—the building manipulation process that slants the prim toward either the x or y axis

Sizing—the process of changing the length, width, and height of a prim or object

Skin—the visual design of the SL client's interface

SL Exchange—an online system through which users may sell or buy SL items through the Web

SL name (Second Life® Name)—the handle that is unique to a user's avatar; it is composed of a chosen first name combined with a last name picked from a generated list

Snapshot—a screenshot of in-world activity that can be taken by the SL client

Sort (inventory)—an inventory menu feature that changes the cataloging system of an avatar's inventory to assist in inventory management

Sound—a 10-second sound bite that can be uploaded into SL

State (scripting)—a set of behaviors that is declared in a script; every script must have a default state

Statement—a single line of code that ends with a semicolon

Syntax Error—an error that occurs during script compilation due to script elements being written in the wrong order

Taper—the building manipulation process that forces the corners of a prim inward to form a point

Teen Grid—a separate server of SL that houses regions specifically geared toward Second Life® users between the ages of 13 and 17

Telehub—a specific location that estate managers may set to force all avatars to rezz into when visiting a region

Teleport—the act of instantly moving from one area of SL to another area of SL; can occur across sims or within the same region

Terms of Service (TOS)—a list of rules that every SL user must abide

Terraform—to make adjustments or modifications to the actual land of a region or parcel

Terrain—terrain refers to the actual virtual land that a user can terraform

Text Chat—the mode of communication where users can talk through text

Textures—images that are uploaded into SL to use for building or sharing information

Transparency—the building feature that changes the opacity of a prim or object

Trash (inventory)—the folder where deleted inventory items are sent

Variable—a scripting element that stores information

Virtual world (VW)—a 3-D computer-based platform that allows users to interact with each other in real time
Synonym: virtual environment (VE)

Voice Chat—the mode of communication where users can verbally talk

Walk—the action that an avatar performs when the directional keys or ASWD keys are pressed on the user's keyboard

Appendix E

Automatic Script Viewer Explanation

In Chapter 8, we used the following script to turn a prim into an automatic picture viewer. This page explains the elements of that script.

Automatic Picture Viewer Script

```
integer totalimage = 0;
integer currentimage = 0;
float wait = 5.0;
float counter = 0.0;
integer face = 5;
default
{
    state_entry()
    {
        totalimage  = llGetInventoryNumber(INVENTORY_TEXTURE);
        llSetTimerEvent(wait);
    }
    timer()
    {
        counter = counter + wait;
        llSetTexture(llGetInventoryName(INVENTORY_TEXTURE,
            currentimage), face);
        if (currentimage < totalimage- 1)
            currentimage++;
        else
            currentimage = 0;
    }
    changed(integer change)
    {
        if (change & CHANGED_INVENTORY)
            llResetScript();
    }
}
```

In the beginning of the script, you will see a series of variables. These variables are called global variables because they are declared before the default state. Global variables apply across the entire script. Variables can also be declared locally. Local variables are defined within an event. You can use global and local variables concurrently because sometimes it is necessary to redefine a global variable within the event.

For instance, in the `state_entry` of this script, the variable `totalimage` is redefined from the global value. With this adjustment, the script changes the meaning of the `totalimage` variable when it enters the default state. Instead, upon activating the `state_entry` event the script will begin to inspect the contents of the object to get the total number of textures that are present.

When declaring variables, you must declare its type and the variable name, and you must include the informational equivalent that you want the script to hold.

The second function in the `state_entry` event is the function that tells the object it is to perform an action at a set interval. This function must be used in coordination with the `timer()` event. The `timer()` event is where you define the action to be done at every interval. In this script, the action we tell the script to do is to change the image from the `currentimage` to the next image listed in the object inventory. In the `timer()` event the function `llSetTexture` is the scripting element that actually performs the action of changing the texture.

Defined within this function is a type of flow control called an if–else statement. This statement tells the object that there are specific conditions under which it should change the texture. In the first half of the conditional statement, we are telling the object that if the number of the current displayed image is less than the number of total images minus one, then it should move onto the next image of the series. If not, then the else statement is called to change the image back to 0, which will then display the first image in the series.

Finally, the `changed()` event accommodates any changes that occur within the object. This event uses an `if` statement to tell the script to perform a certain function if the changed action meets a set of particular parameters. In this instance, the script will tell the object to reset the script if the object experiences a change (the change variable of the changed event) in conjunction with a change in inventory. With this event active, the script will then reset if any textures are added or removed from the object's inventory so that the values the script uses to identify the textures will always be the most recent.

Credits Page

The following figures are courtesy of Linden Research, Inc. Second Life is a trademark of Linden Research, Inc. Certain materials have been reproduced with the permission of Linden Research, Inc.

Introduction   1, 2, 3

Chapter 1   1.1, 1.2

Chapter 2   2.1, 2.3, 2.4, 2.6, 2.7, 2.8, 2.9, 2.10, 2.11, 2.12, 2.13, 2.14, 2.15, 2.16, 2.17, 2.18, 2.19, 2.20, 2.22, 2.23, 2.24, 2.25, 2.26, 2.27, 2.28, 2,29, 2.30, 2.31, 2.32, 2.33, 2.34, 2.35, 2.36, 2.37, 2.38, 2.39, 2.40, 2.41

Chapter 3   3.1, 3.2, 3.3, 3.4, 3.5, 3.6, 3.7, 3.8, 3.9, 3.10, 3.12, 3.13, 3.14, 3.15, 3.16, 3.18, 3.19, 3.20, 3.21, 3.22, 3.23, 3.24, 3.25, 3.26, 3.27, 3.28, 3.30, 3.31, 3.32, 3.33, 3.34, 3.35, 3.36, 3.37

Chapter 4   4.1, 4.2, 4.3, 4.4, 4.5, 4.6, 4.7, 4.8, 4.9, 4.10, 4.11, 4.12, 4.13, 4.14, 4.15, 4.16, 4.17, 4.18, 4.19, 4.20, 4.23, 4.24, 4.25, 4.26, 4.27, 4.28, 4.29, 4.30

Chapter 5   5.1, 5.2, 5.3, 5.4, 5.5, 5.6

Chapter 6   6.1, 6.2, 6.3, 6.4, 6.5, 6.6, 6.7, 6.8, 6.9, 6.10, 6.11, 6.12, 6.13, 6.22, 6.24, 6.25, 6.26, 6.27, 6.28, 6.29, 6.30, 6.31, 6.32, 6.35, 6.36, 6.37

Chapter 7   7.1, 7.3, 7.5, 7.6, 7.7, 7.8, 7.9, 7.10, 7.14, 7.17, 7.21, 7.23, 7.24, 7.25, 7.26

Chapter 8   8.4, 8.17

Chapter 9   9.3, 9.5, 9.7, 9.8

Chapter 11   11.5

Chapter 17   17.1, 17.3

The following figures are courtesy of the New Media Consortium:

Preface   1, 2, 3, 4, 5

Chapter 1   Feature Image, 1.3

Chapter 2   Feature Image, 2.14, 2.15, 2.22, 2.23, 2.31

Chapter 3   Feature Image, 3.9, 3.10, 3.16, 3.17, 3.29

Chapter 4   Feature Image, 4.22, 4.23, 4.30, 4.31

Chapter 5   Feature Image, 5.1, 5.2, 5.6

Chapter 6   Feature Image, 6.1, 6.2, 6.3, 6.4, 6.5, 6.6, 6.7, 6.14, 6.22, 6.24, 6.25, 6.26, 6.27, 6.29, 6.31, 6.32, 6.33, 6.34, 6.35, 6.36, 6.37, 6.38

Chapter 7   Feature Image, 7.2, 7.4, 7.5, 7.6, 7.7, 7.8, 7.15, 7.19, 7.20, 7.21

Chapter 8   Feature Image, 8.2, 8.3, 8.4, 8.5

Chapter 9   Feature Image, 9.2, 9.3, 9.4, 9.5, 9.6, 9.7, 9.8

Chapter 11   Feature Image, 11.1, 11.2, 11.5, 11.6

Chapter 12   Feature Image, 12.3, 12.7, 12.8, 12.10, 12.12, 12.13, 12.14

Chapter 17   Feature Image, 17.3

The following figures are screenshots of artwork for the Second Life Viewer, courtesy of Linden Research, Inc. The Second Life Viewer is licensed under the Creative Commons Attribution-ShareAlike 3.0

License. Full version of this license can be found on page 320.

Chapter 6   6.1, 6.2, 6.3, 6.4, 6.5, 6.6, 6.7, 6.8, 6.9, 6.10, 6.11, 6.12, 6.13, 6.22, 6.24, 6.25, 6.26, 6.27, 6.28, 6.29, 6.30, 6.31, 6.32, 6.35, 6.36, 6.37

Chapter 7   7.1, 7.3, 7.5, 7.6, 7.7, 7.8, 7.9, 7.10, 7.14, 7.17, 7.21, 7.23, 7.24, 7.25, 7.26

Chapter 8   8.4, 8.17

Chapter 9   9.3, 9.5, 9.7, 9.8

The following figures are courtesy of the GIMP Documentation Team, under the license of the GNU General Public License. Full version of this license can be found on page 315.

Chapter 8   8.7, 8.8, 8.9, 8.10, 8.11, 8.12, 8.13, 8.14, 8.15, 8.16

Additional Credits

Introduction
Figure IN.3 SLOODLE Blog and Gesture toolbar courtesy of SLOODLE Open Source Management System.

Chapter 1
Figure 1.4 Screenshot of www.activeworlds.com Courtesy of Active Worlds, Inc.

Chapter 2
Figure 2.5 Courtesy of reCAPTCHA.net

Chapter 11
Figure 11.1 Courtesy of Dagmar Kojishi; **Figure 11.2** Courtesy of Simon Kline; **Figure 11.3** Courtesy of SLOODLE Open Source Management System; **Figure 11.4** Courtesy of Ally Aeon, Virtual Art Café; **Figure 11.7** Courtesy of SLOODLE Open Source Management System

Chapter 12
Figure 12.2 Courtesy of Volker Gässler; **Figure 12.3** Courtesy of Simon Kline; **Figure 12.5** Courtesy of Ewan Mureaux, Snap.sl; **Figure 12.6** Courtesy of Jeff Lowe, The Immerse Life; **Figure 12.7** Courtesy of Eloise Pasteur Educational Designs; **Figure 12.8** Courtesy of Dagmar Kojishi; **Figure 12.9** Courtesy of Dagmar Kojishi; **Figure 12.10** Courtesy of Dagmar Kojishi; **Figure 12.11** Courtesy of Jeff Lowe, The Immersive Life; **Figure 12.12** Courtesy of SLOODLE Open Source Management Team; **Figure 12.13** Courtesy of SLOODLE Open Source Management Team; **Figure 12.14** Courtesy of SLOODLE Open Source Management Team

GNU GENERAL PUBLIC LICENSE

Version 3, 29 June 2007

Copyright © 2007 Free Software Foundation, Inc. <http://fsf.org/>

Everyone is permitted to copy and distribute verbatim copies of this license document, but changing it is not allowed.

Preamble

The GNU General Public License is a free, copyleft license for software and other kinds of works.

The licenses for most software and other practical works are designed to take away your freedom to share and change the works. By contrast, the GNU General Public License is intended to guarantee your freedom to share and change all versions of a program--to make sure it remains free software for all its users. We, the Free Software Foundation, use the GNU General Public License for most of our software; it applies also to any other work released this way by its authors. You can apply it to your programs, too.

When we speak of free software, we are referring to freedom, not price. Our General Public Licenses are designed to make sure that you have the freedom to distribute copies of free software (and charge for them if you wish), that you receive source code or can get it if you want it, that you can change the software or use pieces of it in new free programs, and that you know you can do these things.

To protect your rights, we need to prevent others from denying you these rights or asking you to surrender the rights. Therefore, you have certain responsibilities if you distribute copies of the software, or if you modify it: responsibilities to respect the freedom of others.

For example, if you distribute copies of such a program, whether gratis or for a fee, you must pass on to the recipients the same freedoms that you received. You must make sure that they, too, receive or can get the source code. And you must show them these terms so they know their rights.

Developers that use the GNU GPL protect your rights with two steps: (1) assert copyright on the software, and (2) offer you this License giving you legal permission to copy, distribute and/or modify it.

For the developers' and authors' protection, the GPL clearly explains that there is no warranty for this free software. For both users' and authors' sake, the GPL requires that modified versions be marked as changed, so that their problems will not be attributed erroneously to authors of previous versions.

Some devices are designed to deny users access to install or run modified versions of the software inside them, although the manufacturer can do so. This is fundamentally incompatible with the aim of protecting users' freedom to change the software. The systematic pattern of such abuse occurs in the area of products for individuals to use, which is precisely where it is most unacceptable. Therefore, we have designed this version of the GPL to prohibit the practice for those products. If such problems arise substantially in other domains, we stand ready to extend this provision to those domains in future versions of the GPL, as needed to protect the freedom of users.

Finally, every program is threatened constantly by software patents. States should not allow patents to restrict development and use of software on general-purpose computers, but in those that do, we wish to avoid the special danger that patents applied to a free program could make it effectively proprietary. To prevent this, the GPL assures that patents cannot be used to render the program non-free.

The precise terms and conditions for copying, distribution and modification follow.

TERMS AND CONDITIONS

0. Definitions.

"This License" refers to version 3 of the GNU General Public License.

"Copyright" also means copyright-like laws that apply to other kinds of works, such as semiconductor masks.

"The Program" refers to any copyrightable work licensed under this License. Each licensee is addressed as "you". "Licensees" and "recipients" may be individuals or organizations.

To "modify" a work means to copy from or adapt all or part of the work in a fashion requiring copyright permission, other than the making of an exact copy. The resulting work is called a "modified version" of the earlier work or a work "based on" the earlier work.

A "covered work" means either the unmodified Program or a work based on the Program.

To "propagate" a work means to do anything with it that, without permission, would make you directly or secondarily liable for infringement under applicable copyright law, except executing it on a computer or modifying a private copy. Propagation includes copying, distribution (with or without modification), making available to the public, and in some countries other activities as well.

To "convey" a work means any kind of propagation that enables other parties to make or receive copies. Mere interaction with a user through a computer network, with no transfer of a copy, is not conveying.

An interactive user interface displays "Appropriate Legal Notices" to the extent that it includes a convenient and prominently visible feature that (1) displays an appropriate copyright notice, and (2) tells the user that there is no warranty for the work (except to the extent that warranties are provided), that licensees may convey the work under this License, and how to view a copy of this License. If the interface presents a list of user commands or options, such as a menu, a prominent item in the list meets this criterion.

1. Source Code.

The "source code" for a work means the preferred form of the work for making modifications to it. "Object code" means any non-source form of a work.

A "Standard Interface" means an interface that either is an official standard defined by a recognized standards body, or, in the case of interfaces specified for a particular programming language, one that is widely used among developers working in that language.

The "System Libraries" of an executable work include anything, other than the work as a whole, that (a) is included in the normal form of packaging a Major Component, but which is not part of that Major Component, and (b) serves only to enable use of the work with that Major Component, or to implement a Standard Interface for which an implementation is available to the public in source code form. A "Major Component", in this context, means a major essential component (kernel, window system, and so on) of the specific operating system (if any) on which the executable work runs, or a compiler used to produce the work, or an object code interpreter used to run it.

The "Corresponding Source" for a work in object code form means all the source code needed to generate, install, and (for an executable work) run the object code and to modify the work, including scripts to control those activities. However, it does not include the work's System Libraries, or general-purpose tools or generally available free programs which are used unmodified in performing those activities but which are not part of the work. For example, Corresponding Source includes interface definition files associated with source files for the work, and the source code for shared libraries and dynamically linked subprograms that the work is specifically designed to require, such as by intimate data communication or control flow between those subprograms and other parts of the work.

The Corresponding Source need not include anything that users can regenerate automatically from other parts of the Corresponding Source.

The Corresponding Source for a work in source code form is that same work.

2. Basic Permissions.

All rights granted under this License are granted for the term of copyright on the Program, and are irrevocable provided the stated conditions are met. This License explicitly affirms your unlimited permission to run the unmodified Program. The output from running a covered work is covered by this License only if the output, given its content, constitutes a covered work. This License acknowledges your rights of fair use or other equivalent, as provided by copyright law.

You may make, run and propagate covered works that you do not convey, without conditions so long as your license otherwise remains in force. You may convey covered works to others for the sole purpose of having them make modifications exclusively for you, or provide you with facilities for running those works, provided that you comply with the terms of this License in conveying all material for which you do not control copyright. Those thus making or running the covered works for you must do so exclusively on your behalf, under your direction and control, on terms that prohibit them from making any copies of your copyrighted material outside their relationship with you.

Conveying under any other circumstances is permitted solely under the conditions stated below. Sublicensing is not allowed; section 10 makes it unnecessary.

3. Protecting Users' Legal Rights From Anti-Circumvention Law.

No covered work shall be deemed part of an effective technological measure under any applicable law fulfilling obligations under article 11 of the WIPO copyright treaty adopted on 20 December 1996, or similar laws prohibiting or restricting circumvention of such measures.

When you convey a covered work, you waive any legal power to forbid circumvention of technological measures to the extent such circumvention is effected by exercising rights under this License with respect to the covered work, and you disclaim any intention to limit operation or modification of the work as a means of enforcing, against the work's users, your or third parties' legal rights to forbid circumvention of technological measures.

4. Conveying Verbatim Copies.

You may convey verbatim copies of the Program's source code as you receive it, in any medium, provided that you conspicuously and appropriately publish on each copy an appropriate copyright notice; keep intact all notices stating that this License and any non-permissive terms added in accord with section 7 apply to the code; keep intact all notices of the absence of any warranty; and give all recipients a copy of this License along with the Program.

You may charge any price or no price for each copy that you convey, and you may offer support or warranty protection for a fee.

5. Conveying Modified Source Versions.

You may convey a work based on the Program, or the modifications to produce it from the Program, in the form of source code under the terms of section 4, provided that you also meet all of these conditions:

- a) The work must carry prominent notices stating that you modified it, and giving a relevant date.
- b) The work must carry prominent notices stating that it is released under this License and any conditions added under section 7. This requirement modifies the requirement in section 4 to "keep intact all notices".
- c) You must license the entire work, as a whole, under this License to anyone who comes into possession of a copy. This License will therefore apply, along with any applicable section 7 additional terms, to the whole of the work, and all its parts, regardless of how they are packaged. This License gives no permission to license the work in any other way, but it does not invalidate such permission if you have separately received it.
- d) If the work has interactive user interfaces, each must display Appropriate Legal Notices; however, if the Program has interactive interfaces that do not display Appropriate Legal Notices, your work need not make them do so.

A compilation of a covered work with other separate and independent works, which are not by their nature extensions of the covered work, and which are not combined with it such as to form a larger program, in or on a volume of a storage or distribution medium, is called an "aggregate" if the compilation and its resulting copyright are not used to limit the access or legal rights of the compilation's users beyond what the individual works permit. Inclusion of a covered work in an aggregate does not cause this License to apply to the other parts of the aggregate.

6. Conveying Non-Source Forms.

You may convey a covered work in object code form under the terms of sections 4 and 5, provided that you also convey the machine-readable Corresponding Source under the terms of this License, in one of these ways:

- a) Convey the object code in, or embodied in, a physical product (including a physical distribution medium), accompanied by the Corresponding Source fixed on a durable physical medium customarily used for software interchange.
- b) Convey the object code in, or embodied in, a physical product (including a physical distribution medium), accompanied by a written offer, valid for at least three years and valid for as long as you offer spare parts or customer support for that product model, to give anyone who possesses the object code either (1) a copy of the Corresponding Source for all the software in the product that is covered by this License, on a durable physical medium customarily used for software interchange, for a price no more than your reasonable cost of physically performing this conveying of source, or (2) access to copy the Corresponding Source from a network server at no charge.
- c) Convey individual copies of the object code with a copy of the written offer to provide the Corresponding Source. This alternative is allowed only occasionally and noncommercially, and only if you received the object code with such an offer, in accord with subsection 6b.
- d) Convey the object code by offering access from a designated place (gratis or for a charge), and offer equivalent access to the Corresponding Source in the same way through the same place at no further charge. You need not require recipients to copy the Corresponding Source along with the object code. If the place to copy the object code is a network server, the Corresponding Source may be on a different server (operated by you or a third party) that supports equivalent copying facilities, provided you maintain clear directions next to the object code saying where to find the Corresponding Source. Regardless of what server hosts the Corresponding Source, you remain obligated to ensure that it is available for as long as needed to satisfy these requirements.
- e) Convey the object code using peer-to-peer transmission, provided you inform other peers where the object code and Corresponding Source of the work are being offered to the general public at no charge under subsection 6d.

A separable portion of the object code, whose source code is excluded from the Corresponding Source as a System Library, need not be included in conveying the object code work.

A "User Product" is either (1) a "consumer product", which means any tangible personal property which is normally used for personal, family, or household purposes, or (2) anything designed or sold for incorporation into a dwelling. In determining whether a product is a consumer product, doubtful cases shall be resolved in favor of coverage. For a particular product received by a particular user, "normally used" refers to a typical or common use of that class of product, regardless of the status of the particular user or of the way in which the particular user actually uses, or expects or is expected to use, the product. A product is a consumer product regardless of whether the product has substantial commercial, industrial or non-consumer uses, unless such uses represent the only significant mode of use of the product.

"Installation Information" for a User Product means any methods, procedures, authorization keys, or other information required to install and execute modified versions of a covered work in that User Product from a modified version of its Corresponding Source. The information must suffice to ensure that the continued functioning of the modified object code is in no case prevented or interfered with solely because modification has been made.

If you convey an object code work under this section in, or with, or specifically for use in, a User Product, and the conveying occurs as part of a transaction in which the right of possession and use of the User Product is transferred to the recipient in perpetuity or for a fixed term (regardless of how the transaction is characterized), the Corresponding Source conveyed under this section must be accompanied by the Installation Information. But this requirement does not apply if neither you nor any third party retains the ability to install modified object code on the User Product (for example, the work has been installed in ROM).

The requirement to provide Installation Information does not include a requirement to continue to provide support service, warranty, or updates for a work that has been modified or installed by the recipient, or for the User Product in which it has been modified or installed. Access to a network may be denied when the modification itself materially and adversely affects the operation of the network or violates the rules and protocols for communication across the network.

Corresponding Source conveyed, and Installation Information provided, in accord with this section must be in a format that is publicly documented (and with an implementation available to the public in source code form), and must require no special password or key for unpacking, reading or copying.

7. Additional Terms.

"Additional permissions" are terms that supplement the terms of this License by making exceptions from one or more of its conditions. Additional permissions that are applicable to the entire Program shall be treated as though they were included in this License, to the extent that they are valid under applicable law. If additional permissions apply only to part of the Program, that part may be used separately under those permissions, but the entire Program remains governed by this License without regard to the additional permissions.

When you convey a copy of a covered work, you may at your option remove any additional permissions from that copy, or from any part of it. (Additional permissions may be written to require their own removal in certain cases when you modify the work.) You may place additional permissions on material, added by you to a covered work, for which you have or can give appropriate copyright permission.

Notwithstanding any other provision of this License, for material you add to a covered work, you may (if authorized by the copyright holders of that material) supplement the terms of this License with terms:

- a) Disclaiming warranty or limiting liability differently from the terms of sections 15 and 16 of this License; or
- b) Requiring preservation of specified reasonable legal notices or author attributions in that material or in the Appropriate Legal Notices displayed by works containing it; or
- c) Prohibiting misrepresentation of the origin of that material, or requiring that modified versions of such material be marked in reasonable ways as different from the original version; or
- d) Limiting the use for publicity purposes of names of licensors or authors of the material; or
- e) Declining to grant rights under trademark law for use of some trade names, trademarks, or service marks; or
- f) Requiring indemnification of licensors and authors of that material by anyone who conveys the material (or modified versions of it) with contractual assumptions of liability to the recipient, for any liability that these contractual assumptions directly impose on those licensors and authors.

All other non-permissive additional terms are considered "further restrictions" within the meaning of section 10. If the Program as you received it, or any part of it, contains a notice stating that it is governed by this License along with a term that is a further restriction, you may remove that term. If a license document contains a further restriction but permits relicensing or conveying under this License, you may add to a covered work material governed by the terms of that license document, provided that the further restriction does not survive such relicensing or conveying.

If you add terms to a covered work in accord with this section, you must place, in the relevant source files, a statement of the additional terms that apply to those files, or a notice indicating where to find the applicable terms.

Additional terms, permissive or non-permissive, may be stated in the form of a separately written license, or stated as exceptions; the above requirements apply either way.

8. Termination.

You may not propagate or modify a covered work except as expressly provided under this License. Any attempt otherwise to propagate or modify it is void, and will automatically terminate your rights under this License (including any patent licenses granted under the third paragraph of section 11).

However, if you cease all violation of this License, then your license from a particular copyright holder is reinstated (a) provisionally, unless and until the copyright holder explicitly and finally terminates your license, and (b) permanently, if the copyright holder fails to notify you of the violation by some reasonable means prior to 60 days after the cessation.

Moreover, your license from a particular copyright holder is reinstated permanently if the copyright holder notifies you of the violation by some reasonable means, this is the first time you have received notice of violation of this License (for any work) from that copyright holder, and you cure the violation prior to 30 days after your receipt of the notice.

Termination of your rights under this section does not terminate the licenses of parties who have received copies or rights from you under this License. If your rights have been terminated and not permanently reinstated, you do not qualify to receive new licenses for the same material under section 10.

9. Acceptance Not Required for Having Copies.

You are not required to accept this License in order to receive or run a copy of the Program. Ancillary propagation of a covered work occurring solely as a consequence of using peer-to-peer transmission to receive a copy likewise does not require acceptance. However, nothing other than this License grants you permission to propagate or modify any covered work. These actions infringe copyright if you do not accept this License. Therefore, by modifying or propagating a covered work, you indicate your acceptance of this License to do so.

10. Automatic Licensing of Downstream Recipients.

Each time you convey a covered work, the recipient automatically receives a license from the original licensors, to run, modify and propagate that work, subject to this License. You are not responsible for enforcing compliance by third parties with this License.

An "entity transaction" is a transaction transferring control of an organization, or substantially all assets of one, or subdividing an organization, or merging organizations. If propagation of a covered work results from an entity transaction, each party to that transaction who receives a copy of the work also receives whatever licenses to the work the party's predecessor in interest had or could give under the previous paragraph, plus a right to possession of the Corresponding Source of the work from the predecessor in interest, if the predecessor has it or can get it with reasonable efforts.

You may not impose any further restrictions on the exercise of the rights granted or affirmed under this License. For example, you may not impose a license fee, royalty, or other charge for exercise of rights granted under this License, and you may not initiate litigation (including a cross-claim or counterclaim in a lawsuit) alleging that any patent claim is infringed by making, using, selling, offering for sale, or importing the Program or any portion of it.

11. Patents.

A "contributor" is a copyright holder who authorizes use under this License of the Program or a work on which the Program is based. The work thus licensed is called the contributor's "contributor version".

A contributor's "essential patent claims" are all patent claims owned or controlled by the contributor, whether already acquired or hereafter acquired, that would be infringed by some manner, permitted by this License, of making, using, or selling its contributor version, but do not include claims that would be infringed only as a consequence of further modification of the contributor version. For purposes of this definition, "control" includes the right to grant patent sublicenses in a manner consistent with the requirements of this License.

Each contributor grants you a non-exclusive, worldwide, royalty-free patent license under the contributor's essential patent claims, to make, use, sell, offer for sale, import and otherwise run, modify and propagate the contents of its contributor version.

In the following three paragraphs, a "patent license" is any express agreement or commitment, however denominated, not to enforce a patent (such as an express permission to practice a patent or covenant not to sue for patent infringement). To "grant" such a patent license to a party means to make such an agreement or commitment not to enforce a patent against the party.

If you convey a covered work, knowingly relying on a patent license, and the Corresponding Source of the work is not available for anyone to copy, free of charge and under the terms of this License, through a publicly available network server or other readily accessible means, then you must either (1) cause the Corresponding Source to be so available, or (2) arrange to deprive yourself of the benefit of the patent license for this particular work, or (3) arrange, in a manner consistent with the requirements of this License, to extend the patent license to downstream recipients. "Knowingly relying" means you have actual knowledge that, but for the patent license, your conveying the covered work in a country, or your recipient's use of the covered work in a country, would infringe one or more identifiable patents in that country that you have reason to believe are valid.

If, pursuant to or in connection with a single transaction or arrangement, you convey, or propagate by procuring conveyance of, a covered work, and grant a patent license to some of the parties receiving the covered work authorizing them to use, propagate, modify or convey a specific copy of the covered work, then the patent license you grant is automatically extended to all recipients of the covered work and works based on it.

A patent license is "discriminatory" if it does not include within the scope of its coverage, prohibits the exercise of, or is conditioned on the non-exercise of one or more of the rights that are specifically granted under this License. You may not convey a covered work if you are a party to an arrangement with a third party that is in the business of distributing software, under which you make payment to the third party based on the extent of your activity of conveying the work, and under which the third party grants, to any of the parties who would receive the covered work from you, a discriminatory patent license (a) in connection with copies of the covered work conveyed by you (or copies made from those copies), or (b) primarily for and in connection with specific products or compilations that contain the covered work, unless you entered into that arrangement, or that patent license was granted, prior to 28 March 2007.

Nothing in this License shall be construed as excluding or limiting any implied license or other defenses to infringement that may otherwise be available to you under applicable patent law.

12. No Surrender of Others' Freedom.

If conditions are imposed on you (whether by court order, agreement or otherwise) that contradict the conditions of this License, they do not excuse you from the conditions of this License. If you cannot convey a covered work so as to satisfy simultaneously your obligations under this License and any other pertinent obligations, then as a consequence you may not convey it at all. For example, if you agree to terms that obligate you to collect a royalty for further conveying from those to whom you convey the Program, the only way you could satisfy both those terms and this License would be to refrain entirely from conveying the Program.

13. Use with the GNU Affero General Public License.

Notwithstanding any other provision of this License, you have permission to link or combine any covered work with a work licensed under version 3 of the GNU Affero General Public License into a single combined work, and to convey the resulting work. The terms of this License will continue to apply to the part which is the covered work, but the special requirements of the GNU Affero General Public License, section 13, concerning interaction through a network will apply to the combination as such.

14. Revised Versions of this License.

The Free Software Foundation may publish revised and/or new versions of the GNU General Public License from time to time. Such new versions will be similar in spirit to the present version, but may differ in detail to address new problems or concerns.

Each version is given a distinguishing version number. If the Program specifies that a certain numbered version of the GNU General Public License "or any later version" applies to it, you have the option of following the terms and conditions either of that numbered version or of any later version published by the Free Software Foundation. If the Program does not specify a version number of the GNU General Public License, you may choose any version ever published by the Free Software Foundation.

If the Program specifies that a proxy can decide which future versions of the GNU General Public License can be used, that proxy's public statement of acceptance of a version permanently authorizes you to choose that version for the Program.

Later license versions may give you additional or different permissions. However, no additional obligations are imposed on any author or copyright holder as a result of your choosing to follow a later version.

15. Disclaimer of Warranty.

THERE IS NO WARRANTY FOR THE PROGRAM, TO THE EXTENT PERMITTED BY APPLICABLE LAW. EXCEPT WHEN OTHERWISE STATED IN WRITING THE COPYRIGHT HOLDERS AND/OR OTHER PARTIES PROVIDE THE PROGRAM "AS IS" WITHOUT WARRANTY OF ANY KIND, EITHER EXPRESSED OR IMPLIED, INCLUDING, BUT NOT LIMITED TO, THE IMPLIED WARRANTIES OF MERCHANTABILITY AND FITNESS FOR A PARTICULAR PURPOSE. THE ENTIRE RISK AS TO THE QUALITY AND PERFORMANCE OF THE PROGRAM IS WITH YOU. SHOULD THE PROGRAM PROVE DEFECTIVE, YOU ASSUME THE COST OF ALL NECESSARY SERVICING, REPAIR OR CORRECTION.

16. Limitation of Liability.

IN NO EVENT UNLESS REQUIRED BY APPLICABLE LAW OR AGREED TO IN WRITING WILL ANY COPYRIGHT HOLDER, OR ANY OTHER PARTY WHO MODIFIES AND/OR CONVEYS THE PROGRAM AS PERMITTED ABOVE, BE LIABLE TO YOU FOR DAMAGES, INCLUDING ANY GENERAL, SPECIAL, INCIDENTAL OR CONSEQUENTIAL DAMAGES ARISING OUT OF THE USE OR INABILITY TO USE THE PROGRAM (INCLUDING BUT NOT LIMITED TO LOSS OF DATA OR DATA BEING RENDERED INACCURATE OR LOSSES SUSTAINED BY YOU OR THIRD PARTIES OR A FAILURE OF THE PROGRAM TO OPERATE WITH ANY OTHER PROGRAMS), EVEN IF SUCH HOLDER OR OTHER PARTY HAS BEEN ADVISED OF THE POSSIBILITY OF SUCH DAMAGES.

17. Interpretation of Sections 15 and 16.

If the disclaimer of warranty and limitation of liability provided above cannot be given local legal effect according to their terms, reviewing courts shall apply local law that most closely approximates an absolute waiver of all civil liability in connection with the Program, unless a warranty or assumption of liability accompanies a copy of the Program in return for a fee.

END OF TERMS AND CONDITIONS

How to Apply These Terms to Your New Programs

If you develop a new program, and you want it to be of the greatest possible use to the public, the best way to achieve this is to make it free software which everyone can redistribute and change under these terms.

To do so, attach the following notices to the program. It is safest to attach them to the start of each source file to most effectively state the exclusion of warranty; and each file should have at least the "copyright" line and a pointer to where the full notice is found.

```
<one line to give the program's name and a brief idea of what it does.>
Copyright (C) <year>  <name of author>

This program is free software: you can redistribute it and/or modify
it under the terms of the GNU General Public License as published by
the Free Software Foundation, either version 3 of the License, or
(at your option) any later version.

This program is distributed in the hope that it will be useful,
but WITHOUT ANY WARRANTY; without even the implied warranty of
MERCHANTABILITY or FITNESS FOR A PARTICULAR PURPOSE.  See the
GNU General Public License for more details.

You should have received a copy of the GNU General Public License
along with this program.  If not, see <http://www.gnu.org/licenses/>.
```

Also add information on how to contact you by electronic and paper mail.

If the program does terminal interaction, make it output a short notice like this when it starts in an interactive mode:

```
<program>  Copyright (C) <year>  <name of author>
This program comes with ABSOLUTELY NO WARRANTY; for details type `show w'.
This is free software, and you are welcome to redistribute it
under certain conditions; type `show c' for details.
```

The hypothetical commands `show w' and `show c' should show the appropriate parts of the General Public License. Of course, your program's commands might be different; for a GUI interface, you would use an "about box".

You should also get your employer (if you work as a programmer) or school, if any, to sign a "copyright disclaimer" for the program, if necessary. For more information on this, and how to apply and follow the GNU GPL, see <http://www.gnu.org/licenses/>.

The GNU General Public License does not permit incorporating your program into proprietary programs. If your program is a subroutine library, you may consider it more useful to permit linking proprietary applications with the library. If this is what you want to do, use the GNU Lesser General Public License instead of this License. But first, please read <http://www.gnu.org/philosophy/why-not-lgpl.html>.

CREATIVE COMMONS LICENSE

License

THE WORK (AS DEFINED BELOW) IS PROVIDED UNDER THE TERMS OF THIS CREATIVE COMMONS PUBLIC LICENSE ("CCPL" OR "LICENSE"). THE WORK IS PROTECTED BY COPYRIGHT AND/OR OTHER APPLICABLE LAW. ANY USE OF THE WORK OTHER THAN AS AUTHORIZED UNDER THIS LICENSE OR COPYRIGHT LAW IS PROHIBITED.

BY EXERCISING ANY RIGHTS TO THE WORK PROVIDED HERE, YOU ACCEPT AND AGREE TO BE BOUND BY THE TERMS OF THIS LICENSE. TO THE EXTENT THIS LICENSE MAY BE CONSIDERED TO BE A CONTRACT, THE LICENSOR GRANTS YOU THE RIGHTS CONTAINED HERE IN CONSIDERATION OF YOUR ACCEPTANCE OF SUCH TERMS AND CONDITIONS.

1. Definitions

a. **"Adaptation"** means a work based upon the Work, or upon the Work and other pre-existing works, such as a translation, adaptation, derivative work, arrangement of music or other alterations of a literary or artistic work, or phonogram or performance and includes cinematographic adaptations or any other form in which the Work may be recast, transformed, or adapted including in any form recognizably derived from the original, except that a work that constitutes a Collection will not be considered an Adaptation for the purpose of this License. For the avoidance of doubt, where the Work is a musical work, performance or phonogram, the synchronization of the Work in timed-relation with a moving image ("synching") will be considered an Adaptation for the purpose of this License.

b. **"Collection"** means a collection of literary or artistic works, such as encyclopedias and anthologies, or performances, phonograms or broadcasts, or other works or subject matter other than works listed in Section 1(f) below, which, by reason of the selection and arrangement of their contents, constitute intellectual creations, in which the Work is included in its entirety in unmodified form along with one or more other contributions, each constituting separate and independent works in themselves, which together are assembled into a collective whole. A work that constitutes a Collection will not be considered an Adaptation (as defined below) for the purposes of this License.

c. **"Creative Commons Compatible License"** means a license that is listed at http://creativecommons.org/compatiblelicenses that has been approved by Creative Commons as being essentially equivalent to this License, including, at a minimum, because that license: (i) contains terms that have the same purpose, meaning and effect as the License Elements of this License; and, (ii) explicitly permits the relicensing of adaptations of works made available under that license under this License or a Creative Commons jurisdiction license with the same License Elements as this License.

d. **"Distribute"** means to make available to the public the original and copies of the Work or Adaptation, as appropriate, through sale or other transfer of ownership.

e. **"License Elements"** means the following high-level license attributes as selected by Licensor and indicated in the title of this License: Attribution, ShareAlike.

f. **"Licensor"** means the individual, individuals, entity or entities that offer(s) the Work under the terms of this License.

g. **"Original Author"** means, in the case of a literary or artistic work, the individual, individuals, entity or entities who created the Work or if no individual or entity can be identified, the publisher; and in addition (i) in the case of a performance the actors, singers, musicians, dancers, and other persons who act, sing, deliver, declaim, play in, interpret or otherwise perform literary or artistic works or expressions of folklore; (ii) in the case of a phonogram the producer being the person or legal entity who first fixes the sounds of a performance or other sounds; and, (iii) in the case of broadcasts, the organization that transmits the broadcast.

h. **"Work"** means the literary and/or artistic work offered under the terms of this License including without limitation any production in the literary, scientific and artistic domain, whatever may be the mode or form of its expression including digital form, such as a book, pamphlet and other writing; a lecture, address, sermon or other work of the same nature; a dramatic or dramatico-musical work; a choreographic work or entertainment in dumb show; a musical composition with or without words; a cinematographic work to which are assimilated works expressed by a process analogous to cinematography; a work of drawing, painting, architecture, sculpture, engraving or lithography; a photographic work to which are assimilated works expressed by a process analogous to photography; a work of applied art; an illustration, map, plan, sketch or three-dimensional work relative to geography, topography, architecture or science; a performance; a broadcast; a phonogram; a compilation of data to the extent it is protected as a copyrightable work; or a work performed by a variety or circus performer to the extent it is not otherwise considered a literary or artistic work.

i. **"You"** means an individual or entity exercising rights under this License who has not previously violated the terms of this License with respect to the Work, or who has received express permission from the Licensor to exercise rights under this License despite a previous violation.

j. **"Publicly Perform"** means to perform public recitations of the Work and to communicate to the public those public recitations, by any means or process, including by wire or wireless means or public digital performances; to make available to the public Works in such a way that members of the public may access these Works from a place and at a place individually chosen by them; to perform the Work to the public by any means or process and the communication to the public of the performances of the Work, including by public digital performance; to broadcast and rebroadcast the Work by any means including signs, sounds or images.

k. **"Reproduce"** means to make copies of the Work by any means including without limitation by sound or visual recordings and the right of fixation and reproducing fixations of the Work, including storage of a protected performance or phonogram in digital form or other electronic medium.

2. Fair Dealing Rights.
Nothing in this License is intended to reduce, limit, or restrict any uses free from copyright or rights arising from limitations or exceptions that are provided for in connection with the copyright protection under copyright law or other applicable laws.

3. License Grant.
Subject to the terms and conditions of this License, Licensor hereby grants You a worldwide, royalty-free, non-exclusive, perpetual (for the duration of the applicable copyright) license to exercise the rights in the Work as stated below:

a. to Reproduce the Work, to incorporate the Work into one or more Collections, and to Reproduce the Work as incorporated in the Collections;

b. to create and Reproduce Adaptations provided that any such Adaptation, including any translation in any medium, takes reasonable steps to clearly label, demarcate or otherwise identify that changes were made to the original Work. For example, a translation could be marked "The original work was translated from English to Spanish," or a modification could indicate "The original work has been modified.";

c. to Distribute and Publicly Perform the Work including as incorporated in Collections; and,

d. to Distribute and Publicly Perform Adaptations.

e. For the avoidance of doubt:

    i. **Non-waivable Compulsory License Schemes.** In those jurisdictions in which the right to collect royalties through any statutory or compulsory licensing scheme cannot be waived, the Licensor reserves the exclusive right to collect such royalties for any exercise by You of the rights granted under this License;

    ii. **Waivable Compulsory License Schemes.** In those jurisdictions in which the right to collect royalties through any statutory or compulsory licensing scheme can be waived, the Licensor waives the exclusive right to collect such royalties for any exercise by You of the rights granted under this License; and,

    iii. **Voluntary License Schemes.** The Licensor waives the right to collect royalties, whether individually or, in the event that the Licensor is a member of a collecting society that administers voluntary licensing schemes, via that society, from any exercise by You of the rights granted under this License.

The above rights may be exercised in all media and formats whether now known or hereafter devised. The above rights include the right to make such modifications as are technically necessary to exercise the rights in other media and formats. Subject to Section 8(f), all rights not expressly granted by Licensor are hereby reserved.

4. Restrictions

The license granted in Section 3 above is expressly made subject to and limited by the following restrictions:

a. You may Distribute or Publicly Perform the Work only under the terms of this License. You must include a copy of, or the Uniform Resource Identifier (URI) for, this License with every copy of the Work You Distribute or Publicly Perform. You may not offer or impose any terms on the Work that restrict the terms of this License or the ability of the recipient of the Work to exercise the rights granted to that recipient under the terms of the License. You may not sublicense the Work. You must keep intact all notices that refer to this License and to the disclaimer of warranties with every copy of the Work You Distribute or Publicly Perform. When You Distribute or Publicly Perform the Work, You may not impose any effective technological measures on the Work that restrict the ability of a recipient of the Work from You to exercise the rights granted to that recipient under the terms of the License. This Section 4(a) applies to the Work as incorporated in a Collection, but this does not require the Collection apart from the Work itself to be made subject to the terms of this License. If You create a Collection, upon notice from any Licensor You must, to the extent practicable, remove from the Collection any credit as required by Section 4(c), as requested. If You create an Adaptation, upon notice from any Licensor You must, to the extent practicable, remove from the Adaptation any credit as required by Section 4(c), as requested.

b. You may Distribute or Publicly Perform an Adaptation only under the terms of: (i) this License; (ii) a later version of this License with the same License Elements as this License; (iii) a Creative Commons jurisdiction license (either this or a later license version) that contains the same License Elements as this License (e.g., Attribution-ShareAlike 3.0 US)); (iv) a Creative Commons Compatible License. If you license the Adaptation under one of the licenses mentioned in (iv), you must comply with the terms of that license. If you license the Adaptation under the terms of any of the licenses mentioned in (i), (ii) or (iii) (the "Applicable License"), you must comply with the terms of the Applicable License generally and the following provisions: (I) You must include a copy of, or the URI for, the Applicable License with every copy of each Adaptation You Distribute or Publicly Perform; (II) You may not offer or impose any terms on the Adaptation that restrict the terms of the Applicable License or the ability of the recipient of the Adaptation to exercise the rights granted to that recipient under the terms of the Applicable License; (III) You must keep intact all notices that refer to the Applicable License and to the disclaimer of warranties with every copy of the Work as included in the Adaptation You Distribute or Publicly Perform; (IV) when You Distribute or Publicly Perform the Adaptation, You may not impose any effective technological measures on the Adaptation that restrict the ability of a recipient of the Adaptation from You to exercise the rights granted to that recipient under the terms of the Applicable License. This Section 4(b) applies to the Adaptation as incorporated in a Collection, but this does not require the Collection apart from the Adaptation itself to be made subject to the terms of the Applicable License.

c. If You Distribute, or Publicly Perform the Work or any Adaptations or Collections, You must, unless a request has been made pursuant to Section 4(a), keep intact all copyright notices for the Work and provide, reasonable to the medium or means You are utilizing: (i) the name of the Original Author (or pseudonym, if applicable) if supplied, and/or if the Original Author and/or Licensor designate another party or parties (e.g., a sponsor institute, publishing entity, journal) for attribution ("Attribution Parties") in Licensor's copyright notice, terms of service or by other reasonable means, the name of such party or parties; (ii) the title of the Work if supplied; (iii) to the extent reasonably practicable, the URI, if any, that Licensor specifies to be associated with the Work, unless such URI does not refer to the copyright notice or licensing information for the Work; and (iv) , consistent with Section 3(b), in the case of an Adaptation, a credit identifying the use of the Work in the Adaptation (e.g., "French translation of the Work by Original Author," or "Screenplay based on original Work by Original Author"). The credit required by this Section 4(c) may be implemented in any reasonable manner; provided, however, that in the case of a Adaptation or Collection, at a minimum such credit will appear, if a credit for all contributing authors of the Adaptation or Collection appears, then as part of these credits and in a manner at least as prominent as the credits for the other contributing authors. For the avoidance of doubt, You may only use the credit required by this Section for the purpose of attribution in the manner set out above and, by exercising Your rights under this License, You may not implicitly or explicitly assert or imply any connection with, sponsorship or endorsement by the Original Author, Licensor and/or Attribution Parties, as appropriate, of You or Your use of the Work, without the separate, express prior written permission of the Original Author, Licensor and/or Attribution Parties.

d. Except as otherwise agreed in writing by the Licensor or as may be otherwise permitted by applicable law, if You Reproduce, Distribute or Publicly Perform the Work either by itself or as part of any Adaptations or Collections, You must not distort, mutilate, modify or take other derogatory action in relation to the Work which would be prejudicial to the Original Author's honor or reputation. Licensor agrees that in those jurisdictions (e.g. Japan), in which any exercise of the right granted in Section 3(b) of this License (the right to make Adaptations) would be deemed to be a distortion, mutilation, modification or other derogatory action prejudicial to the Original Author's honor and reputation, the Licensor will waive or not assert, as appropriate, this Section, to the fullest extent permitted by the applicable national law, to enable You to reasonably exercise Your right under Section 3(b) of this License (right to make Adaptations) but not otherwise.

5. Representations, Warranties and Disclaimer

UNLESS OTHERWISE MUTUALLY AGREED TO BY THE PARTIES IN WRITING, LICENSOR OFFERS THE WORK AS-IS AND MAKES NO REPRESENTATIONS OR WARRANTIES OF ANY KIND CONCERNING THE WORK, EXPRESS, IMPLIED, STATUTORY OR OTHERWISE, INCLUDING, WITHOUT LIMITATION, WARRANTIES OF TITLE, MERCHANTIBILITY, FITNESS FOR A PARTICULAR PURPOSE, NONINFRINGEMENT, OR THE ABSENCE OF LATENT OR OTHER DEFECTS, ACCURACY, OR THE PRESENCE OF ABSENCE OF ERRORS, WHETHER OR NOT DISCOVERABLE. SOME JURISDICTIONS DO NOT ALLOW THE EXCLUSION OF IMPLIED WARRANTIES, SO SUCH EXCLUSION MAY NOT APPLY TO YOU.

6. Limitation on Liability

EXCEPT TO THE EXTENT REQUIRED BY APPLICABLE LAW, IN NO EVENT WILL LICENSOR BE LIABLE TO YOU ON ANY LEGAL THEORY FOR ANY SPECIAL, INCIDENTAL, CONSEQUENTIAL, PUNITIVE OR EXEMPLARY DAMAGES ARISING OUT OF THIS LICENSE OR THE USE OF THE WORK, EVEN IF LICENSOR HAS BEEN ADVISED OF THE POSSIBILITY OF SUCH DAMAGES.

7. Termination

a. This License and the rights granted hereunder will terminate automatically upon any breach by You of the terms of this License. Individuals or entities who have received Adaptations or Collections from You under this License, however, will not have their licenses terminated provided such individuals or entities remain in full compliance with those licenses. Sections 1, 2, 5, 6, 7, and 8 will survive any termination of this License.

b. Subject to the above terms and conditions, the license granted here is perpetual (for the duration of the applicable copyright in the Work). Notwithstanding the above, Licensor reserves the right to release the Work under different license terms or to stop distributing the Work at any time; provided, however that any such election will not serve to withdraw this License (or any other license that has been, or is required to be, granted under the terms of this License), and this License will continue in full force and effect unless terminated as stated above.

8. Miscellaneous

a. Each time You Distribute or Publicly Perform the Work or a Collection, the Licensor offers to the recipient a license to the Work on the same terms and conditions as the license granted to You under this License.

b. Each time You Distribute or Publicly Perform an Adaptation, Licensor offers to the recipient a license to the original Work on the same terms and conditions as the license granted to You under this License.

c. If any provision of this License is invalid or unenforceable under applicable law, it shall not affect the validity or enforceability of the remainder of the terms of this License, and without further action by the parties to this agreement, such provision shall be reformed to the minimum extent necessary to make such provision valid and enforceable.

d. No term or provision of this License shall be deemed waived and no breach consented to unless such waiver or consent shall be in writing and signed by the party to be charged with such waiver or consent.

e. This License constitutes the entire agreement between the parties with respect to the Work licensed here. There are no understandings, agreements or representations with respect to the Work not specified here. Licensor shall not be bound by any additional provisions that may appear in any communication from You. This License may not be modified without the mutual written agreement of the Licensor and You.

Index

Symbols and Numbers